History of American Economy:
Studies and Material for Study

A series of reprints of important studies and source books relating
to the growth of the American economic system.

GENERAL EDITORS
William N. Parker, *Professor of Economics, Yale University*
Harry N. Scheiber, *Professor of History, University of California,
San Diego*

JOHNSON REPRINT CORPORATION
New York • London
1972

Library of Congress Cataloging in Publication Data:

Lord, Clifford Lee, 1912–
  Historical atlas of the United States.

  (History of American economy)
  Reprint of the 1953 ed.
  Bibliography: p.
  1. U.S.—Historical geography—Maps. 2. U.S.—Economic conditions—
Maps. 3. U.S.—Population—Maps. I. Lord, Elizabeth Sniffen (Hubbard)
1912–   joint author. II. Title.
G1201.S1L6   1972   911'.73   72-10004
ISBN 0-384-33650-7

This volume was reproduced from an original copy in the collection of the
New York State Library, Albany
Reprinted with the permission of the original publisher
First reprinting 1969
Second reprinting 1972
All rights reserved
Johnson Reprint Corporation, 111 Fifth Avenue, New York, New York 10003
Printed in the United States of America

HISTORICAL ATLAS

OF THE

UNITED STATES

REVISED EDITION

By CLIFFORD L. LORD
and ELIZABETH H. LORD

COMMITTEE FOR
TECHNICAL EDUCATION

NEW YORK : HENRY HOLT AND COMPANY

Preface

Any attempt at the serious study of historical development without a somewhat meticulous regard for geographical factors has long been regarded as an educational venture of dubious value. The map, with its own peculiar usefulness, is an established tool for the student both inside and outside the classroom.

The startlingly rapid growth and development of the United States make its history particularly susceptible to visual portrayal. The animated cartoon-map is certainly the most vivid way of showing, for instance, the tentacles of our railroad system reaching out year by year across the country, or of portraying the spread of our crop areas, the development of manufacturing regions, the westward advance of population. It may be the best way to show the spread of reform, and particularly the evolution of such pillars of our democracy as the free public school, universal suffrage, and the abolition of slavery. But movies have their limitations. They may be seen and heard, but they are difficult to study, even in classrooms. Those who lack photographic memories (and they are many) are more apt to carry away a vague impression than definite knowledge. By mapping developments in particular fields every few years, so that one can almost see them grow or shift, this atlas tries to combine the usefulness of the animated map with the advantages of being able to sit down face to face with the moving panorama of American history for study at such length as need be. That is its first excuse for being.

Its second excuse is derived from the sound increase of emphasis in the last few decades upon social and economic history. The study of geopolitics is being begun in American schools, courses in economic geography have become common, and frequent attempts have been made to study the development of many of the characteristics of our democracy from a geographical basis. Yet, just as much attention has been paid to American government but relatively little to the history of that American government, so history has been slow to adapt the techniques of the economic and political geographer to its own field, and so far has produced no serviceable handbook, sufficiently wide in scope, which so juxtaposes basic social and economic maps against those of our political history as to be useful in a general introduction to the history of the United States. The need in this field cannot be fully met for many years to come, until far more detailed research and compilation has been done in the statistics of early industry, agriculture, and transportation. But much material now exists, and its partial mapping and correlation here gives further reason for this volume.

The authors are firmly convinced of the pedagogical necessity of using such a collection of maps as these in teaching a well-rounded course in American history—are convinced that such a volume would be useful in the hands of every high school or college student of American history.

It should be clearly understood that this volume is not designed to be a reference atlas.[1] It is designed to help every student of American history along the road to that clarified, broader, integrated understanding which is the essence of intelligent education.

Every good teacher has his or her particular ideas on teaching. Therefore no attempt is made here to present any suggested class exercises. Obviously the study of the Granger movement will be enriched by attention to contemporary railroad development, to drought frequency and the major crop belts. One will find intriguing material in correlating the areas of light slaveholding in the South with the areas of Southern opposition to secession in 1860–61; the advancing frontier with the line of Indian land cessions; the routes of westward migration with the existing canals and waterways; the spread of the free public school and the liberalization of the franchise; the growth of crop and manufacturing areas and the increase of foreign trade. Liberal use has been made of the relief map of the United States in maps of exploration, communication, military campaigning, and wherever else it could be used without undue confusion of detail or loss of clarity. The direct correlation of such subjects with the topography of the region opens fur-

---

[1] Students wishing to consult a good reference atlas on American history should refer to C. O. Paullin (ed.), *Atlas of the Historical Geography of the United States* (Washington, 1932), or to the atlas accompanying the *Dictionary of American History.*

ther vistas of interest and comprehension. The imagination of both teacher and student will develop worthwhile and useful correlations along these lines far more satisfactorily than could any arbitrary set of stereotyped exercises.

The authors are indebted to many people for assistance in preparing this volume. George Robertson, of Arlington, Virginia, has contributed greatly to its usefulness by generously permitting us to reproduce the prints, so extensively used, of his revisions of the relief models of both North and South America originally prepared by E. E. Howell. The staffs of the Columbia University, the Boston and New York Public Libraries, and the American Geographical Society have been most helpful. The Carnegie Institution of Washington has graciously permitted the authors to use freely the maps of its *Atlas of the Historical Geography of the United States*, permission which has been used as noted in the section on Sources. The New Jersey Historical Records Survey, Work Projects Administration, generously granted the use, as a basis for the maps in this book, of its plottings of the development of state and territorial borders, the evolution of the federal circuit and district courts, and the maps of the votes of the House and Senate upon certain major issues, prepared for the projected *Atlas of Congressional Roll-Calls*. Elizabeth Smart of the Women's Christian Temperance Union, Laura Lindley of the Anti-Saloon League, Lawrence Martin of the Library of Congress, and Henrietta L. Gordon of the Child Welfare League of America have given valuable aid. Many government officials, particularly those of the Division of Statistical and Historical Research, the Bureau of Agricultural Economics, the Bureau of Plant Industry, the Soil Conservation Service, and the Forest Service in the Department of Agriculture; of the National Park Service in the Interior Department; of the Corps of Engineers, U. S. A.; of the Federal Reserve System; of the Public Roads Division of the Public Works Administration; of the Children's Bureau, the Women's Bureau, and the Office of the Solicitor of the Department of Labor; of the then Civil Aeronautics Commission; the Office of the Attorney-General; and officials of various states, have furnished their full and indispensable cooperation. Col. Robert Henry has previously permitted use of his map representing the actual areas of federal land grants to railroads. Particularly grateful acknowledgement should be made to Amy Wadsworth Wells, whose drawing and lettering of the final copy of the maps insured the attractiveness of their ultimate form; and to many academic friends for help and suggestions.

C.L.L.
E.H.L.

Madison, Wisconsin,
January 25, 1953.

Sources

Government publications have been heavily drawn upon in the preparation of many of the maps of this book. Maps prepared by the Department of Agriculture have been adapted for the general maps of temperature, soil belts, regionalized types of farming, vegetation and forestation belts, drought frequency and the distribution of crops.

The map of regional watersheds was adapted from the December, 1936, *Report* of the National Resources Board, which was also consulted for the maps of rainfall, submarginal land areas, and the land retirement program. The maps of national resources were developed largely from data and maps appearing in publications of the Geological Survey. The irrigation maps were taken from the census volumes on agriculture since 1890.

Population maps, including those showing the distribution of residents of foreign birth, were taken, as were the maps of farm tenancy, from those published in volumes of the *Census Reports* and in some editions of the *Statistical Atlas of the United States*. The map of distribution of racial stocks in 1775 is based on the map in J. T. Adams, *The Record of America*, checked against A. B. Faust, *The German Element in the United States*. Population density in western states and territories for 1860 was based on data from census records and statistics given in the Commonwealth Club of California's *The Population of California*, checked against the Hammond and Hart-Bolton-and-Matteson atlases.

Maps of highways eligible for federal aid were prepared from maps furnished by the Bureau of Public Roads, Federal Works Administration. Maps of the development of the national parks were adapted from maps furnished by the National Park Service. National Monuments were adapted from the wall map of the Department of the Interior, 1940 edition; the dates of establishment were obtained from the Department. The Federal Reserve System furnished the map of the capitals and borders of the Reserve districts, together with data on the negligible border changes since 1914. Newspaper statistics for 1725, 1775 and 1800 were derived from Clarence Brigham's *Bibliography of American Newspapers Published Prior to 1820*; for 1860 from Kenny, *American Newspaper Directory*.

The development of the federal circuit and district courts was worked out by the Historical Records Survey of New Jersey for the projected *Handbook of the Federal Circuit and District Courts*, edited by the author. Maps of votes in both Houses of Congress were compiled by the same project for the author's projected *Atlas of Congressional Roll Calls*. Borders of states and territories used on all maps were also worked out by the New Jersey Historical Records Survey from the *United States Statutes At Large*, federal court decisions, and the reports of boundary commissions.

Colonial period maps were based largely on Shepherd's *Historical Atlas* (by permission of the publisher), with information added from other sources such as the *New International Encyclopaedia*. Charter lines and the colonial wars were to some degree adapted from Paullin's *Atlas of the Historical Geography of the United States* (by permission of the publishers), where an excellent textual summary of each charter appears. Data for the maps of Spanish expansion in the Southwest were taken from H. E. Bolton, *Colonization of North America*, *Spanish Borderlands*, and *Spanish Explorations in the Southwest*, and from W. E. Lowery, *Spanish Settlements Within the Present Limits of the United States*. The map of the exploration of the American West was adapted largely from Shepherd, supplemented by additional data from the *New International Encyclopaedia* and Paullin. Colonial manufacturing maps were based largely on the iron works mapped in V. S. Clark, *History of Manufactures in the United States*. Later manufacturing maps were based on textile and iron and steel statistics in *American State Papers, Finance*, vol. 2, supplemented by Clark. Still later maps are based on census figures.

Maps of abolition, free public schools, compulsory school attendance, hours of men's and women's work, and child labor were worked out from the volumes of state statutes, supplemented, in the case of the latter three, by publications of the Women's Bureau, the Children's Bureau, the Bureau of Labor Statistics, the Bureau of Labor Standards, and the Solicitor of the Department of Labor. Ratification of the Constitution is based on Orin G. Libby's famous and much-used work; ratification of the Amendments is based on the lists of ratification dates in the annotated *Constitution of the United States of America*.

The prohibition maps were worked out from Funk and Wagnalls, *Cyclopaedia of Temperance and Prohibition*; E. H. Cherrington, *Evolution of Prohibition in the United States of America*; and D. L. Colvin, *Prohibition in the United States*. Additional data were furnished by Miss Laura Lindley of the Anti-Saloon League, the officials of many states, and Miss Elizabeth Smart of the Women's Christian Temperance Union. The map of dry territory in 1919 is based on the 1919 *Handbook of the World League Against Alcoholism* (by permission). The franchise maps were compiled from K. H. Porter, *A History of Suffrage in the United States*, and the *Codes* and *Session Laws* of the several states.

The military maps have been adapted largely from Paullin, simplified to show only routes of attack, not retreat, and put on a background of the region's physical features. The maps of the Treaty of 1783, Guadeloupe Hidalgo, post roads, banks and rates of travel were adapted, with permission, from the same source. The maps of the Revolutionary War were adapted from Shepherd, those of the Civil War from the atlas accompanying the *Official Records of the War of the Rebellion*, compiled by Davis, Perry and Kirkley. Maps of American participation in World War I on both the domestic and the French fronts were drawn from a number of maps in L. P. Ayres, Chief of the Statistics Branch of the General Staff, U. S. A., *The War With Germany*. M. F. Steele, *American Campaigns*, was also helpful.

The routes of westward migration, the underground railway and the slave trade were adapted from Shepherd. The map of federal land grants in aid of railroad and wagon road construction was derived from that published by the Bureau of Corporations in *The Lumber Industry*, part 1 (1913).

Canal maps were based on the list of canals and their completion dates in the Census of 1880, vol. 4. Railroad maps for the period 1840–60 were based on V. S. Clark, *History of Manufactures in the United States*, and H. V. Poor, *History of the Railroads and Canals of the United States*; those for 1870–80 on G. W. Colton, *General Atlas*. The 1854 telegraph map was adapted from Disturnell's *New Map of the United States and Canada* (1854). The map of 1922 transmission lines was derived from F. G. Baum, *Atlas of the U. S. A. Electrical Power Industry*; the 1935 lines from the wall map issued by the Federal Power Commission in that year.

The manifest destiny and expansion maps were compiled from the author's course notes, worked up over a number of years, from A. Weinberg's *Manifest Destiny*, from Harper's *Atlas of American History*, and from valuable suggestions by Basil Rauch of the Barnard faculty.

The maps of southern opposition to secession, slaves per slaveholder, and proportion of slaves to total population were prepared from the reports of the State Secession conventions, the *Tribune Almanac and Political Reporter* and the 1860 *Census Reports*.

The college maps were prepared from statistics taken from Frasier, *American Almanac and Depository of Useful Knowledge* for the period 1830–60; from Armatraut, *An Introduction to Education* for the period before 1800; from the *Reports* of the Commissioner of Education for the years 1870–1910; and from the *Bulletins* of the Bureau of Education for the decades 1920–40.

Trade maps and the appendix of trade statistics for 1800 were derived from *American State Papers: Commerce and Navigation*, I; for 1850, from Treasury Department, *Report of the Register of the Treasury*; for 1900 from the Treasury Department, Bureau of Statistics, *Foreign Commerce and Navigation of the United States for the Year Ending June 30, 1900*; for 1938 from the volume of the same title published by the Department of Commerce, Bureau of Foreign and Domestic Commerce for the calendar year, 1938. The figures on American investments abroad are taken from R. W. Dunn, *American Foreign Investments*; and from the 1930 and 1936 surveys published by the Bureau of Foreign and Domestic Commerce; data on subsidized ship lines from P. M. Zeis, *American Shipping Policy*, and J. E. Saugstad, *Shipping and Shipbuilding Subsidies*.

The publications of the National Geographic Society were used for the names of physical features of North and South America, the nomenclature conforming to that used by the U. S. Board of Geographic Names.

CONTENTS

SECTION I. GENERAL MAPS

SECTION II. COLONIAL PERIOD

SECTION III. 1775-1865

SECTION IV. 1865-1950

APPENDICES

HISTORICAL ATLAS

Section I

GENERAL MAPS

The maps presented in this section contain generalized data on the physical features and political boundaries of our own nation and her neighbors of this hemisphere, on climate, soils, and national resources.

The student will constantly want to refer to these maps in connection with his use of the maps of the later sections. Major cities and physical features have been shown as fully as the available space will allow. Climate, soil, and vegetation belts are shown in generalized form, with the elimination of local variations too small to be shown practically on maps of this scale.

The teacher may find it useful, when discussing industrial developments or the opening of new mineral strikes such as those at the Comstock Lode, or Leadville, or the Kettleman Hills field, to refer back to the maps where some of the most important deposits of natural resources are specifically labeled; or, when discussing regional planning or regional problems, to refer back to the relief model on which the watersheds are clearly outlined and labeled with the designations used by the National Resources Board. Discussion of crop belts will almost of necessity recall the student to the maps of rainfall, soil, vegetation, drought frequency, temperature belts and the particularly valuable map on regionalized types of farming. Such cross-reference will immeasurably increase one's knowledge and appreciation of factors in the basic development of the country.

The map of Indian locales is necessarily limited in its usefulness. Many Indian tribes, particularly the Plains Indians and the victims of Iroquois aggression, migrated over vast areas both before and after the coming of the white settlers. Others were forcibly moved to reservations and often subsequently made to change their locale a second or third time. It is impossible on such a map as this to represent all the places where a given Indian group appeared at different times. Accordingly, this map attempts merely to show the location of an Indian group at the period when, in the authors' opinion, that group was most important or prominent in American history. An authority on Indians may quarrel with some of the selections, particularly those made in the cases of the more migratory Indians. The map is designed, however, for general study purposes.

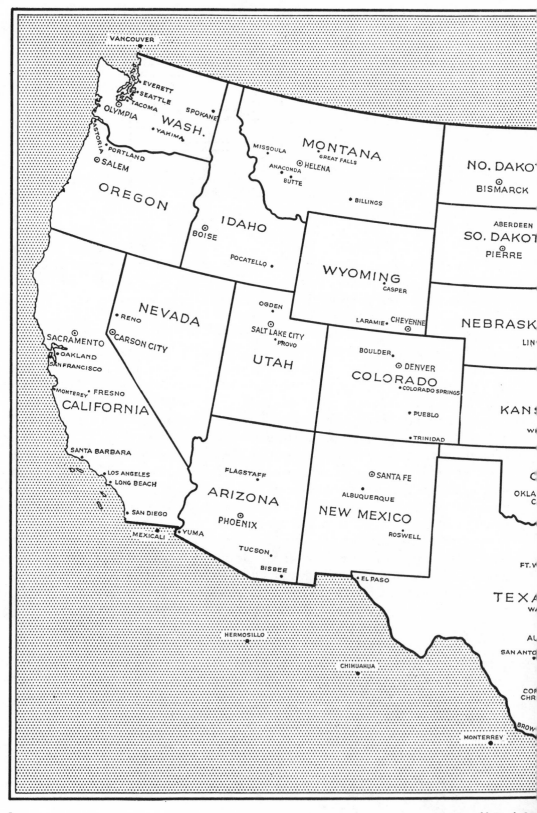

United Sta
Includes some sites of

s and Principal Cities

st not shown on other maps in this atlas

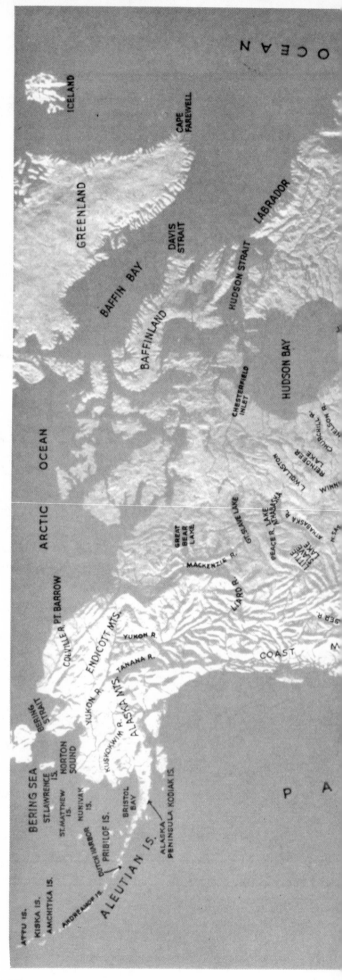

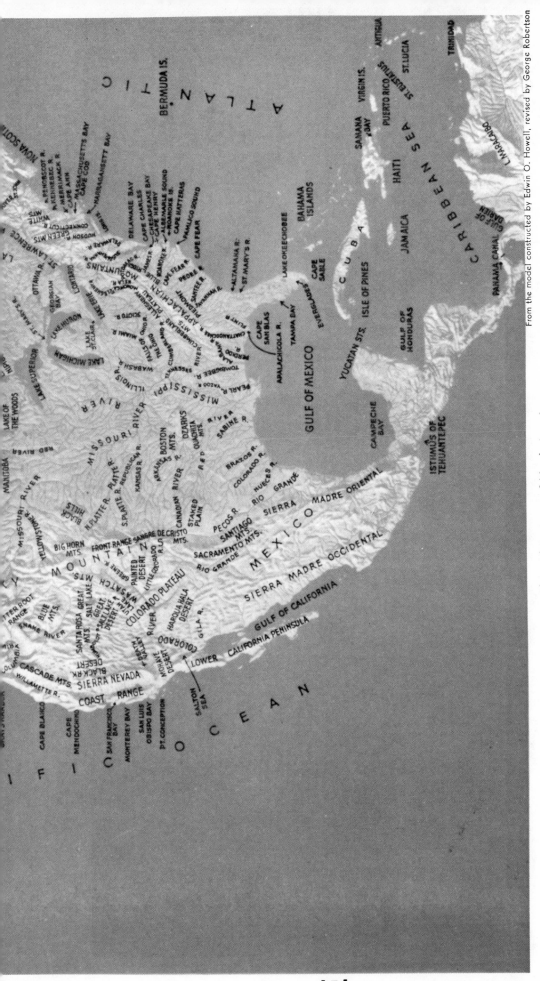

Physical Features of North America

From the model constructed by Edwin O. Howell, revised by George Robertson

2

[5]

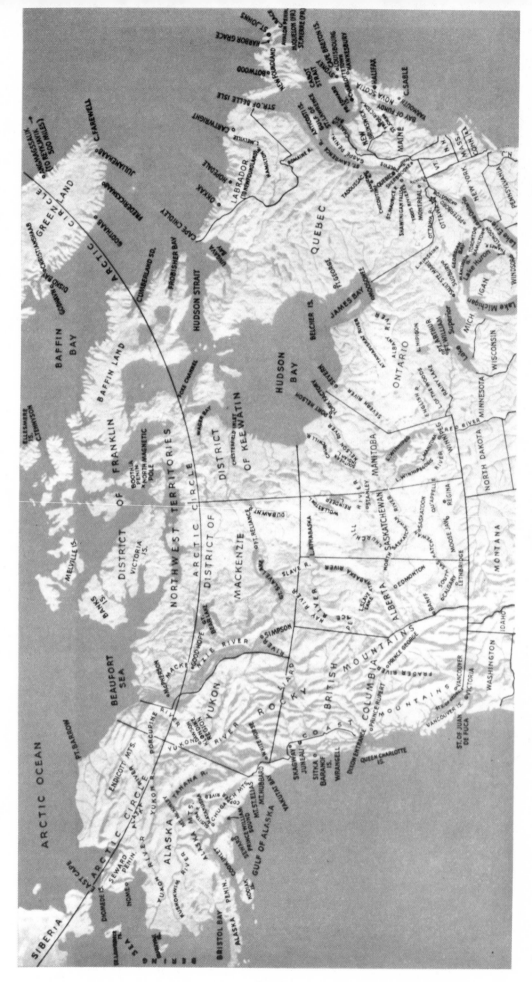

Canada and Alaska

3

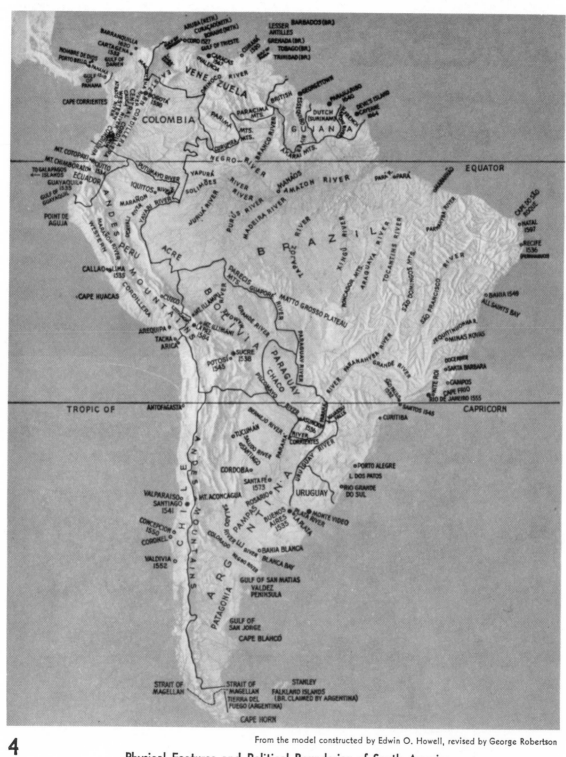

4

From the model constructed by Edwin O. Howell, revised by George Robertson

Physical Features and Political Boundaries of South America
Shows dates of colonial settlement, including those at Panama

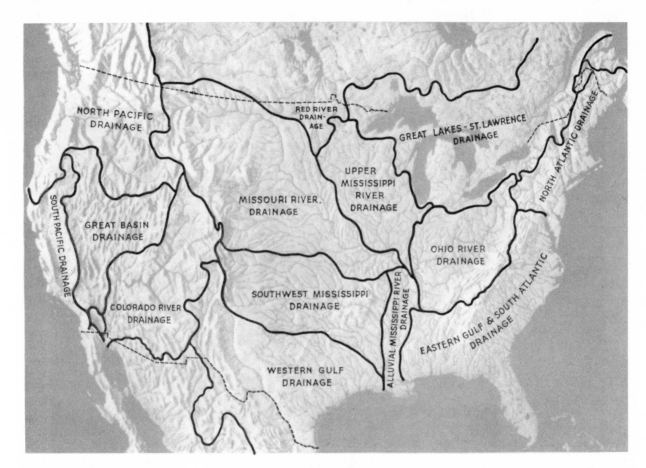

5   Regional Watersheds

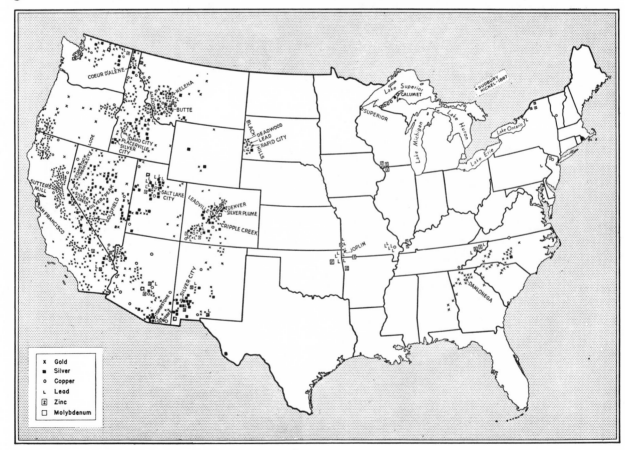

6   Metallic Resources

[8]

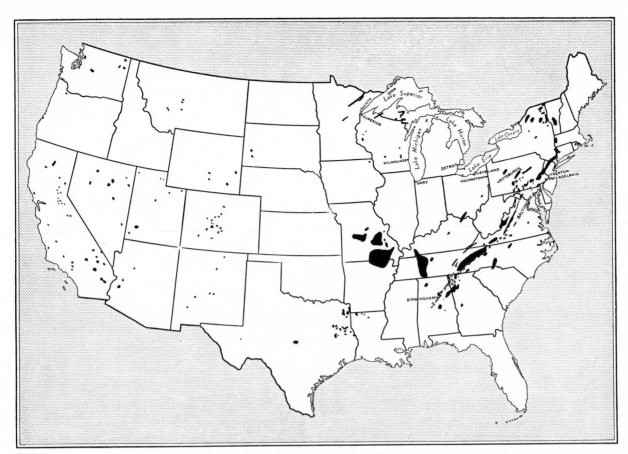

7   Iron Ore Deposits: Hematite, Limonite, and Magnetite

The principal commercial beds are located around Lake Superior, in Pennsylvania, and in Alabama

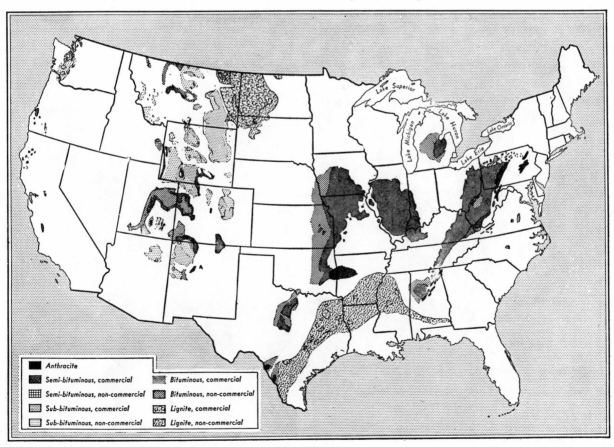

Anthracite

Semi-bituminous, commercial   Bituminous, commercial

Semi-bituminous, non-commercial   Bituminous, non-commercial

Sub-bituminous, commercial   Lignite, commercial

Sub-bituminous, non-commercial   Lignite, non-commercial

8   Coal Deposits

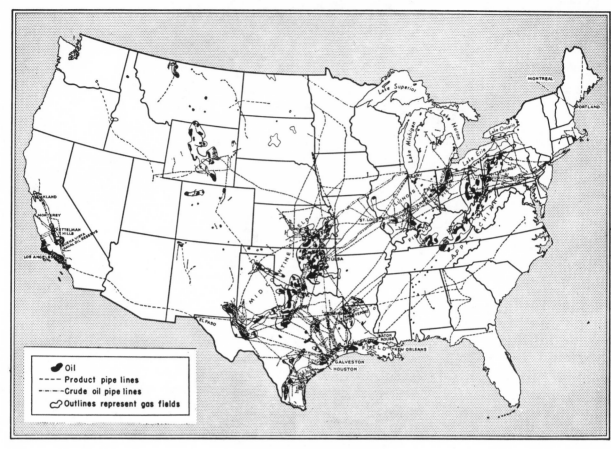

9

Oil and Natural Gas, 1950

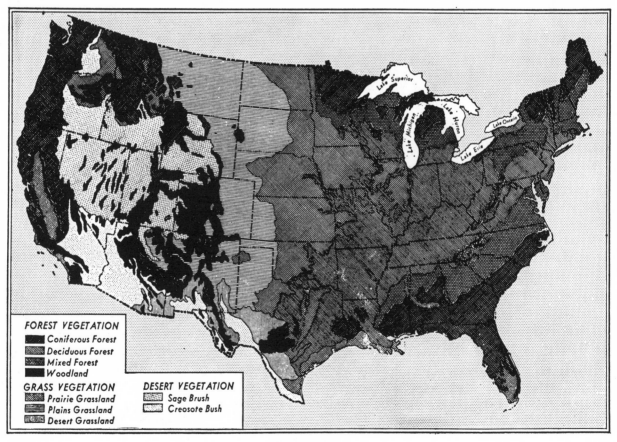

10

Vegetation Belts

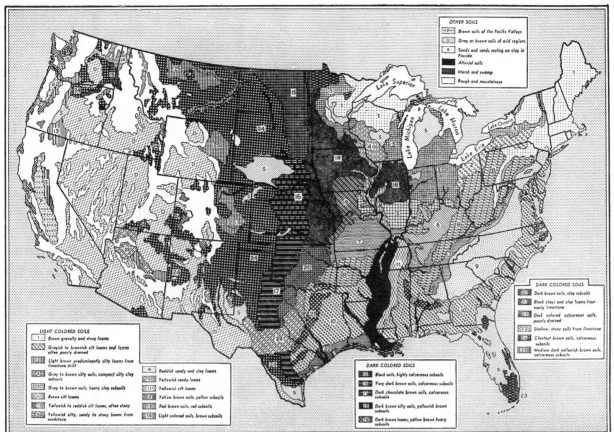

From Map Prepared by C. F. Marbut and Associates in the Soil Survey

Soil Regions

11

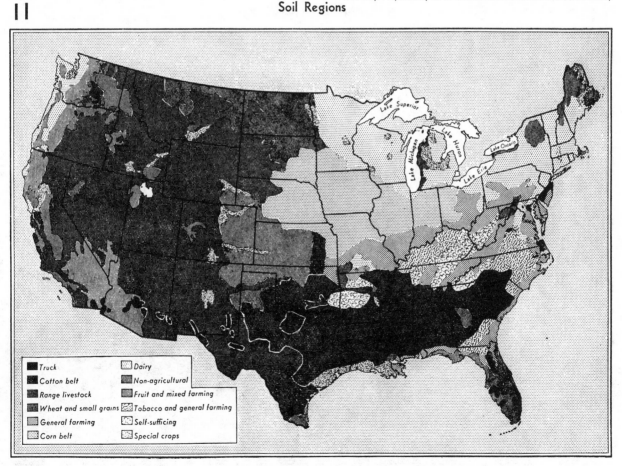

12

Regionalized Types of Farming
(For production of specific commodities see crop and cattle maps)

[11]

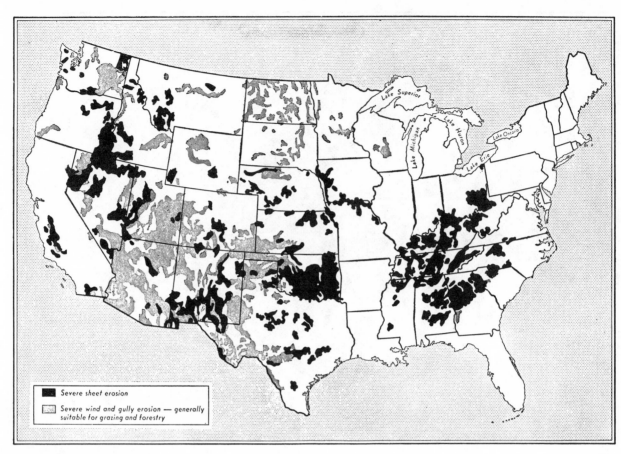

13   Areas of Major Soil Erosion

Severe sheet erosion

Severe wind and gully erosion — generally suitable for grazing and forestry

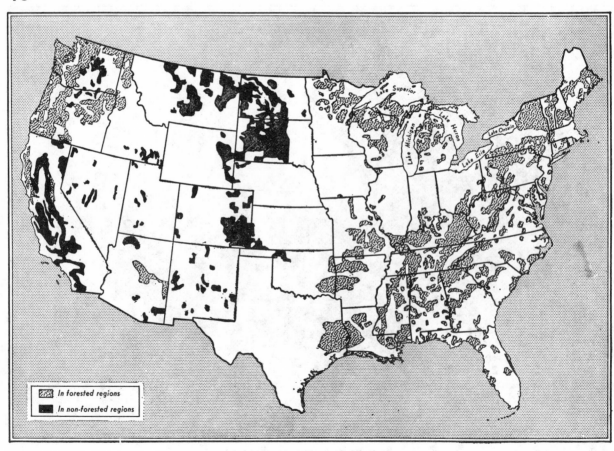

14   Areas Most Suitable for a Land Retirement Program

In forested regions

In non-forested regions

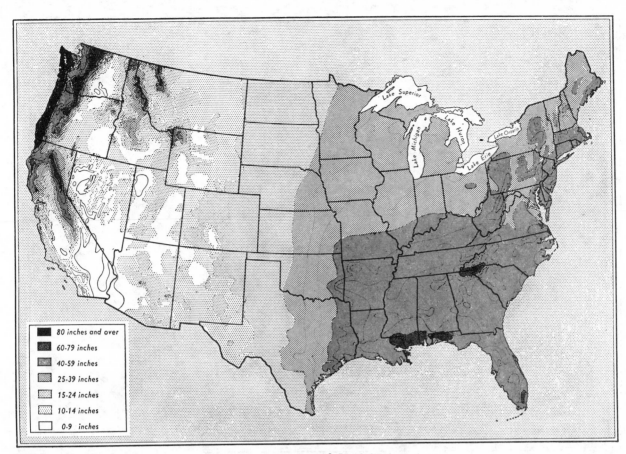

15   Average Annual Precipitation

Legend:
- 80 inches and over
- 60-79 inches
- 40-59 inches
- 25-39 inches
- 15-24 inches
- 10-14 inches
- 0-9 inches

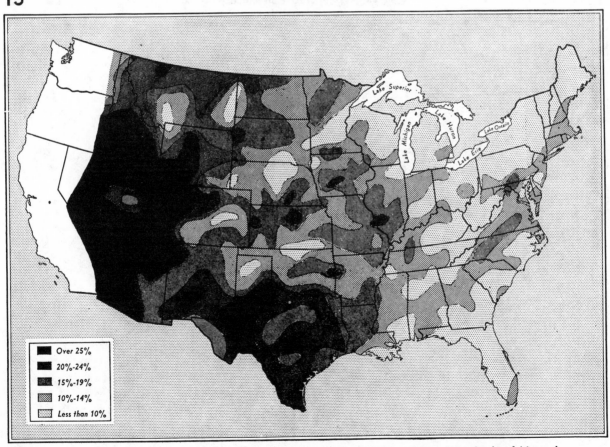

16   Drought Frequency: Percentage of Years in which Rainfall is Less than Two-thirds of Normal
from May through August (East of the Pacific Coast Mountain Ranges)

Legend:
- Over 25%
- 20%-24%
- 15%-19%
- 10%-14%
- Less than 10%

[13]

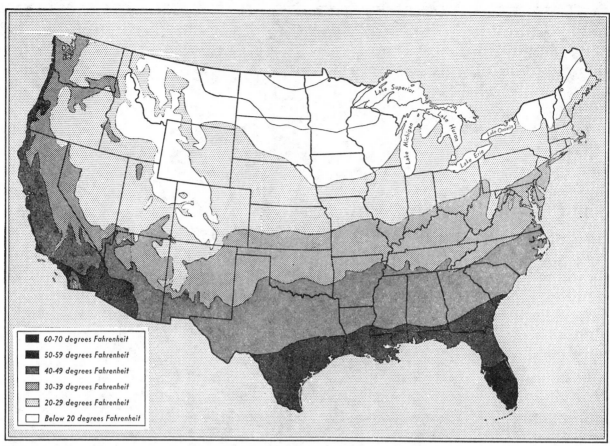

17   Average Temperature in January

Legend for map 17:
- 60-70 degrees Fahrenheit
- 50-59 degrees Fahrenheit
- 40-49 degrees Fahrenheit
- 30-39 degrees Fahrenheit
- 20-29 degrees Fahrenheit
- Below 20 degrees Fahrenheit

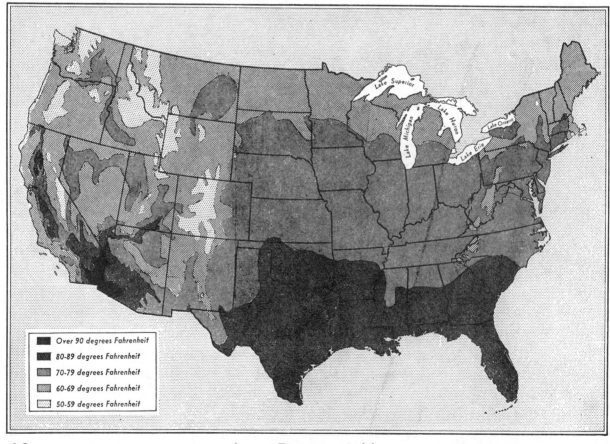

18   Average Temperature in July

Legend for map 18:
- Over 90 degrees Fahrenheit
- 80-89 degrees Fahrenheit
- 70-79 degrees Fahrenheit
- 60-69 degrees Fahrenheit
- 50-59 degrees Fahrenheit

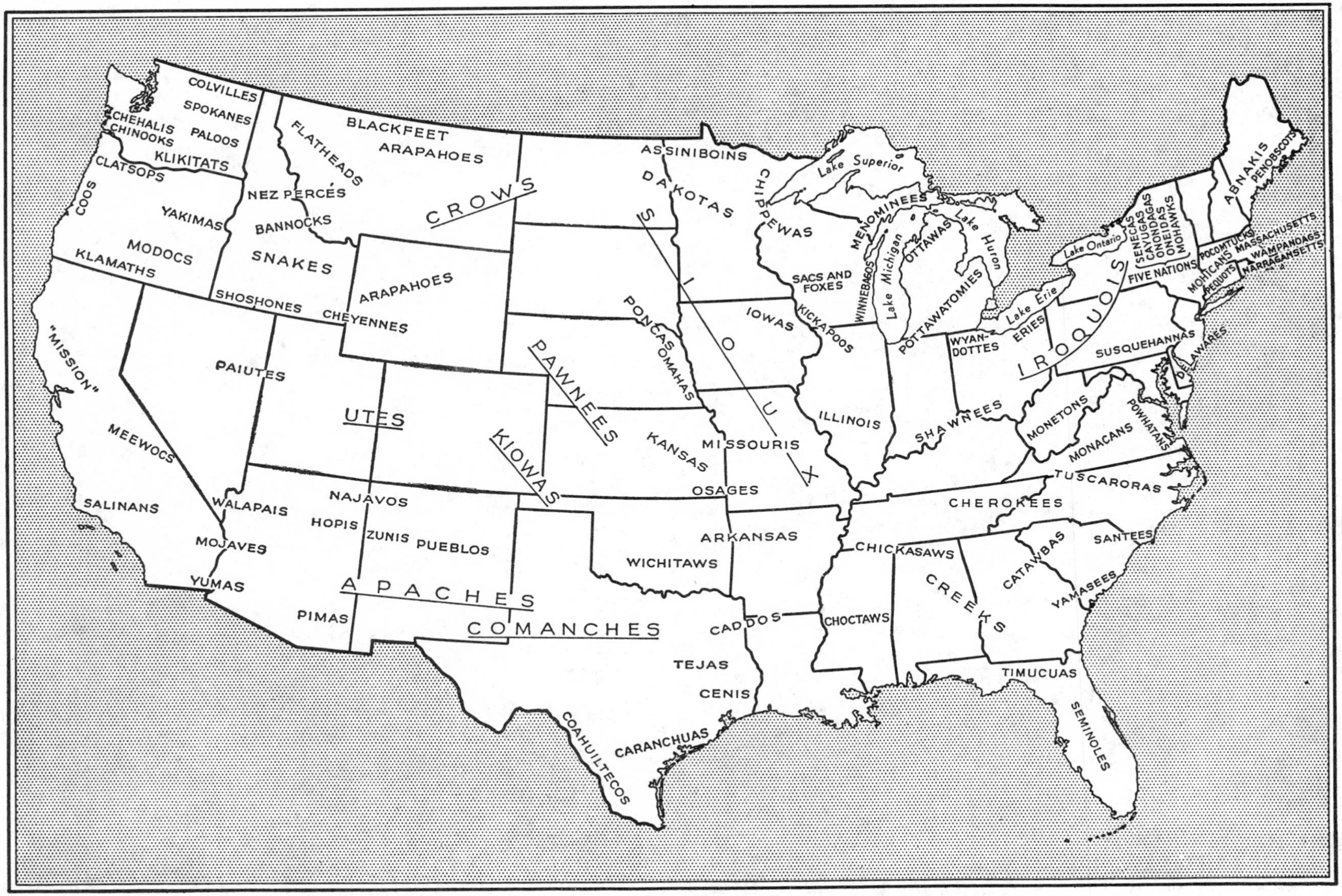

The American Indian: Approximate Location of Indians at the Period of Their Greatest Significance in the Westward Movement of the Frontier

The more prominent names are underlined

19

[15]

Section II

COLONIAL PERIOD

The days of exploration, early settlement, and gradual growth of the colonies and provinces prior to the Revolution constitute one of the most interesting and vital parts of our history. Too often in classroom and textbook this receives the treatment reserved for "early childhood" in most biographies. Unhappily, the lack of time and space which cramps its presentation in introductory courses is a restricting factor even here. Another is that full and reliable statistics for the period are largely unavailable, so that the economic maps are necessarily limited both in number and usefulness.

After the age of exploration and the founding of Spain's enormous colonial empire, the English began the permanent settlements along the Atlantic Coast which were to become the direct forebears of the United States.

The growth of the English colonies is shown first in the charter grants, the advancing line of population, and the expansion of frontier forts and settlements. International rivalries, determining the future course of empire, were present from the outset, though the earlier ones were destined to be somewhat dwarfed by the magnitude of the century of struggle between France and England.

Here one can see France and Spain clash from Georgia to Texas. One can watch the fingers of settlement move out dramatically from New Netherland, absorbing New Sweden, meeting the more rapidly moving tentacles of New England in Long Island, in the Connecticut Valley and on the mouth of the Delaware. The final absorption of the Dutch settlements by the English only paved the way for the ensuing conflict for mastery of the continent between the French and the English. Few more effective methods may be found for presenting the meaning of this conflict and its course than to study the expansion of French and English posts and forts between 1688 and 1763, and to correlate the military campaigns of the four wars with this expansion and its attempt to establish hegemony of the Ohio, the Mississippi, the Great Lakes, and, of course, the fur trade. Spain meanwhile was pressing her expansion northward, but neither so far nor so fast as to come into serious conflict with the British colonials, moving westward. Trouble in that area was to wait on American independence, the Jay-Gardoqui negotiations, the Louisiana Purchase, the Texan Revolution and the Mexican War.

Franchise laws show the close restriction of the suffrage prior to the Revolution. The limits of free district school legislation mark the difficulty, despite the promise of the Massachusetts Act of 1649, which the son of the man of modest means encountered in obtaining a rudimentary education. Restricted by British legislation and far more effectively checked by transportation difficulties, manufacturing was limited largely to production for local markets. Commerce, influenced appreciably by British policies of enumeration, subsidy and empire trade, was an extremely important factor in the colonial economy in the period preceding the establishment of independence. Restrictions upon that commerce, on westward expansion, and on local self-determination, were to contribute largely to the outbreak of revolt against the government of George III. Some of the commodities, their countries of origin, and the much abused and oversimplified "triangular" routes are indicated on the map of colonial trade.

The diverse nationalities which were eventually to constitute the American nation were already in evidence prior to the Revolution, English, Dutch, Scotch-Irish and German predominating. Newspapers, always useful vehicles, as well as significant criteria, of the spread of knowledge and literacy, were already long established by the time the Revolution came to give birth to new Tory and Patriot sheets. Though many provincials relied on English institutions for higher learning, by 1775 American colleges, beginning with Harvard College in 1636, included many of our best-known universities. Many of the foundation stones of modern America were in place by April, 1775.

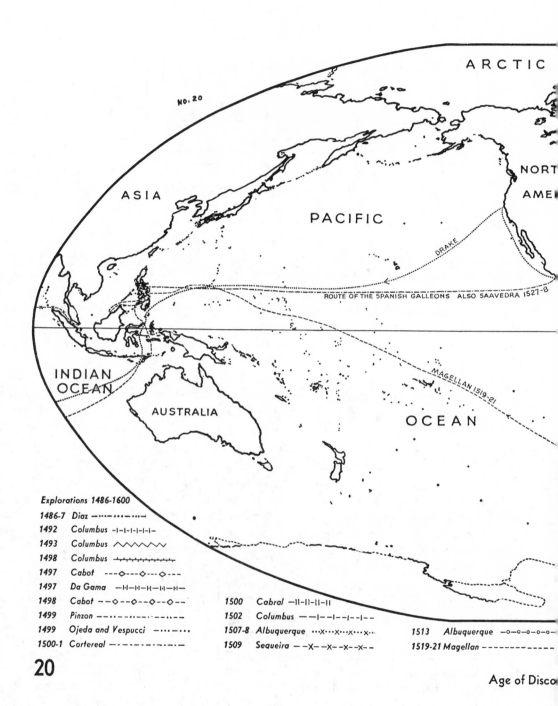

ARCTIC

NORT
AME

ASIA

PACIFIC

DRAKE

ROUTE OF THE SPANISH GALLEONS ALSO SAAVEDRA 1527-8

MAGELLAN 1519-21

INDIAN
OCEAN

AUSTRALIA

OCEAN

Explorations 1486-1600

1486-7	Diaz — · — · · · — ·			
1492	Columbus –ı–ı–ı–ı–ı–			
1493	Columbus ⌃⌃⌃⌃⌃⌃			
1498	Columbus +++++++			
1497	Cabot ---◇---◇---			
1497	Da Gama —ıı—ıı—ıı—ıı—ıı—			
1498	Cabot – –◇– –◇– –◇– –			
1499	Pinzon — — · · — · · · — · — · —	1500	Cabral —ıı–ıı–ıı–ıı	1513	Albuquerque –o–o–o–o–
1499	Ojeda and Vespucci — · · · — · ·	1502	Columbus — —ı— ı— ı— ı— —	1519-21 Magellan — — — — — — — —
1500-1	Cortereal — — · — · · — · — ·	1507-8	Albuquerque ···x···x···x···x··		
		1509	Sequeira — —x— —x— —x— —x— —		

20

Age of Disco

OCEAN

No. 20

ASIA

EUROPE

WILLOUGHBY
& CHANCELLOR
1553

JENKINSON 1557-8

DAVIS 1587
DAVIS 1585
ORTEREALL
1500-1
DAVIS 1586
FROBISHER 1576-8
CABOT 1497
CABOT 1498
CARTIER 1534-5
CARTIER
FAGUNDES 1521

VERRAZANO 1524
COLUMBUS 1493

ATLANTIC
COLUMBUS 1492

ALBUQUERQUE 1507-8

AFRICA

COLUMBUS 1493
GALLEONS
COLUMBUS 1502
COLUMBUS 1498 VESPUCCI 1499
OJEDA

ALBUQUERQUE 1513

SEQUEIRA 1509

PINZON 1499

SOUTH
AMERICA

INDIAN

DA GAMA 1497

OCEAN

OCEAN

DRAKE 1577-80

DRAKE 1577-80

CABRAL 1500

ELCANO (MAGELLAN) 1521-3

DIAZ 1486-7

ANTARCTICA

1553	Willoughby and Chancellor	-----------
1557-8	Jenkinson	—※—※—※
1576-8	Frobisher	···III···III···III···III
1577-80	Drake	···········

1526	Guevara	—··—··—··—··—
1527-8	Saavedra	—··—··—··—··—
1534-5	Cartier	—=—=—=—=—=
1535-6	Cartier	—+—+—+—+—+—

1585	Davis	—II—II—II—II—
1586	Davis	—II·II—II·II—
1587	Davis	···o····o····o···
Galleons		—··—··—··—

Fagundes ∿∿∿∿∿∿∿

Verrazano -----·-----·-----

-1600

Case Map by Permission of Denoyer-Geppert Company, Chicago

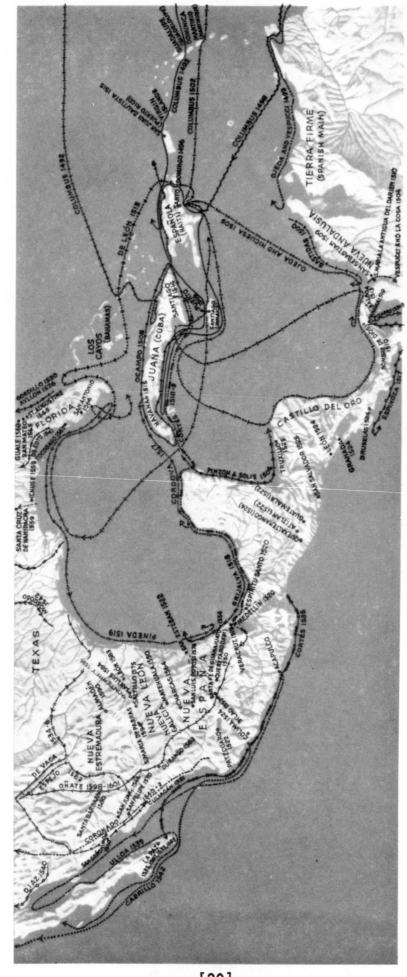

21 Spanish Exploration and Expansion in the Caribbean and Central America—1492-1600

Dates in parentheses are dates of capitulation of native towns to the Spanish conquerors. Dates without parentheses are dates of Spanish settlement

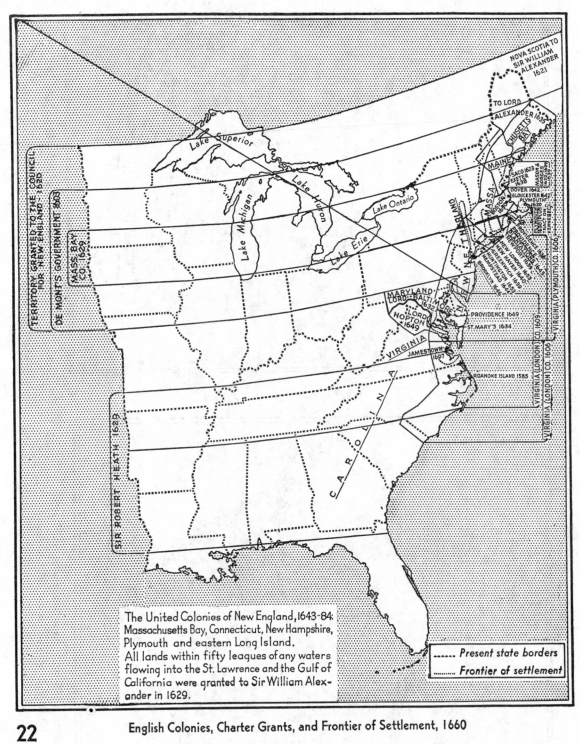

NOVA SCOTIA TO
SIR WILLIAM
ALEXANDER
1621

TO LORD
ALEXANDER 1635

Lake Superior

TERRITORY GRANTED TO THE COUNCIL
FOR NEW ENGLAND 1620

DE MONT'S GOVERNMENT 1603

MASS. BAY
CO. 1629

Lake Michigan

Lake Huron

Lake Ontario

Lake Erie

MAINE

CHUSETTS
BAY

SACO 1623
EXETER
1638
DOVER 1642
GLOUCESTER 1642
PLYMOUTH
1620

MASONS
GORGES
1629

KENNEBEC

NEW HAMPSHIRE

PLYMOUTH
PROVINCE 1621
KENNEBEC

PROVIDENCE 1636
NEW HAVEN 1638
HARTFORD 1635
WETHERSFIELD 1633
BROOKFIELD 1660

NEW NETHERLAND

MARYLAND
LORD BALTIMORE 1632

LORD
HOPTON
1649

PROVIDENCE 1649

ST. MARY'S 1634

VIRGINIA

JAMESTOWN
1607

VIRGINIA (PLYMOUTH) CO. 1606

VIRGINIA (LONDON) CO. 1609

VIRGINIA (LONDON) CO. 1606

ROANOKE ISLAND 1585

VIRGINIA (LONDON) CO. 1606

SIR ROBERT HEATH 1629

C A R O L I N A

The United Colonies of New England, 1643-84:
Massachusetts Bay, Connecticut, New Hampshire,
Plymouth and eastern Long Island.
All lands within fifty leagues of any waters
flowing into the St. Lawrence and the Gulf of
California were granted to Sir William Alex-
ander in 1629.

.... Present state borders
.... Frontier of settlement

22   English Colonies, Charter Grants, and Frontier of Settlement, 1660

[21]

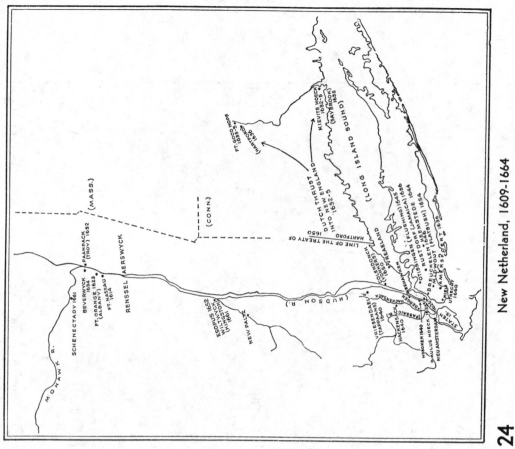

24 New Netherland, 1609-1664

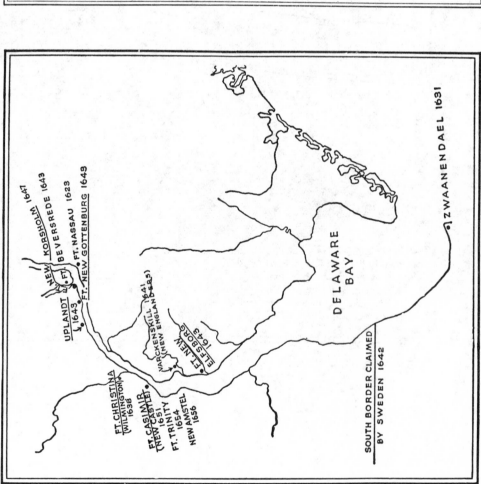

23 New Sweden, 1638-1655; New Netherland, 1655-1664
Names of Swedish settlements are underscored

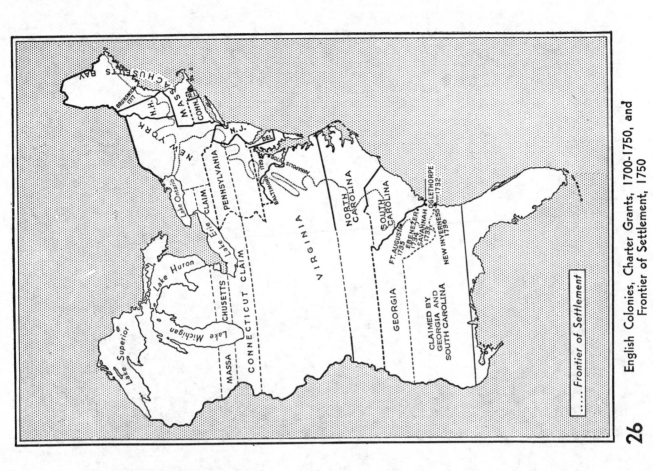

26 English Colonies, Charter Grants, 1700-1750, and
Frontier of Settlement, 1750

..... Frontier of Settlement

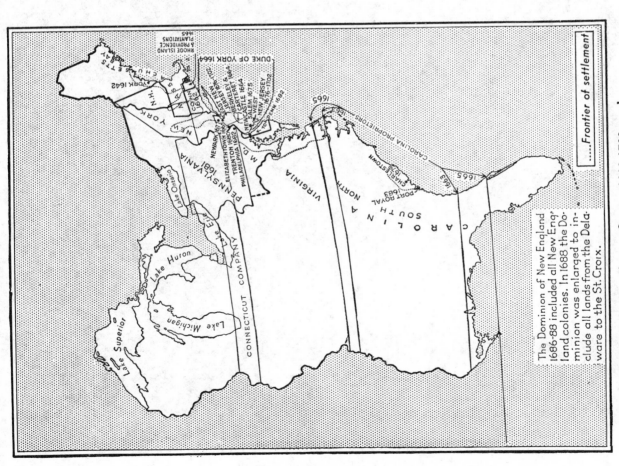

The Dominion of New England 1686-88 included all New England colonies. In 1688 the Dominion was enlarged to include all lands from the Delaware to the St. Croix.

..... Frontier of settlement

25 English Colonies, Charter Grants, 1660-1700, and
Frontier of Settlement, 1700

27   English Expansion to 1697

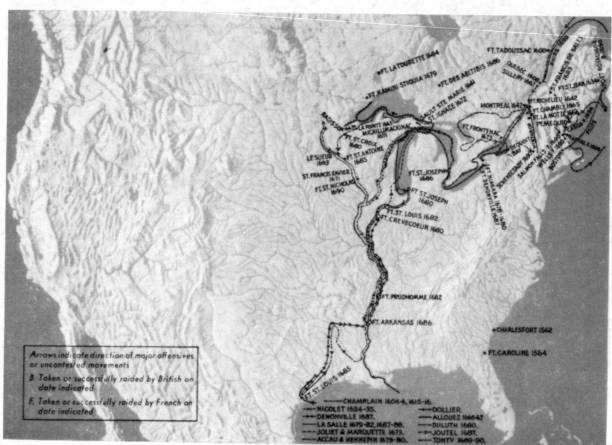

Arrows indicate direction of major offensives
or uncontested movements

B Taken or successfully raided by British on
date indicated

F Taken or successfully raided by French on
date indicated

CHAMPLAIN 1604-6, 1615-16.   DOLLIER.
NICOLET 1634-35.   ALLOUEZ 1666-67.
DENONVILLE 1687.   DULUTH 1680.
LA SALLE 1679-82, 1687-88.   JOUTEL 1687.
JOLIET & MARQUETTE 1673.   TONTY 1689-90.
ACCAU & HENNEPIN 1679-80.

28   French Expansion to 1697: American Campaigns of King William's War or the
War of the League of Augsburg

Dates approximate first settlement of sometimes ephemeral posts
For maps 27-34 the same base is used to show the relative positions of the French and the British

[24]

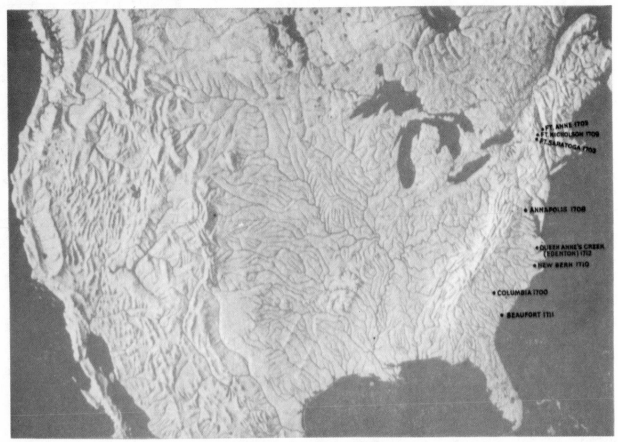

29   English Expansion, 1698-1713

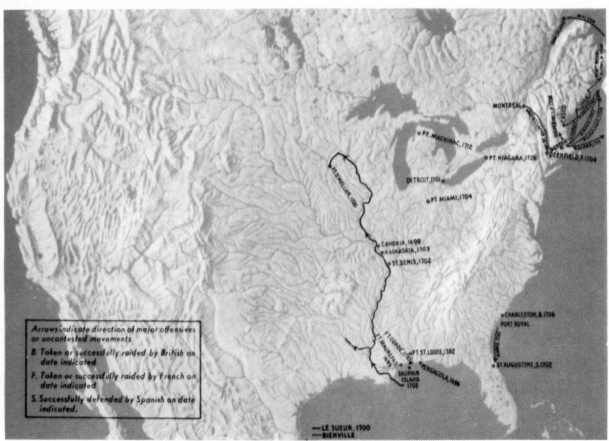

30   French Expansion, 1698-1713: American Campaigns of Queen Anne's War or the
War of the Spanish Succession
Dates approximate first settlement of sometimes ephemeral posts

31   English Expansion, 1714-1744

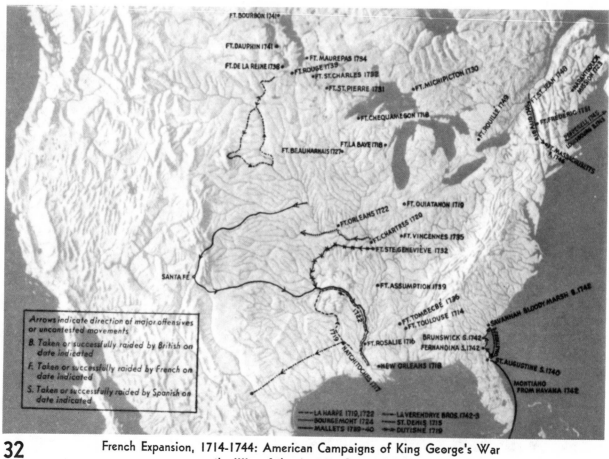

Arrows indicate direction of major offensives
or uncontested movements

B. Taken or successfully raided by British on
date indicated

F. Taken or successfully raided by French on
date indicated

S. Taken or successfully raided by Spanish on
date indicated

FT.BOURBON 1741
FT.DAUPHIN 1741
FT.DE LA REINE 1738
FT.ROUGE 1739
FT.MAUREPAS 1734
FT.ST.CHARLES 1732
FT.ST.PIERRE 1731
FT.MICHIPICTON 1730
FT.CHEQUAMEGON 1718
FT.LA BAYE 1718
FT.BEAUHARNAIS 1727
FT.OUIATANON 1719
FT.ORLEANS 1722
FT.CHARTRES 1720
FT.VINCENNES 1735
FT.STE.GENEVIÈVE 1732
SANTA FÉ
FT.ASSUMPTION 1739
FT.TOMBECBÉ 1736
FT.TOULOUSE 1714
FT.ROSALIE 1716
NATCHITOCHES 1717
NEW ORLEANS 1718
SAVANNAH BLOODY MARSH S.1742
BRUNSWICK S.1742
FERNANDINA S.1742
ST.AUGUSTINE S.1740
MONTIANO FROM HAVANA 1742

FT.ROUILLÉ 1749
FT.ST.JEAN 1748
FT.FREDERIC 1731
FORT MASSACHUSETTS

LA HARPE 1719, 1722   LA VERENDRYE BROS. 1742-3
BOURGEMONT 1724   ST. DENIS 1715
MALLETS 1739-40   DUTISNE 1719

32   French Expansion, 1714-1744: American Campaigns of King George's War
or the War of the Austrian Succession
Dates approximate first establishment of sometimes ephemeral posts

[26]

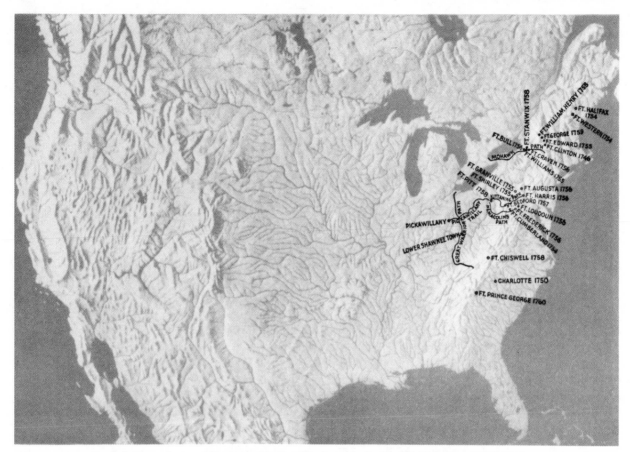

33   English Expansion and Routes of Indian Trade with the English Colonies, 1744-1763

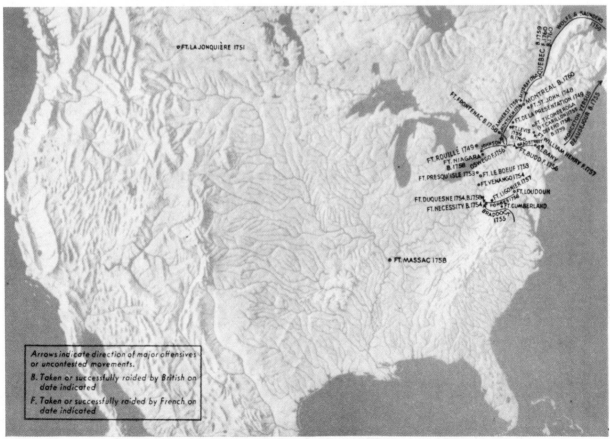

34   French Expansion, 1745-1763: American Campaigns of the French and Indian War, or
the Seven Years' War

Dates approximate first establishment of sometimes ephemeral posts

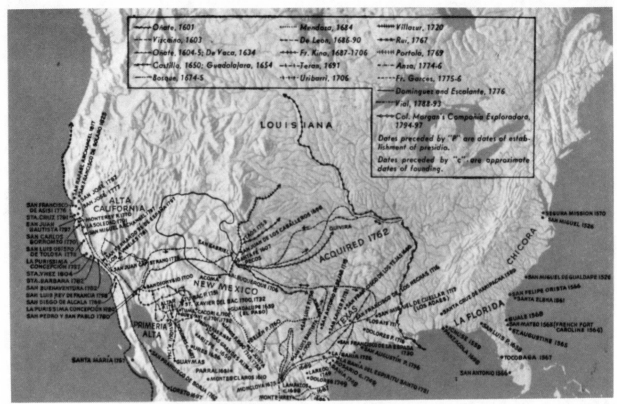

35 **Spanish Exploration and Expansion in and Near the Present Territorial Limits
of the United States, 1600-1823**
Dates approximate first Spanish settlements
(See also Maps 49-51 for Spanish military expeditions in this area during the Revolution)

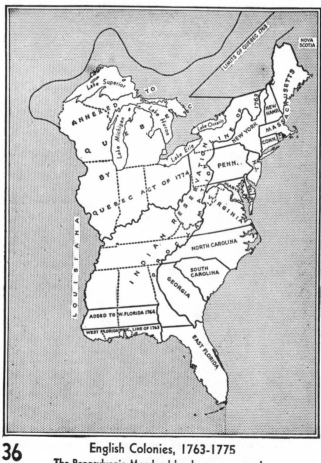

36 **English Colonies, 1763-1775**
The Pennsylvania-Maryland border was surveyed
by Mason and Dixon in 1767

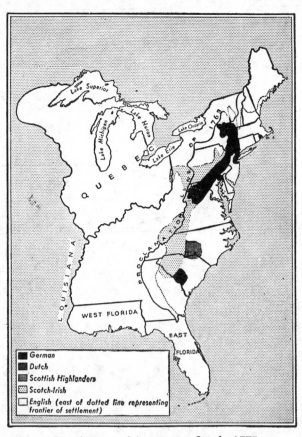

37 Distribution of Immigrant Stock, 1775

Legend:
- German
- Dutch
- Scottish Highlanders
- Scotch-Irish
- English (east of dotted line representing frontier of settlement)

38 Manufacturing Areas (Iron Works), 1775

39 Generalized Crop Areas, 1700

Legend:
- Grain
- Tobacco
- Cattle

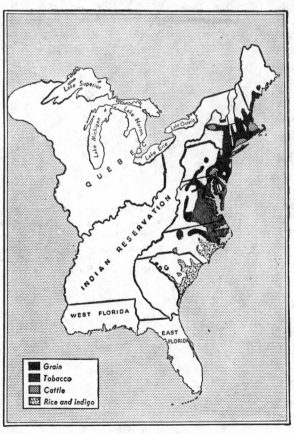

40 Generalized Crop Areas, 1775

Legend:
- Grain
- Tobacco
- Cattle
- Rice and indigo

Maps on this page give data only for the future Thirteen Original States

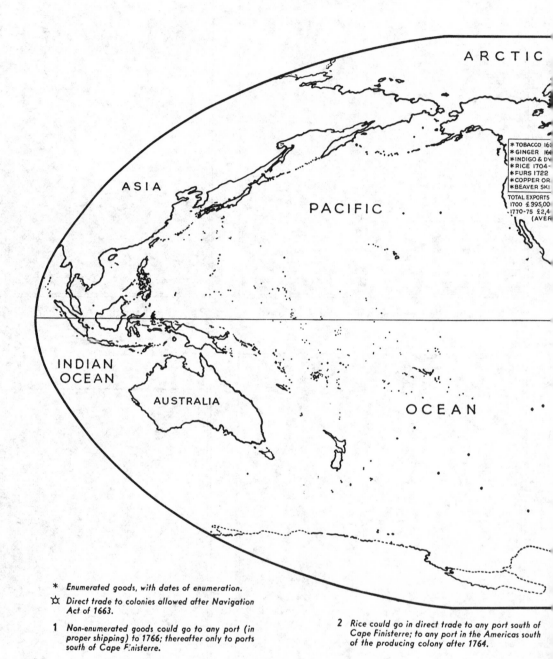

ARCTIC

ASIA

PACIFIC

INDIAN
OCEAN

AUSTRALIA

OCEAN

*   *Enumerated goods, with dates of enumeration.*

☆ *Direct trade to colonies allowed after Navigation Act of 1663.*

1 *Non-enumerated goods could go to any port (in proper shipping) to 1766; thereafter only to ports south of Cape Finisterre.*

2 *Rice could go in direct trade to any port south of Cape Finisterre; to any port in the Americas south of the producing colony after 1764.*

41

Colonia

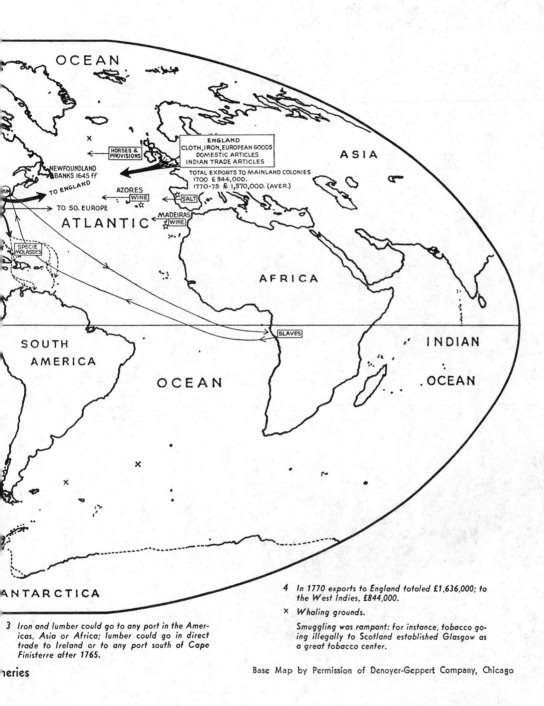

OCEAN

ASIA

×

ENGLAND
CLOTH, IRON, EUROPEAN GOODS
DOMESTIC ARTICLES
INDIAN TRADE ARTICLES

HORSES &
PROVISIONS

TOTAL EXPORTS TO MAINLAND COLONIES
1700 £344,000.
1770-75 £ 1,370,000. (AVER.)

NEWFOUNDLAND
BANKS 1645 ff

TO ENGLAND

AZORES
WINE

SALT

TO SO. EUROPE

ATLANTIC

MADEIRAS
WINE

SPECIE
MOLASSES

AFRICA

SLAVES

INDIAN

SOUTH
AMERICA

OCEAN

OCEAN

×

×

ANTARCTICA

4 In 1770 exports to England totaled £1,636,000; to
   the West Indies, £844,000.

× Whaling grounds.

Smuggling was rampant: for instance, tobacco go-
ing illegally to Scotland established Glasgow as
a great tobacco center.

3 Iron and lumber could go to any port in the Americas, Asia or Africa; lumber could go in direct
  trade to Ireland or to any port south of Cape
  Finisterre after 1765.

heries

Base Map by Permission of Denoyer-Geppert Company, Chicago

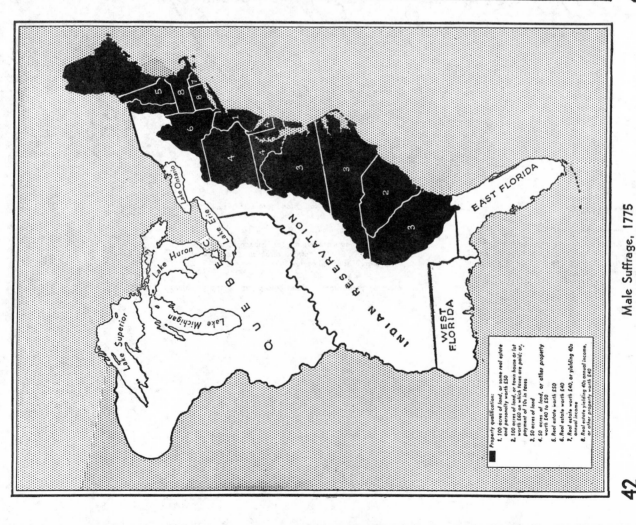

Male Suffrage, 1775

Maine had the same qualifications as Massachusetts; those for Vermont
were not yet fully established

This map gives data only for the future thirteen original states

Property qualification:

1. 100 acres of land, or some real estate
   and personally worth £50

2. 100 acres of land, or town house or lot
   worth £60 on which taxes are paid; or,
   payment of 10s in taxes

3. 50 acres of land

4. 50 acres of land, or other property
   worth £40 to £50

5. Real estate worth £50

6. Real estate worth £40

7. Real estate worth £40, or yielding 40s
   annual income

8. Real estate yielding 40s annual income,
   or other property worth £40

42

Colleges, 1775

Each dot, with date of charter, represents one college

43

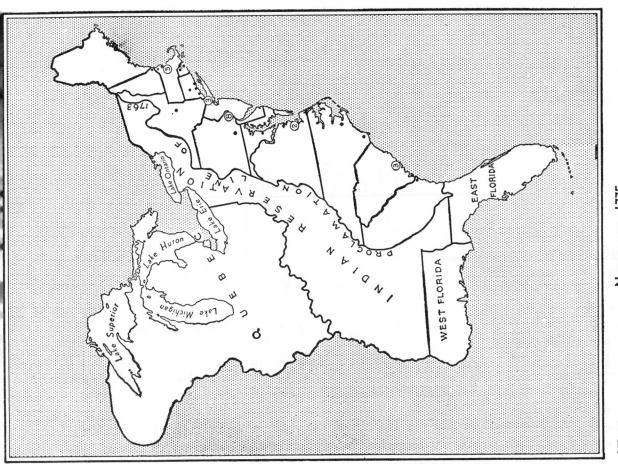

45 Newspapers, 1775

Each dot represents one paper. Circled numerals indicate number of newspapers in a given community

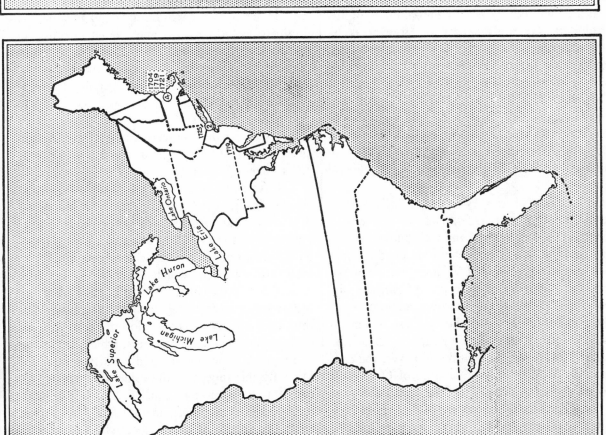

44 Newspapers, 1725

Each dot, with date of founding, represents one newspaper. Circled numerals indicate number of newspapers in a given community

Section III

1775-1865

The question of the West, including the vital problem of defense against the Indians and the corollary right of settlement along the ever mobile frontier, was to continue to absorb much of the interest and effort of the country for another hundred years after the achievement of independence. Important early developments were: (1) the removal of the legal restrictions imposed on westward migration by the Proclamation of 1763 and the "psychological" restrictions imposed by the Quebec Act of 1774; (2) the grants of huge tracts of "western" lands to the veterans of the Revolution; (3) the purchase of large areas by land companies from the Confederation Congresses; and (4) the cession by seven states of their western land claims to create the great public domain. This land, with the subsequent continental acquisitions, was to be split successively into territories whose governments were modeled closely on that of the original Northwest Territory and sold to private owners under unusually liberal terms.

Explorations of the West were followed by the migration of settlers, moving, on the whole, along certain well-marked and well-known routes. This movement, graphically visible on the population maps, precipitated friction with uneasy neighbors—with Spain over the delicate Mississippi Question; with England over sections of the Canadian border. It led to the purchase of Louisiana, the seizure of West Florida, the acquisition of East Florida, the annexation of Texas, the conflict with Mexico, and the division of Oregon. It also influenced America's entrance into the War of 1812. Perforce the expansion of the whites bred conflict with the Indian, whose territory rapidly diminished, as shown by the retreat of the line of Indian cession on the population maps.

With the advancing population marched not only the political organization of states and territories, but also the crops and manufactures by which the nation made its collective living. The growth of the West was also to contribute substantially to the democratization of the American experiment. This development may be partially studied in the maps showing the evolution of franchise qualifications from high property qualifications to universal white manhood suffrage before the Civil War. Extension of the suffrage brought marked changes to our political structure and system. It acted as a catalytic agent in making the "ferment" of the 1830's and 1840's effective in the drive for free public schools. It gave force to the various reform movements of abolition, prohibition, prison management and penology, education for the blind and the handicapped, and the peace and feminist crusades—the great social counterpart of the "flowering" of New England and the extraordinary literary, cultural and religious fluxes of the day.

The American economy underwent phenomenal changes in the period between the Revolution and the Civil War. Agriculture witnessed the preliminary phases of the so-called Agricultural Revolution, spurred by the rich markets for American farm products which developed during the period, and by the county fairs of Elkanah Watson. Industry moved from the domestic handicraft era, through the early mechanization of the textile industry, to the era of big business, which, beginning in the 1850's, advanced rapidly during the Civil War. By this time, too, the value of our manufactured products came to equal that of our agricultural goods. Favorable market conditions, the enormous supply of cheap labor which successive waves of immigration furnished, attractive investment possibilities, and the sudden advent of a national market through the spread of the transportation network, made possible this spectacular development. Banks, many of them wildcat institutions, grew proportionately, and already individual Americans were beginning to invest their capital outside the national borders—in Canada, Mexico and Cuba. Business and the development of the country were aided by the democratization of the mail system, whose rates were rapidly lowered until the act of 1851 established a basic first-class rate of three cents for the first 3,000 miles. The rapid expansion of the facilities of the postal system reached what seemed a climax in the 1850's with the establishment of the Overland Mail and the Pony Express, while mail contracts gave effective government subsidy successively to stage, canal, railroad, steamship—and later airplane—companies.

With the growth of the national economy came an enormous increase in trade with Europe, the overwhelming bulk of it being carried in the rapidly growing American merchant marine. Accurate figures on the non-English trade were perforce the product of independence and the end of the British mercantilistic restrictions. But independence brought its problems for our traders as well as its advantages. Removal of Empire preference, loss of the protection of the British navy (which was to lead to unofficial naval war with France in 1797-1800, to war with the Barbary states under Jefferson, and to war with England in 1812-14), and the trade wars with England culminating in the commercial treaties of 1816 and 1830, cost many individuals dearly. On the other hand, independence enabled us to capitalize on the trading opportunities presented by the Napoleonic Wars, to enter the Oriental trade in 1784 in competition with the powerful East India Company, and to lay the foundations for the greatest period of our merchant marine—and for nearly a hundred years of friction with England in worldwide commercial rivalry.

The phenomenal growth of free public schools and private academies was partially reflected in the growth of the college facilities of the country, while the number of newspapers and the advent of the penny press symbolized the everspreading power of an expanding press.

Our worldwide commerce, the desires of some national figures to balance the growing power of the North by southward expansion into areas where slavery would be possible and profitable, and the efforts of other leaders to escape the impending conflict by a vigorous policy of expansion, produced the era of Manifest Destiny. This concept was ideologically reinforced by a deep-rooted American belief, present throughout our history, in a national mission to "expand the areas of freedom," as Andrew Jackson phrased it—an idea which received much encouragement from the French Revolution, the achievement of Latin American independence, the liberal revolts of 1848 in Europe, the Texan Revolution and the revolts of Papineau and Mackenzie in Canada. The scenes of our commercial and physical expansion during this period constitute one of the most revealing maps of the entire period.

But throughout the thirty years between the appearance of the *Liberator*, the rebellion of Nat Turner, and the firing on Fort Sumter, the increasingly ominous clouds of civil strife more and more obscured the less dramatic outlines of our history. The appearance of a southern cultural nationalism buttressed the rise of a southern economic nationalism, which increasingly manifested itself in debates over expansion, the tariff, slavery in the territories, land policy, railroad construction and subsidy, the role of Yankee capital, and shipping. Through attempts to foster southern enterprise, the series of trade conventions which marked the decades of the forties and fifties vividly emphasized the growing economic, social, and political cleavage of the sections. The conflict was to culminate in secession and four years of the costliest, bloodiest, and bitterest fighting the world had seen up to that time. Yet it is interesting to note the opposition to secession in the South itself prior to Lincoln's call for volunteers, and the relationship of that opposition to the number of slaves per slaveholder and the proportion of slaves to the total population of the South, county by county.

The issue of the war was not to be decided exclusively on the field of battle, but rather in the inner councils of the Republican party, and in the prolonged and bitter struggle between the Reconstructionists (the Radical Republicans) and the Restorationists (Democrats and Conservative Republicans). That struggle, and the predominance of Republican counsel favoring the combination of northern big business and western farming, was greatly to influence the development of the country in the succeeding sixty-five years.

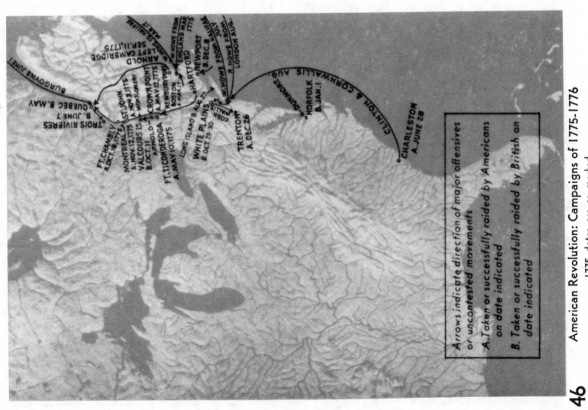

47 American Revolution: Campaigns of 1777

Arrows indicate direction of major offensives or uncontested movements
A. Taken or successfully raided by Americans on date indicated
B. Taken or successfully raided by British on date indicated
Evac. Taken after evacuation by the enemy

46 American Revolution: Campaigns of 1775-1776
1775 dates are so marked

Arrows indicate direction of major offensives or uncontested movements
A. Taken or successfully raided by Americans on date indicated
B. Taken or successfully raided by British on date indicated

[37]

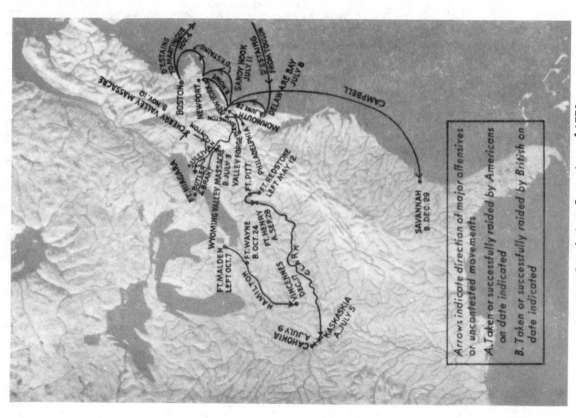

Arrows indicate direction of major offensives
or uncontested movements

A. Taken or successfully raided by Americans
on date indicated

B. Taken, defended or successfully raided
by British on date indicated

Evac. Taken after evacuation by the enemy

S. Taken or successfully raided by Spanish on
date indicated

1. PICKENS
2. LINCOLN
3. ASHE
4. CAMPBELL
5. PREVOST
6. MOULTRIE (JAN) LINCOLN (SEP)

49   American Revolution: Campaigns of 1779

Arrows indicate direction of major offensives
or uncontested movements

A. Taken or successfully raided by Americans
on date indicated

B. Taken or successfully raided by British on
date indicated

48   American Revolution: Campaigns of 1778

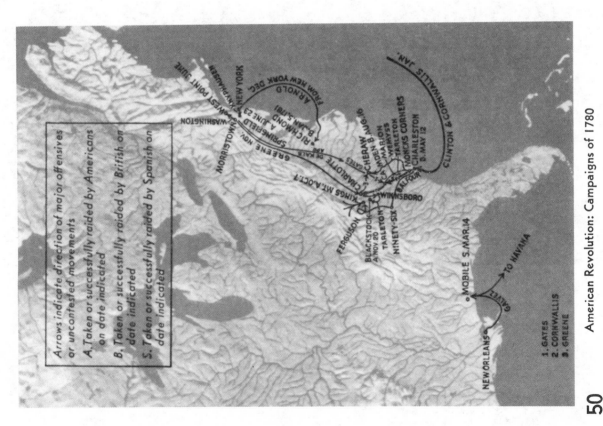

Arrows indicate direction of major offensives,
or uncontested movements

A. Taken or successfully raided by Americans
on date indicated

B. Taken or successfully raided by British on
date indicated

Evac. Taken after evacuation by the enemy

S. Taken or successfully raided by Spanish on
date indicated

American Revolution: Campaigns of 1781

51

Arrows indicate direction of major offensives,
or uncontested movements

A. Taken or successfully raided by Americans
on date indicated

B. Taken or successfully raided by British on
date indicated

S. Taken or successfully raided by Spanish on
date indicated

1. GATES
2. CORNWALLIS
3. GREENE

American Revolution: Campaigns of 1780

50

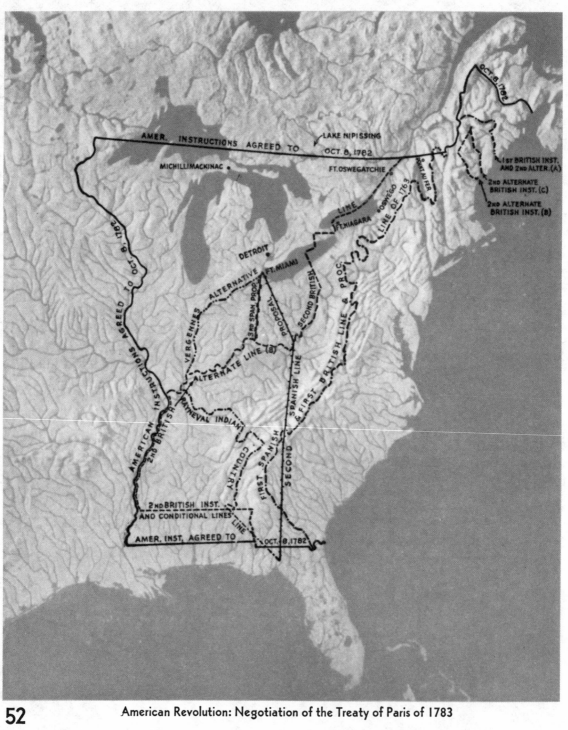

52   American Revolution: Negotiation of the Treaty of Paris of 1783

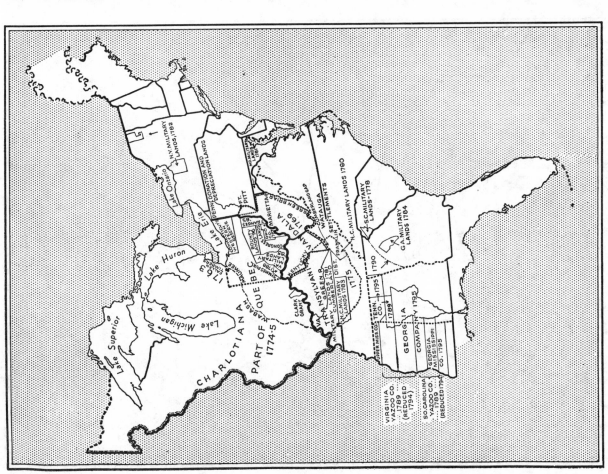

54 Creation of the National Domain: Cessions by New York of Western Land Claims and Relinquishment of the Claim to Vermont

(See Maps 25-26)

53 Western Lands, 1763-1795

(See Maps 25-26)

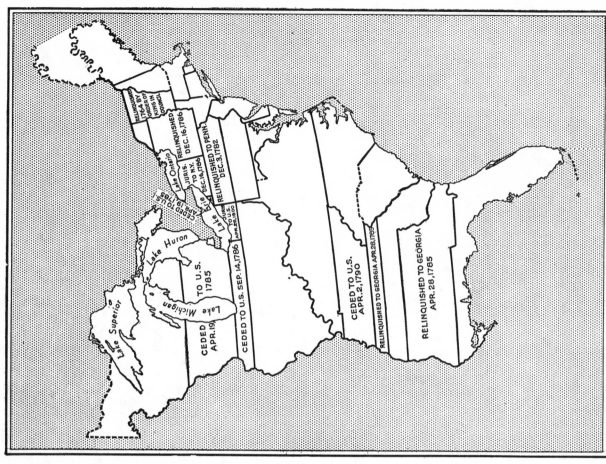

56 Creation of the National Domain: Cessions by New Hampshire, Massachusetts, Connecticut, North Carolina, and South Carolina of Western

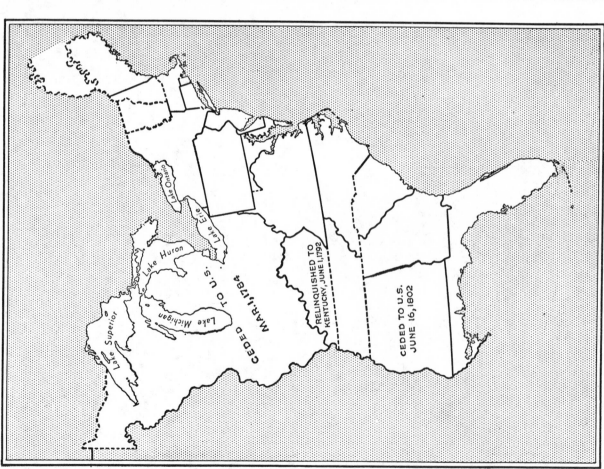

55 Creation of the National Domain: Cessions by Virginia and Georgia of Western Land Claims

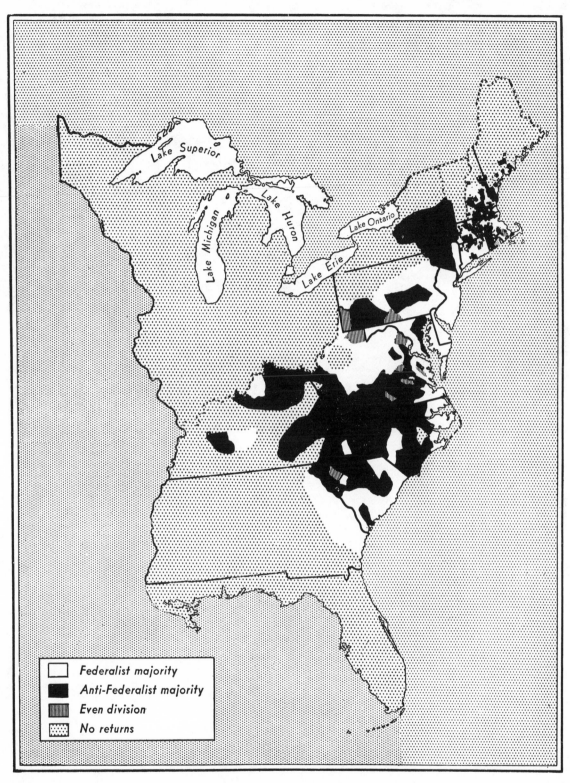

57   Ratification of the Constitution

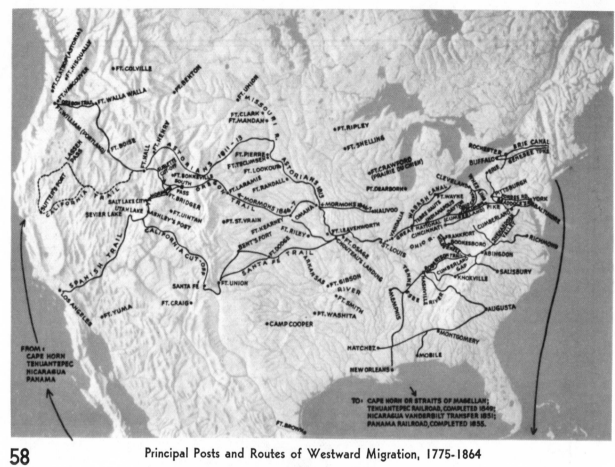

58   Principal Posts and Routes of Westward Migration, 1775-1864

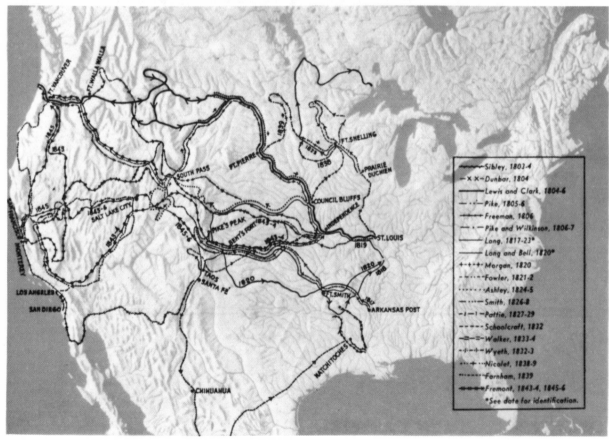

59   American Explorations of the West, 1803-1846

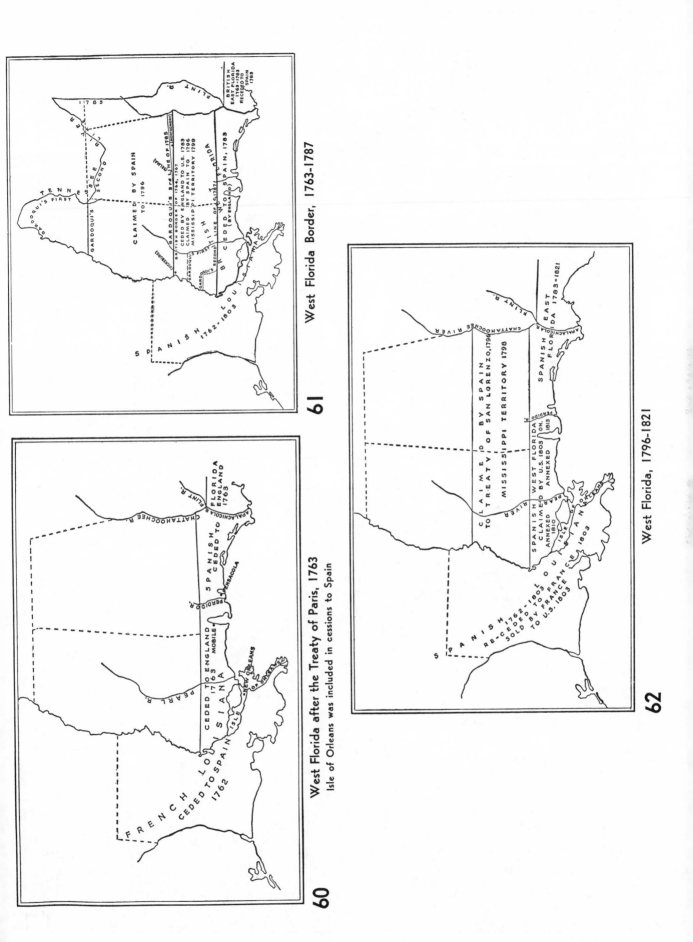

60 West Florida after the Treaty of Paris, 1763

Isle of Orleans was included in cessions to Spain

61 West Florida Border, 1763-1787

62 West Florida, 1796-1821

[45]

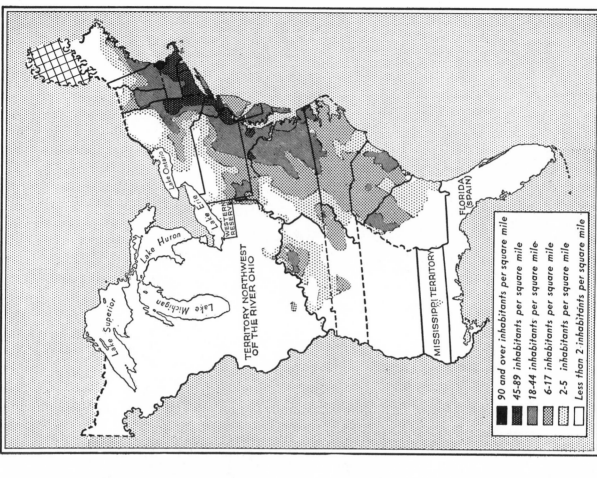

64 Population Density, 1800

Legend (map 64):
- 90 and over inhabitants per square mile
- 45-89 inhabitants per square mile
- 18-44 inhabitants per square mile-
- 6-17 inhabitants per square mile
- 2-5 inhabitants per square mile
- Less than 2 inhabitants per square mile

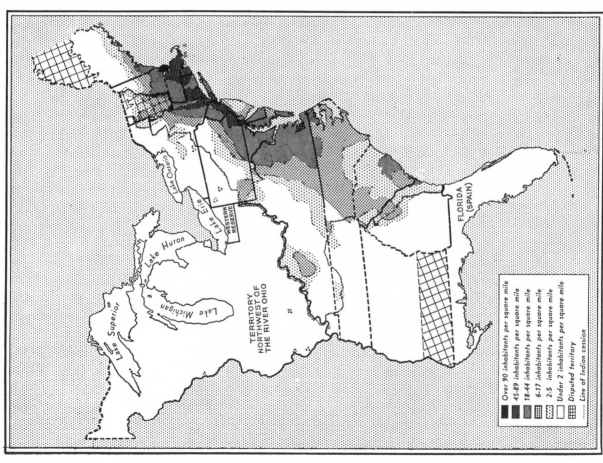

63 Population Density, 1790; Line of Indian Cessions, 1783

Legend (map 63):
- Over 90 inhabitants per square mile
- 45-89 inhabitants per square mile
- 18-44 inhabitants per square mile
- 6-17 inhabitants per square mile;
- 2-5 inhabitants per square mile
- Under 2 inhabitants per square mile
- Disputed territory
- Line of Indian cession

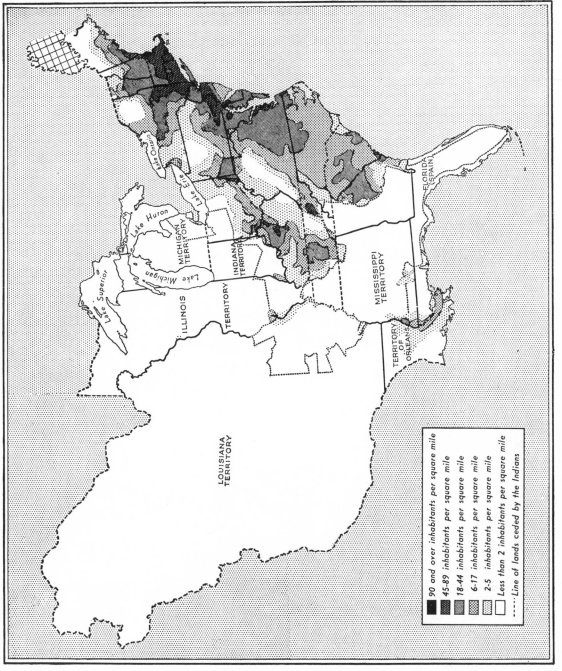

Population Density, Line of Indian Cessions, 1810

65

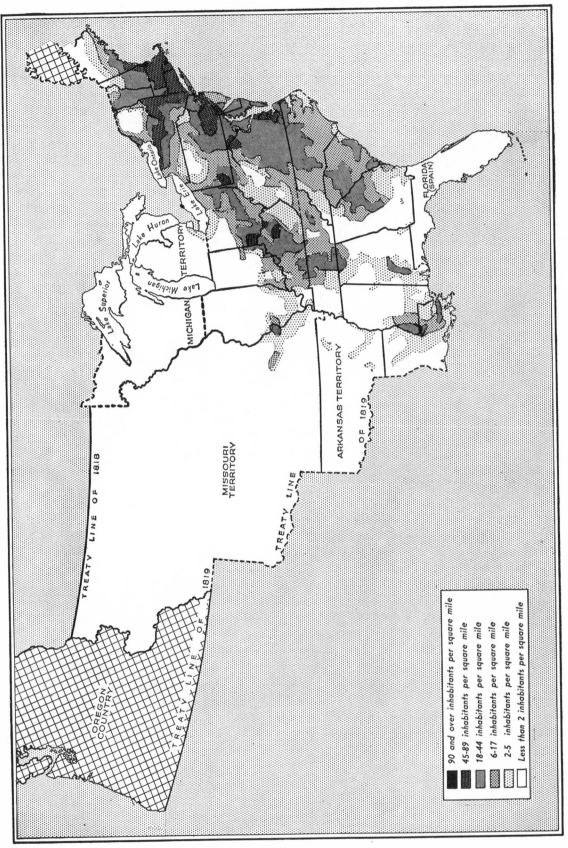

Population Density, 1820

90 and over inhabitants per square mile
45-89 inhabitants per square mile
18-44 inhabitants per square mile
6-17 inhabitants per square mile
2-5 inhabitants per square mile
Less than 2 inhabitants per square mile

OREGON COUNTRY

MISSOURI TERRITORY

MICHIGAN TERRITORY

ARKANSAS TERRITORY OF 1819

FLORIDA (SPAIN)

Lake Superior
Lake Michigan
Lake Huron
Lake Erie
Lake Ontario

TREATY LINE OF 1818

TREATY LINE

TREATY LINE OF 1819

66

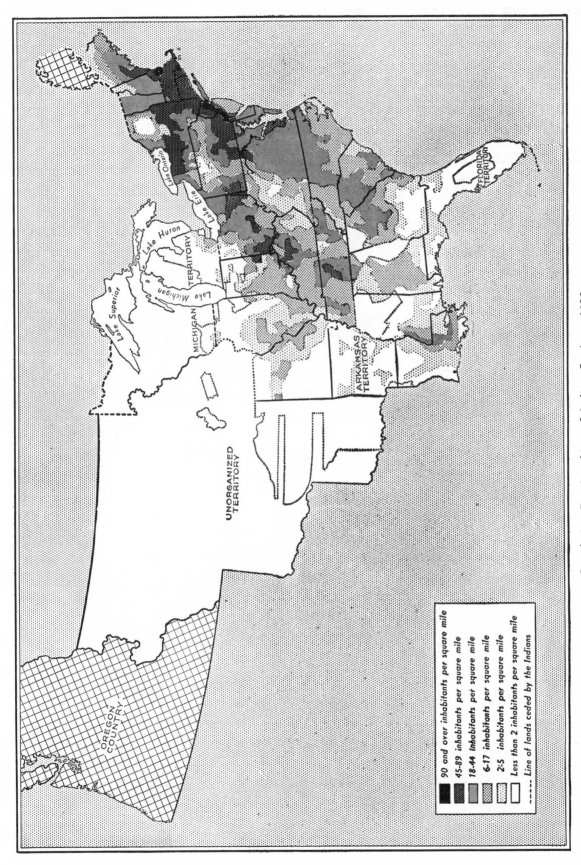

Population Density, Line of Indian Cessions, 1830

90 and over inhabitants per square mile
45-89 inhabitants per square mile
18-44 inhabitants per square mile
6-17 inhabitants per square mile
2-5 inhabitants per square mile
Less than 2 inhabitants per square mile
Line of lands ceded by the Indians

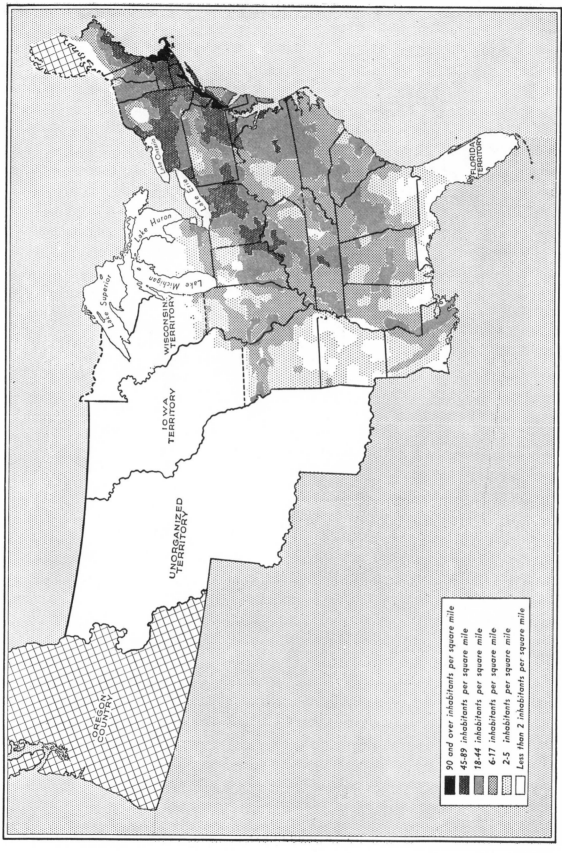

Population Density, 1840

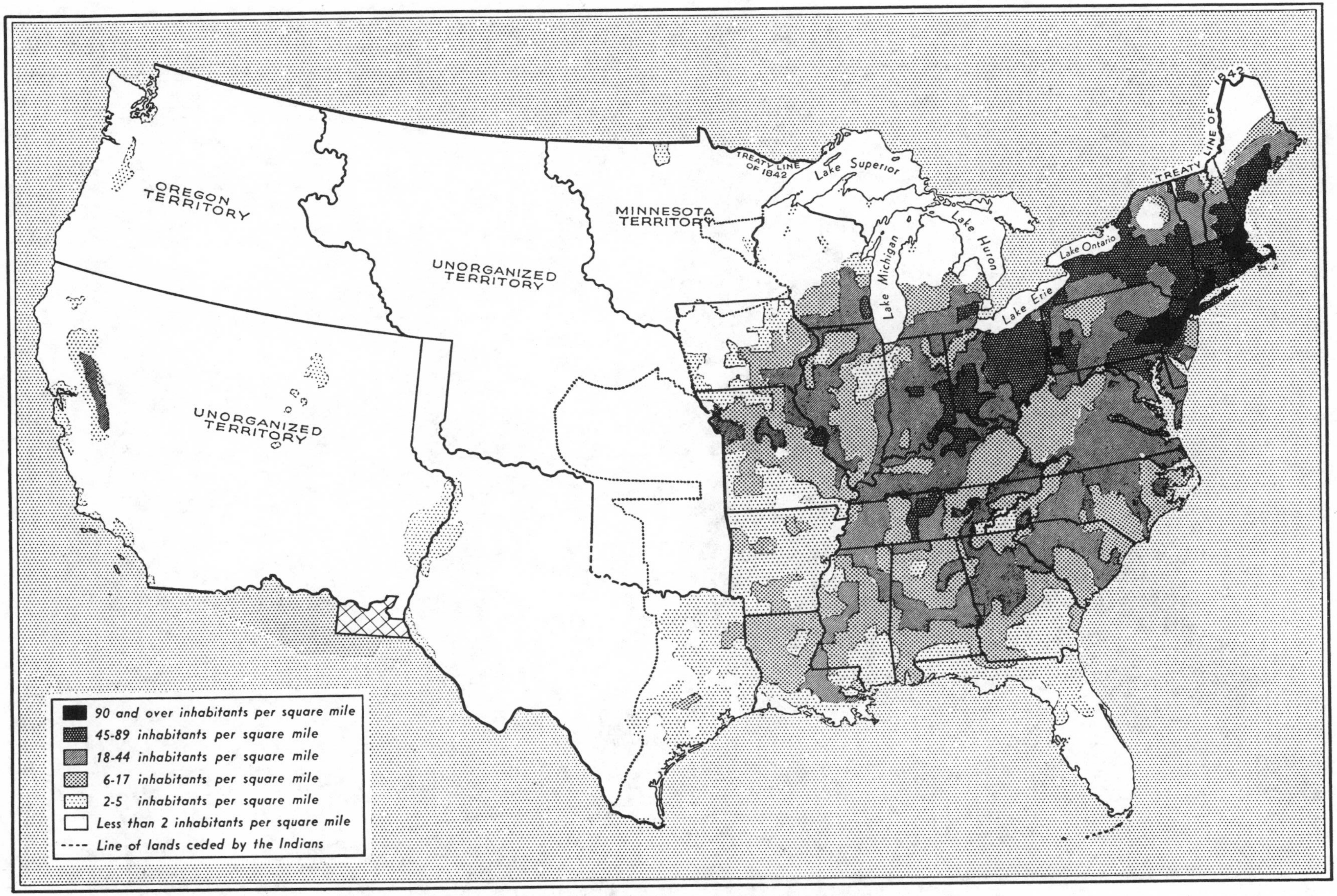

Population Density, Line of Indian Cessions, 1850

Legend:

- 90 and over inhabitants per square mile
- 45-89 inhabitants per square mile
- 18-44 inhabitants per square mile
- 6-17 inhabitants per square mile
- 2-5 inhabitants per square mile
- Less than 2 inhabitants per square mile
- --- Line of lands ceded by the Indians

OREGON TERRITORY

UNORGANIZED TERRITORY

UNORGANIZED TERRITORY

MINNESOTA TERRITORY

TREATY LINE OF 1842

LINE OF 1842 TREATY

Lake Superior

Lake Michigan

Lake Huron

Lake Erie

Lake Ontario

69

[51]

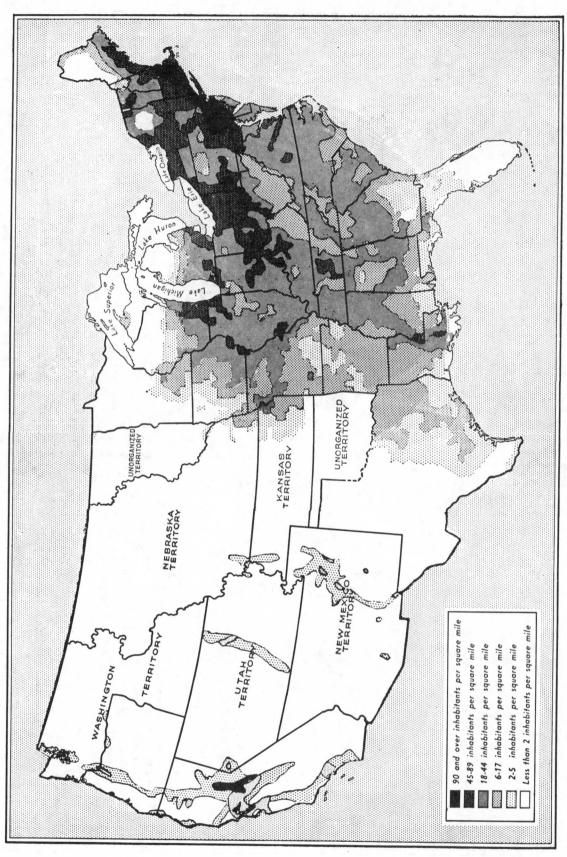

Population Density, 1860

70

Oregon Border Dispute, 1826-1872

72

Lake Superior-Rainy Lake Border Dispute, 1826-1842

73

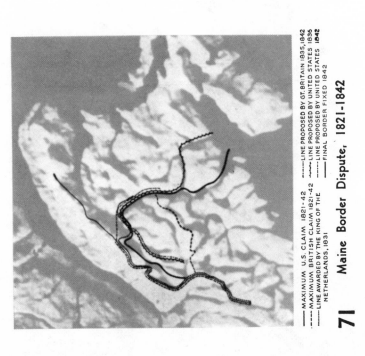

MAXIMUM U.S. CLAIM 1821-42 ———— LINE PROPOSED BY GT. BRITAIN 1835, 1842
MAXIMUM BRITISH CLAIM 1821-42 ———— LINE PROPOSED BY UNITED STATES 1836
LINE AWARDED BY THE KING OF THE ———— LINE PROPOSED BY UNITED STATES 1842
NETHERLANDS, 1831 ———— FINAL BORDER FIXED 1842

71 Maine Border Dispute, 1821-1842

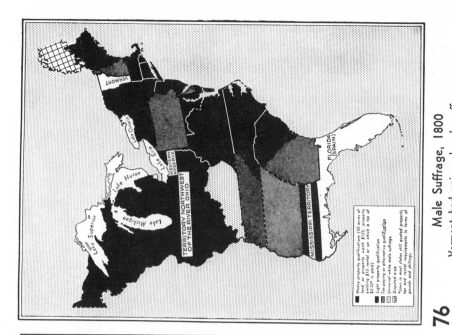

Male Suffrage, 1800
Vermont had universal male suffrage

76

Heavy property qualification (50 acres of
land or property worth $125; property
yielding $10 rental or on which a tax of
$1.50* is paid)

Light property qualification

Tax-paying or alternative qualification

Universal white male suffrage

Disputed area

*Laws in most states still quoted property
tax and rental requirements in terms of
pounds and shillings.

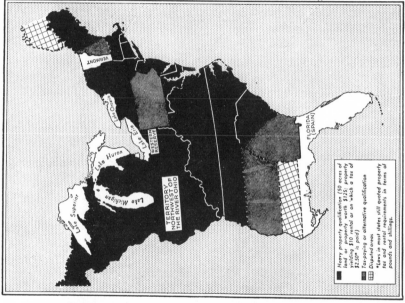

Male Suffrage, 1790
Vermont had universal male suffrage

75

Heavy property qualification (50 acres of
land or property worth $125; property
yielding $10 rental or on which a tax of
$2.50* is paid)

Tax-paying or alternative qualification

Disputed areas

*Laws in most states still quoted property
tax and rental requirements in terms of
pounds and shillings.

Male Suffrage, 1780

74

Heavy property qualification (50 acres of
land or property worth $125; property
yielding $10 rental, or on which a tax of
$2.50 is paid)*

Tax-paying or alternative qualification

Disputed area

*Laws in most states still quoted property
tax and rental requirements in terms of
pounds and shillings.

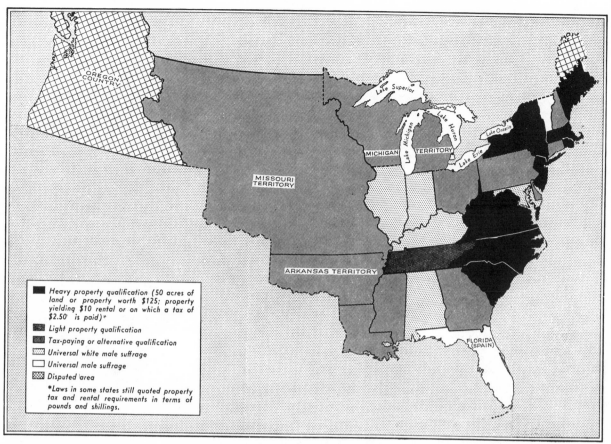

77   Male Suffrage, 1820

78   Male Suffrage, 1830

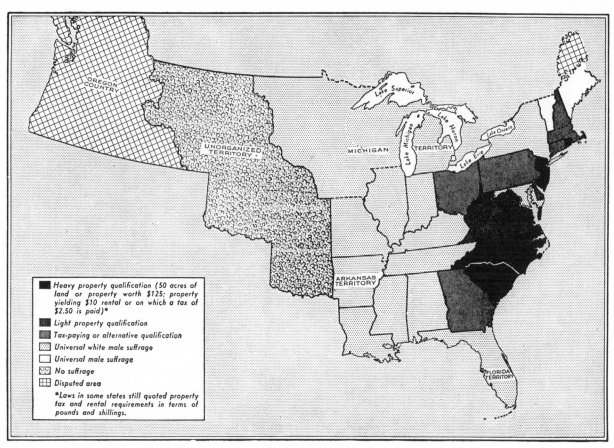

79   Male Suffrage, 1840

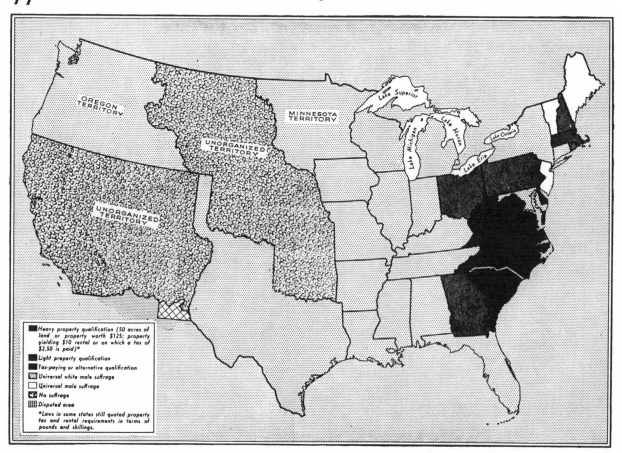

80   Male Suffrage, 1850

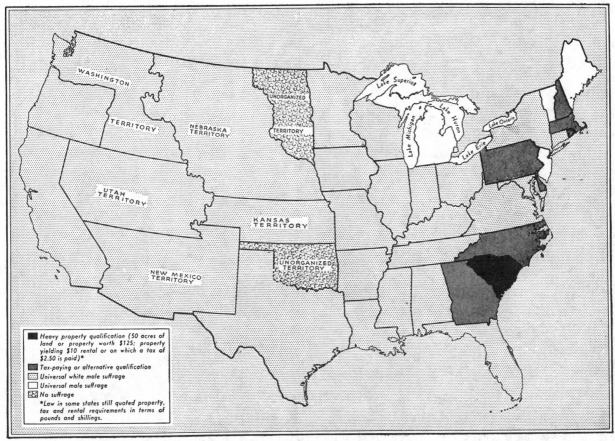

Heavy property qualification (50 acres of land or property worth $125; property yielding $10 rental or on which a tax of $2.50 is paid)*
Tax-paying or alternative qualification
Universal white male suffrage
Universal male suffrage
No suffrage
*Law in some states still quoted property, tax and rental requirements in terms of pounds and shillings.

Male Suffrage, 1860

81

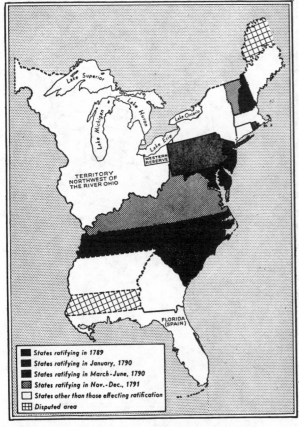

States ratifying in 1789
States ratifying in January, 1790
States ratifying in March-June, 1790
States ratifying in Nov.-Dec., 1791
States other than those effecting ratification
Disputed area

82 States Effecting the Ratification of the First Ten Amendments to the Constitution, 1791

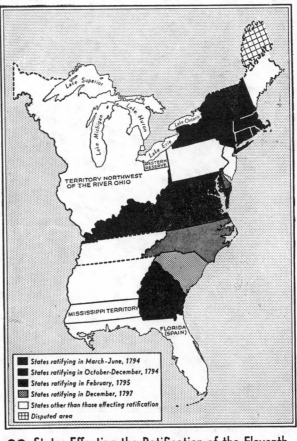

States ratifying in March-June, 1794
States ratifying in October-December, 1794
States ratifying in February, 1795
States ratifying in December, 1797
States other than those effecting ratification
Disputed area

83 States Effecting the Ratification of the Eleventh Amendment to the Constitution, 1798

[57]

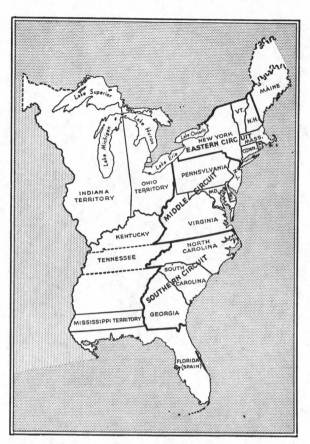

84 Organization of the Federal Circuit and District Courts by Act of September 24, 1789

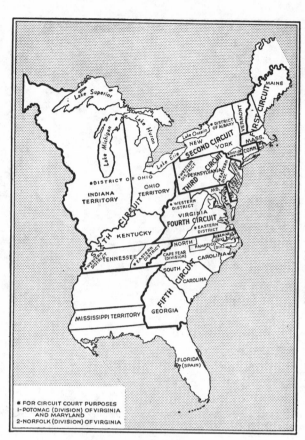

85 Federal Circuit and District Courts, 1801

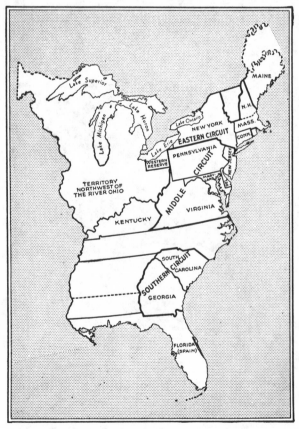

86 Organization of the Federal Circuit and District Courts by Act of March 8, 1802

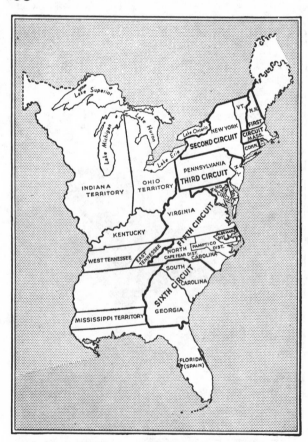

87 Federal Circuit and District Courts, 1802

In maps on this page circuit court borders are marked by heavy lines; district court borders by medium lines; division borders by light lines

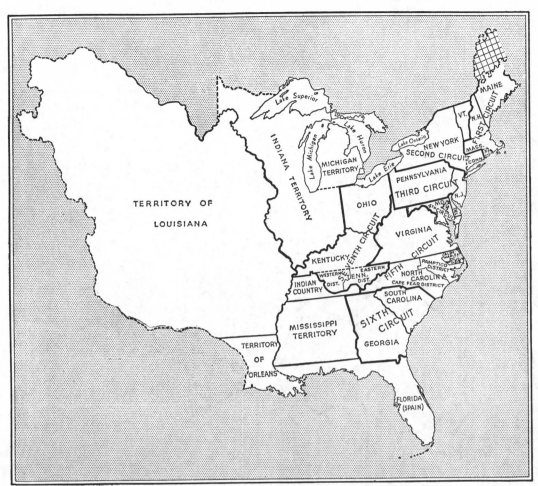

88 Federal Circuit and District Courts, 1807

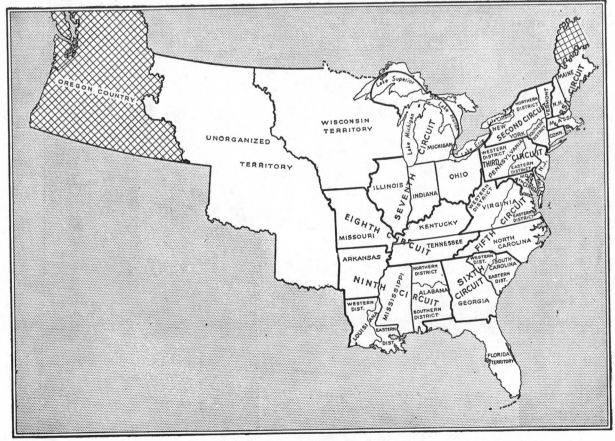

89 **Federal Circuit and District Courts, 1837**
In maps on this page circuit court borders are marked by heavy lines; district court borders by medium lines

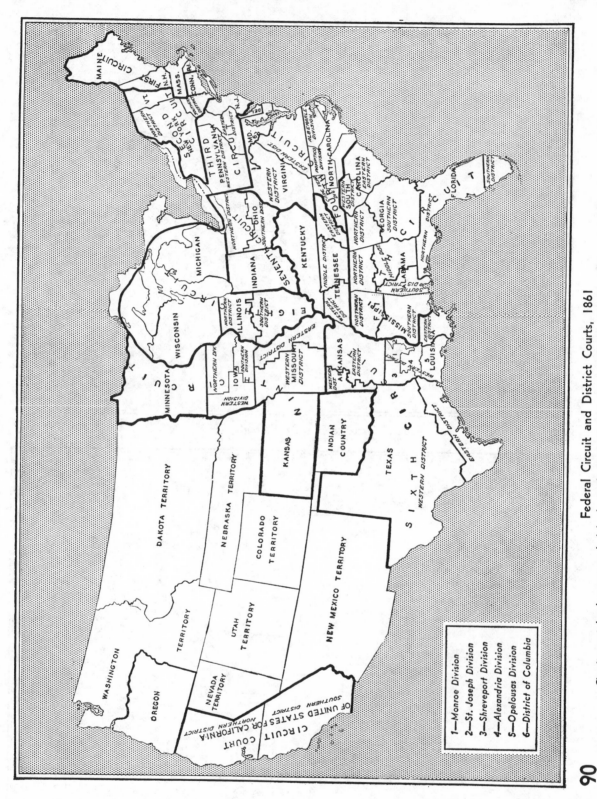

Federal Circuit and District Courts, 1861

Circuit court borders are marked by heavy lines; division borders by medium lines; district court borders by light lines.

1—Monroe Division
2—St. Joseph Division
3—Shreveport Division
4—Alexandria Division
5—Opelousas Division
6—District of Columbia

90

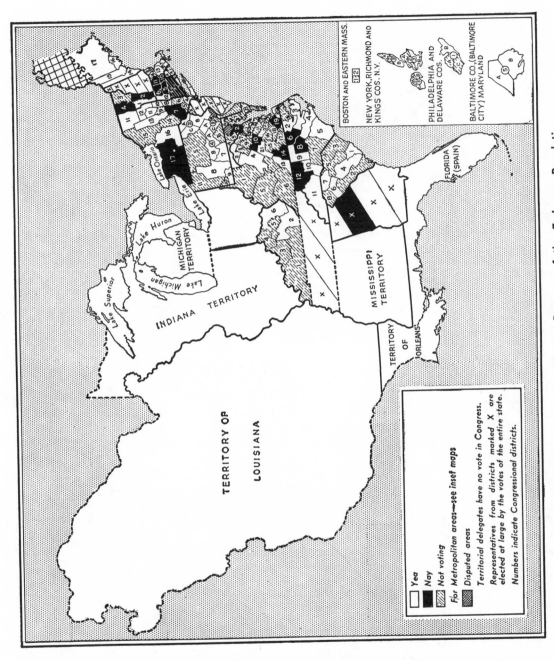

91

House Vote of January 2, 1808, on Passage of the Embargo Resolution

In cases where a number is repeated in the same state, it indicates two parts of the same district

Legend:
- Yea
- Nay
- Not voting
- For Metropolitan areas—see inset maps
- Disputed areas

Territorial delegates have no vote in Congress. Representatives from districts marked X are elected at large by the votes of the entire state. Numbers indicate Congressional districts.

Inset maps:
- BOSTON AND EASTERN MASS.
- NEW YORK, RICHMOND AND KINGS COS. N.Y.
- PHILADELPHIA AND DELAWARE COS.
- BALTIMORE CO.,(BALTIMORE CITY) MARYLAND

TERRITORY OF LOUISIANA

INDIANA TERRITORY

MICHIGAN TERRITORY

MISSISSIPPI TERRITORY

TERRITORY OF ORLEANS

FLORIDA (SPAIN)

Lake Superior

Lake Huron

Lake Michigan

Lake Erie

Lake Ontario

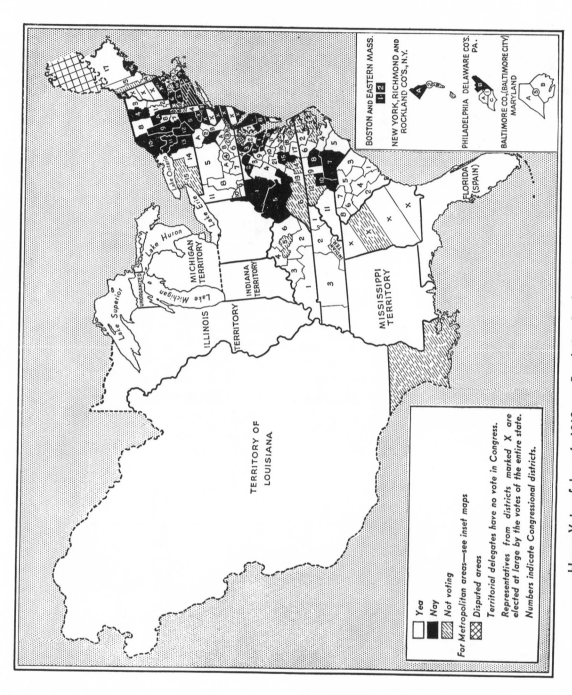

92 House Vote of June 4, 1812, on Resolution Declaring War on Great Britain

In cases where a number appears twice in the same state, it indicates two geographically separated parts of the same congressional district

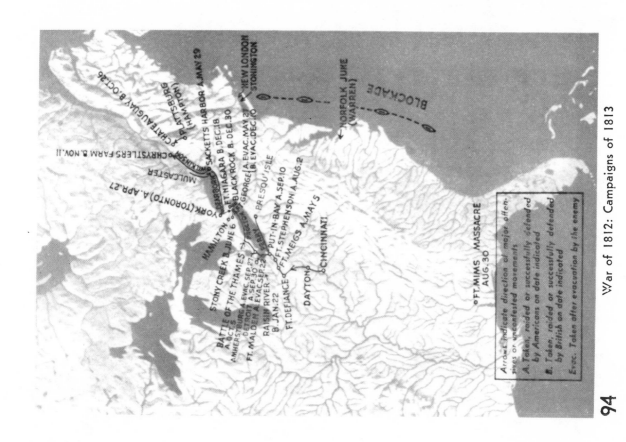

War of 1812: Campaigns of 1813

Arrows indicate direction of major offensives or uncontested movements

A. Taken, raided or successfully defended by Americans on date indicated

B. Taken, raided or successfully defended by British on date indicated

Evac. Taken after evacuation by the enemy

94

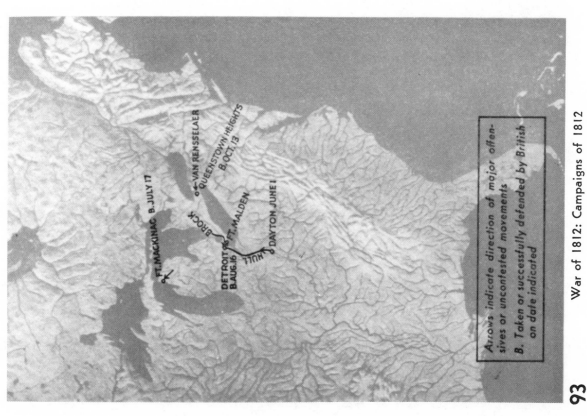

War of 1812: Campaigns of 1812

Arrows indicate direction of major offensives or uncontested movements

B. Taken or successfully defended by British on date indicated

93

95

EASTERN MAINE HELD BY BRITISH

BANGOR HAMPDEN
BELFAST
GLOUCESTER
PLATTSBURG SCITUATE
PREVOST & A.SEP.11 MARSHFIELD
DOWNIE BOSTON PLYMOUTH
NEW BEDFORD
MONTREAL STONINGTON B.AUG.12
BROWN-WILKINSON NEW LONDON

LUNDY'S LANE CHIPPEWA A.JULY 5
A.JULY 15 ERIE BUFFALO
FT.JUN 3
B.AUG.21
A.SEP.21

HAVRE DE GRACE
FREDERICKTON

FT.McHENRY
BALTIMORE NORFOLK ROSS AND
A.SEP.13 COCKBURN
WASHINGTON
B.AUG.25
ALEXANDRIA
B.AUG.28

TO PACKENHAM AT JAMAICA

BLOCKADE

HUNTSVILLE
HORSESHOE BEND A.MAR.27
FT.JACKSON APR.1B FT.SCOTT A.MAR.9,1818
ST.MARKS A.APR.17,1818
SUWANEE RIVER A.APR.17,1818
FT.GADSDEN A.MAR.16,1818
MOBILE
PENSACOLA A.NOV.7,1814,MAY 24,1918
LAKE BORGNE B.DEC.14 NICHOLLS
PACKENHAM FROM JAMAICA
NEW ORLEANS
A.DEC.14 FT.ST.PHILLIP
JAN.8,1815 A.JAN.18,1815

VETERANS BOUNTY LANDS
VETERANS BOUNTY LANDS

Arrows indicate direction of major offensives or
uncontested movements

A. Taken or successfully raided by Americans on
date indicated

B. Taken or successfully raided by British on date
indicated

----- Borders of Federal bounty lands for veterans

War of 1812: Campaigns of 1814; Jackson's Florida Expedition of 1818

[64]

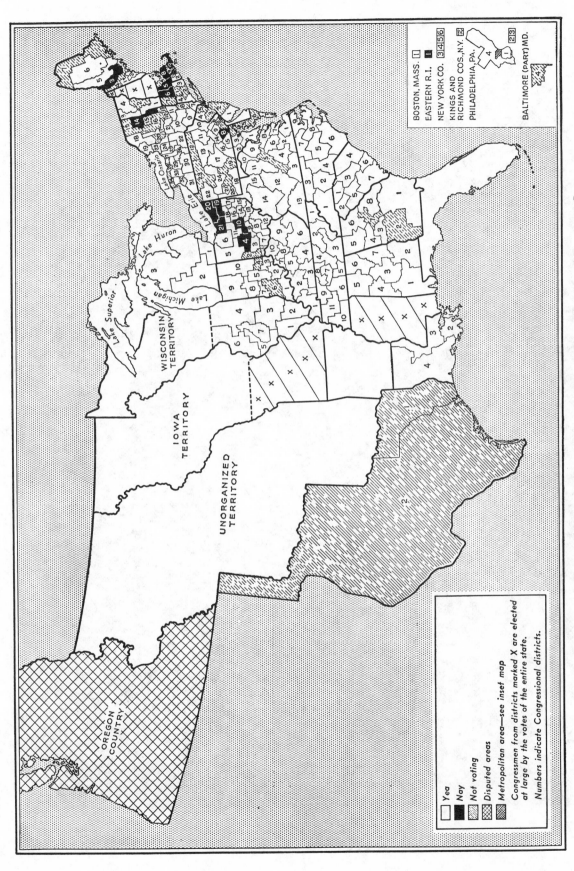

BOSTON, MASS. ☐
EASTERN R.I. ■
NEW YORK CO. ③④⑤⑥
KINGS AND
RICHMOND COS., N.Y. ⑫
PHILADELPHIA, PA.
BALTIMORE (PART) MD.

Lake Superior
Lake Michigan
Lake Huron
Lake Erie
Lake Ontario

WISCONSIN TERRITORY

IOWA TERRITORY

UNORGANIZED TERRITORY

OREGON COUNTRY X

Yea
Nay
Not voting
Disputed areas
Metropolitan area—see inset map

Congressmen from districts marked X are elected at large by the votes of the entire state.
Numbers indicate Congressional districts.

96   House Vote of May 11, 1846, Authorizing the President to Use Military and Naval Forces to Prosecute the Existing War with Mexico

[65]

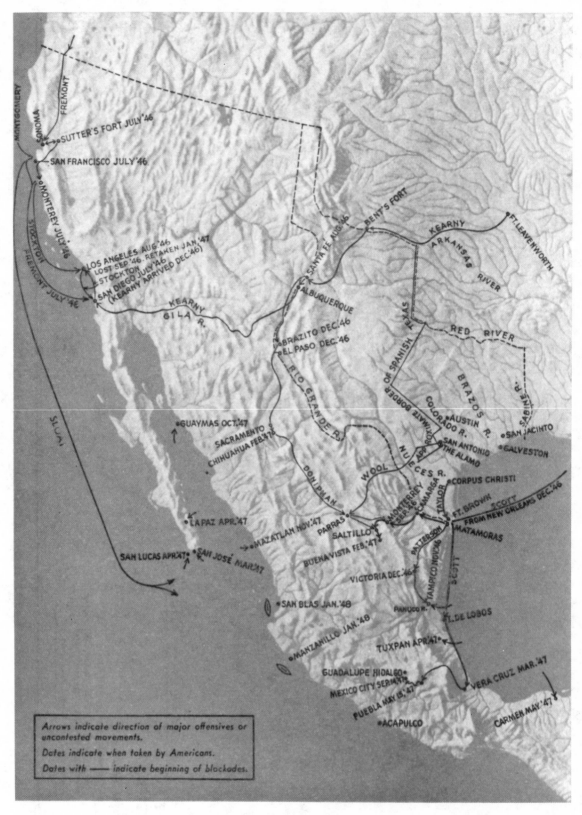

MONTGOMERY

FREMONT

SONOMA

SUTTER'S FORT JULY '46

SAN FRANCISCO JULY '46

STOCKTON

MONTEREY JULY '46

FREMONT JULY '46

LOS ANGELES AUG. '46
LOST SEP. '46. RETAKEN JAN. '47
STOCKTON JULY '46
SAN DIEGO JULY '46
(KEARNY ARRIVED DEC. '46)

SANTA FE AUG. '46

BENT'S FORT

KEARNY

ARKANSAS RIVER

FT. LEAVENWORTH

KEARNY

GILA R.

ALBUQUERQUE

BRAZITO DEC. '46

EL PASO DEC. '46

RED RIVER

SABINE R.

APPROXIMATE BORDER OF SPANISH TEXAS

BRAZOS R.

SLOAT

GUAYMAS OCT. '47

SACRAMENTO

CHIHUAHUA FEB. '47

RIO GRANDE R.

COLORADO R.

AUSTIN

SAN JACINTO

SAN ANTONIO

GALVESTON

THE ALAMO

NUECES R.

WOOL

DONIPHAN

CORPUS CHRISTI

LA PAZ APR. '47

MAZATLAN NOV. '47

PARRAS

MONTERREY
SEP. '46

CAMARGA

TAYLOR

FT. BROWN

SCOTT

FROM NEW ORLEANS DEC. '46

SALTILLO

PATTERSON

MATAMORAS

SAN LUCAS APR. '47

SAN JOSÉ MAR. '47

BUENA VISTA FEB. '47

VICTORIA DEC. '46

TAMPICO NOV. '46

SCOTT

SAN BLAS JAN. '48

PANUCO R.

FT. DE LOBOS

MANZANILLO JAN. '48

TUXPAN APR. '47

GUADALUPE HIDALGO

VERA CRUZ MAR. '47

MEXICO CITY SEP. 14, '47

PUEBLA MAY 15, '47

ACAPULCO

CARMEN MAY '47

Arrows indicate direction of major offensives or
uncontested movements.

Dates indicate when taken by Americans.

Dates with ——— indicate beginning of blockades.

97   The Mexican War

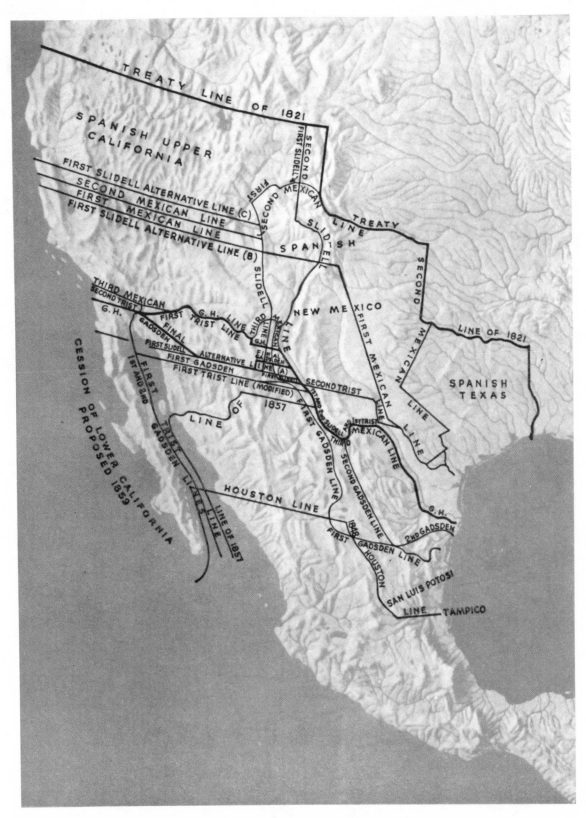

The Mexican Border, 1821-1857

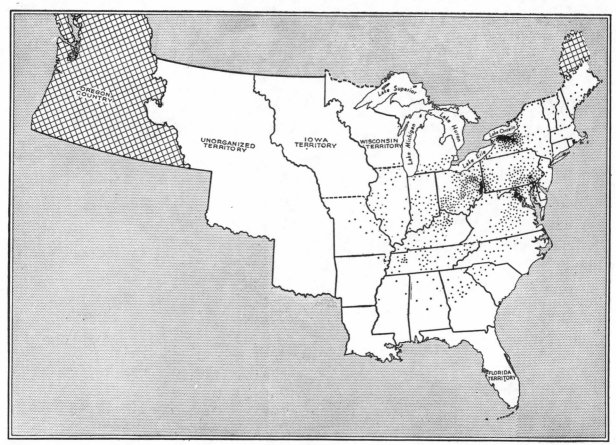

99   Wheat Production, 1840
Each dot represents 100,000 bushels; total crop, 84,823,272 bushels

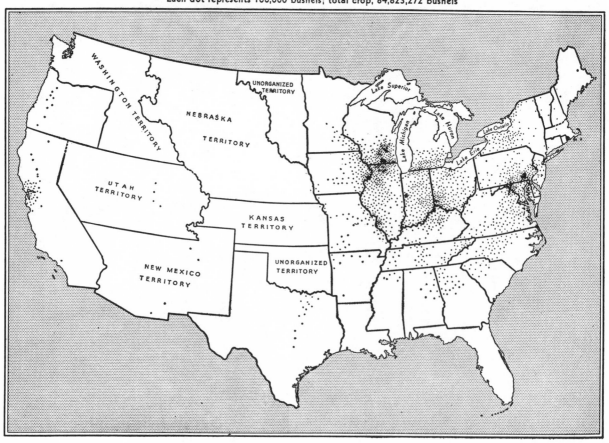

100   Wheat Production, 1860
Each dot represents 100,000 bushels; total crop, 173,104,924 bushels

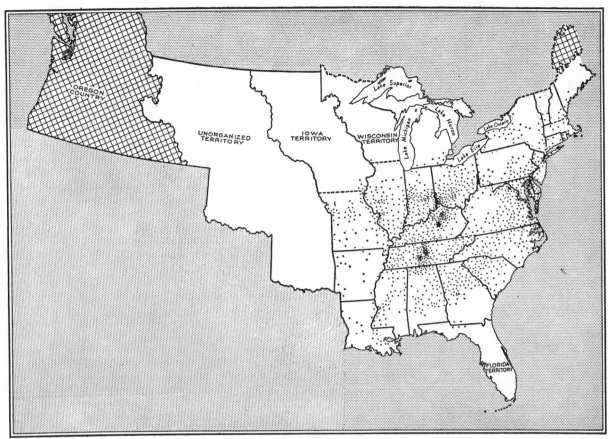

101

Corn Production, 1840
Each dot represents 300,000 bushels; total crop, 377,531,875 bushels

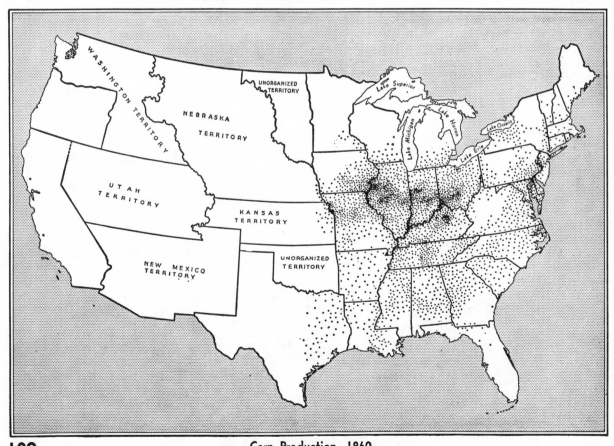

102

Corn Production, 1860
Each dot represents 300,000 bushels; total crop, 838,792,740 bushels

103 Cotton Production, 1840
Each dot represents 4,000 500-lb. bales;
total crop, 1,976,198 500-lb. bales

104 Cotton Production, 1860
Each dot represents 4,000 500-lb. bales;
total crop, 4,309,641 500-lb. bales

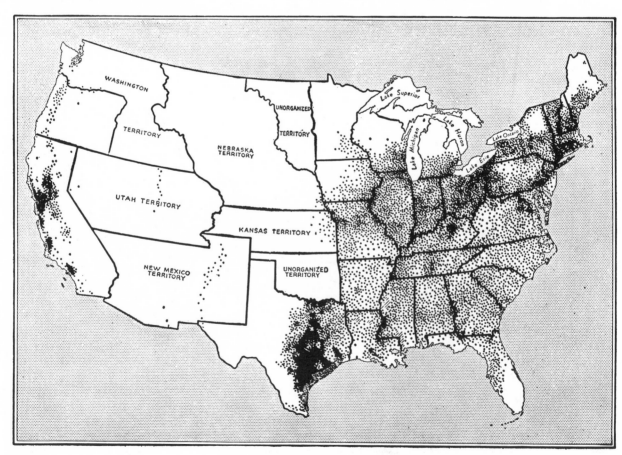

105 Cattle (Excluding Dairy Cows), 1860
Each dot represents 2,000 head; total, 8,585,735 head

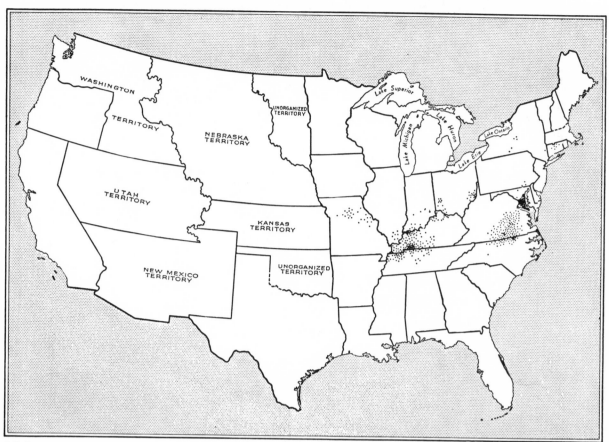

106   Tobacco Production, 1860
Each dot represents 1,000,000 lbs.; total crop, 434,209,461 lbs.

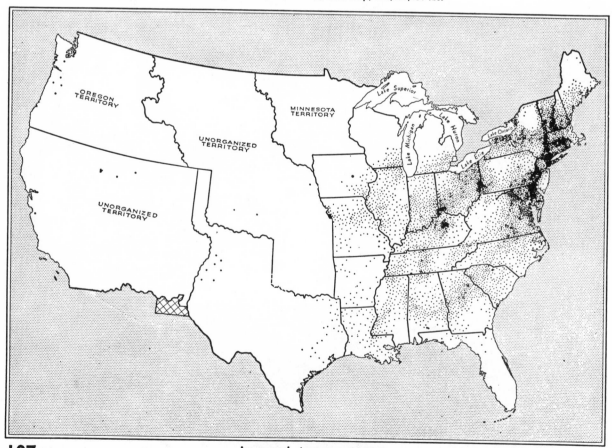

107   Improved Acreage, 1850
Each dot represents 25,000 acres; total, 113,632,614 acres

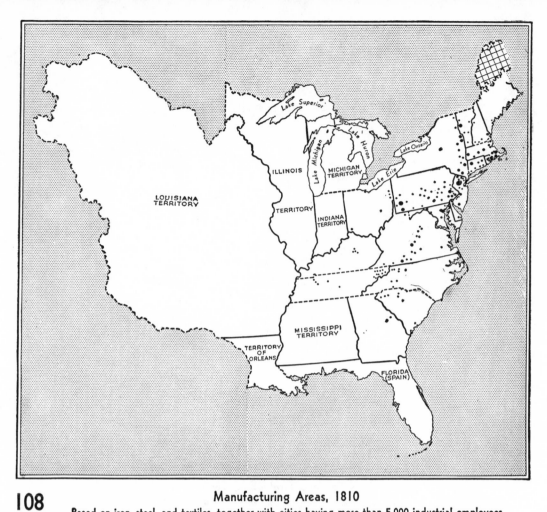

108

Manufacturing Areas, 1810

Based on iron, steel, and textiles, together with cities having more than 5,000 industrial employees

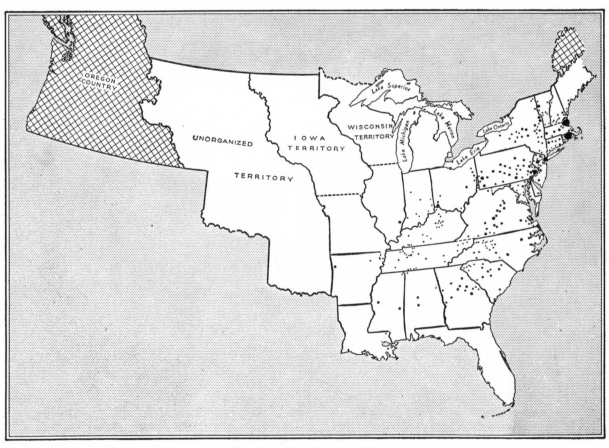

Manufacturing Areas, 1840

109

Based on iron, steel, and textiles, together with cities having more than 5,000 industrial employees

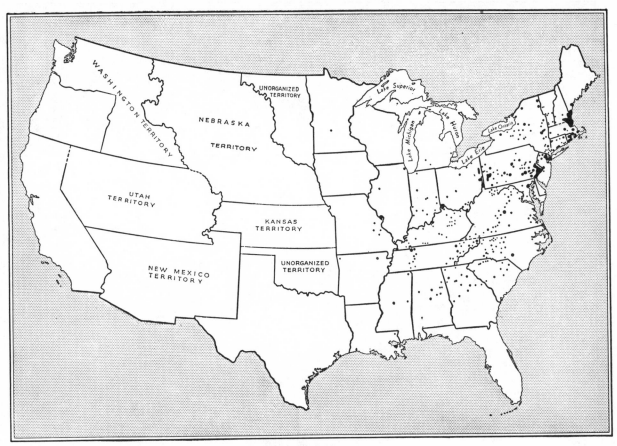

110
Manufacturing Areas, 1860
Based on iron, steel, and textiles, together with cities having more than 5,000 industrial employees

111 Banks of 1800, Including All Branches of
the First Bank of the United States

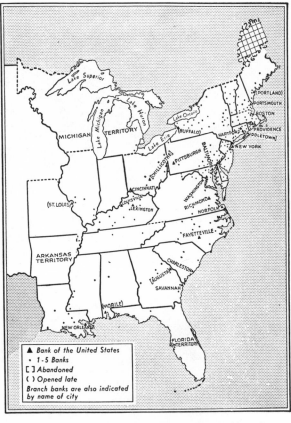

112 Banks of 1830, Including All Branches of
the Second Bank of the United States

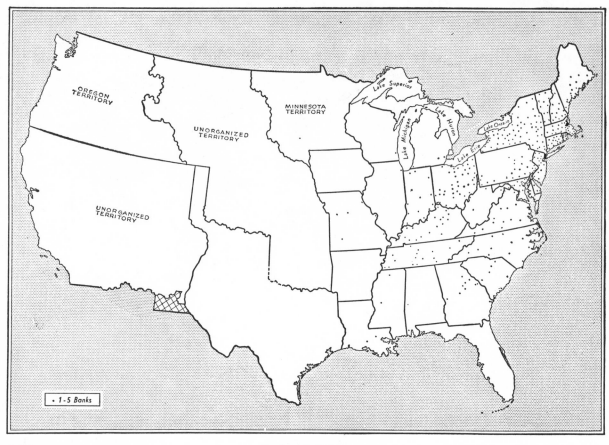

113   Banks of 1850

OREGON TERRITORY

UNORGANIZED TERRITORY

MINNESOTA TERRITORY

UNORGANIZED TERRITORY

Lake Superior

Lake Michigan

Lake Huron

Lake Erie

Lake Ontario

• 1-5 Banks

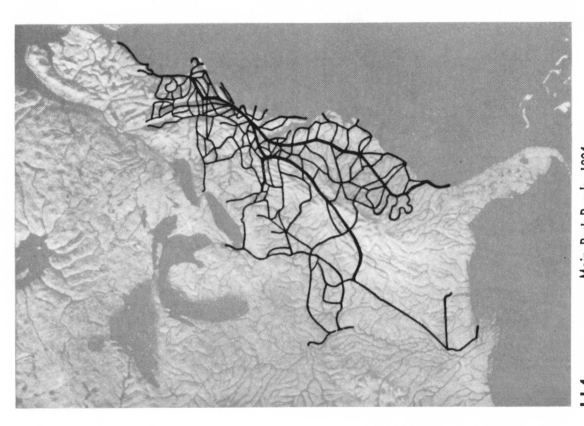

Main Post Roads, 1804
Heavier lines indicate routes most used

114

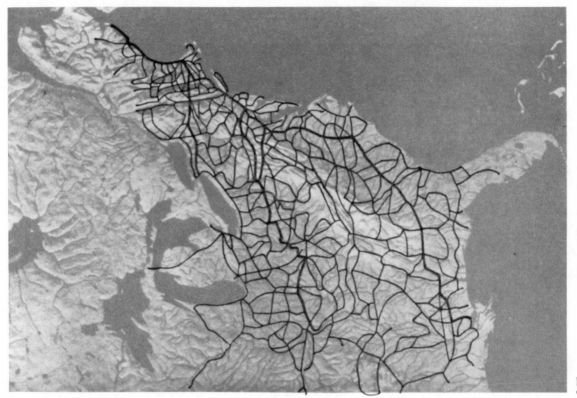

Main Post Roads, 1834
Heavier lines indicate routes most used

115

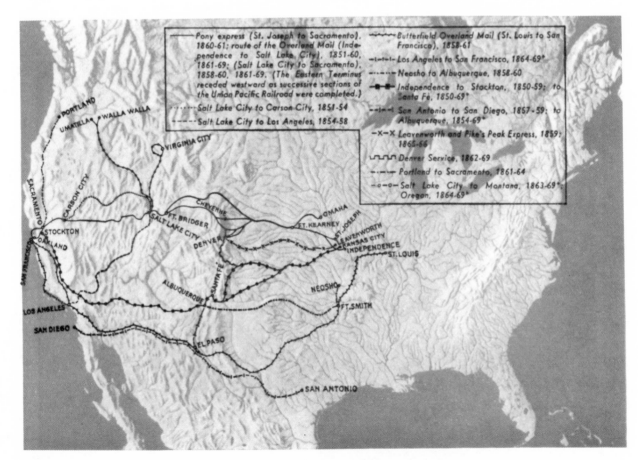

Pony express (St. Joseph to Sacramento), 1860-61; route of the Overland Mail (Independence to Salt Lake City), 1851-60, 1861-69; (Salt Lake City to Sacramento), 1858-60, 1861-69. (The Eastern Terminus receded westward as successive sections of the Union Pacific Railroad were completed.)

Salt Lake City to Carson City, 1851-54

Salt Lake City to Los Angeles, 1854-58

Butterfield Overland Mail (St. Louis to San Francisco), 1858-61

Los Angeles to San Francisco, 1864-69*

Neosho to Albuquerque, 1858-60

Independence to Stockton, 1850-59; to Santa Fé, 1850-69*

San Antonio to San Diego, 1857-59; to Albuquerque, 1854-69*

Leavenworth and Pike's Peak Express, 1859; 1865-66

Denver Service, 1862-69

Portland to Sacramento, 1861-64

Salt Lake City to Montana, 1863-69*; Oregon, 1864-69*

116

Routes of the Overland Mail and the Pony Express

[75]

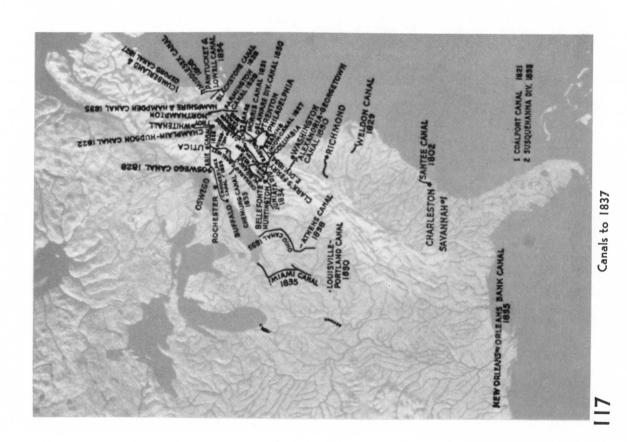

117   Canals to 1837

118   Canals, 1837-1860

[76]

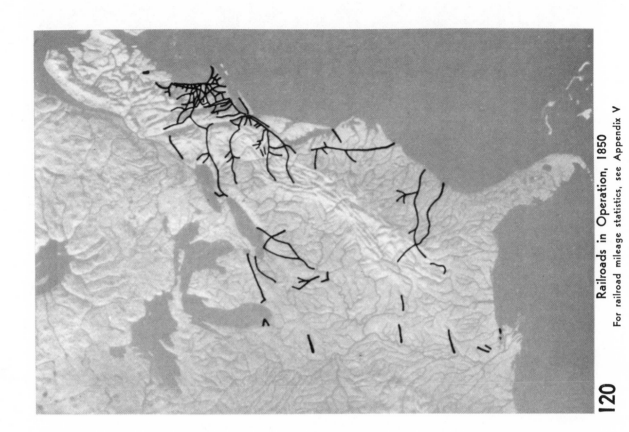

Railroads in Operation, 1850

For railroad mileage statistics, see Appendix V

120

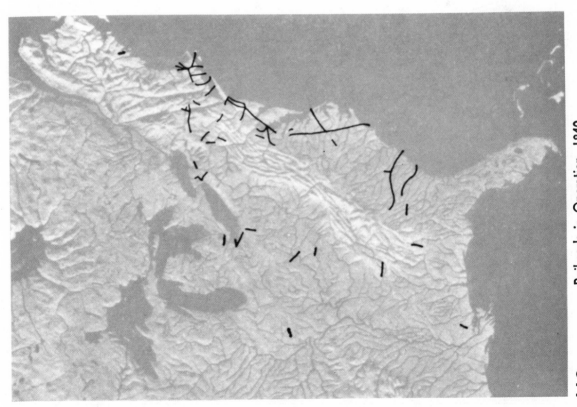

Railroads in Operation, 1840

For railroad mileage statistics, see Appendix V

119

[77]

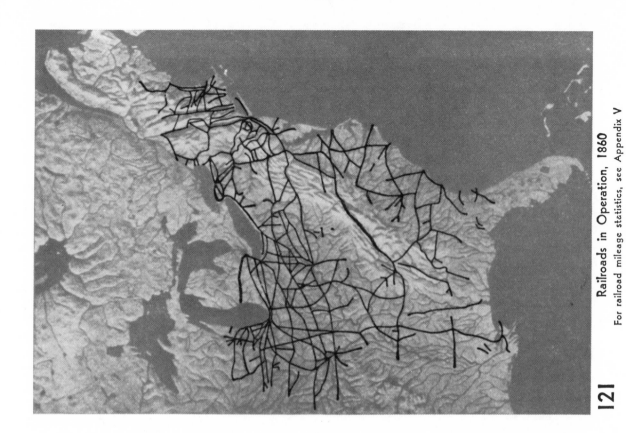

Railroads in Operation, 1860

For railroad mileage statistics, see Appendix V

121

First Ten Years of the Telegraph, 1844-1854

FIRST TRANSCONTINENTAL LINE
COMPLETED 1862

122

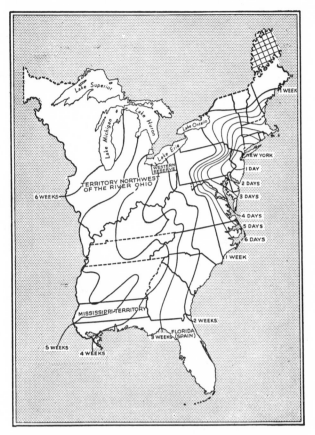

123 Rates of Travel from New York, 1800

124 Rates of Travel from New York, 1830

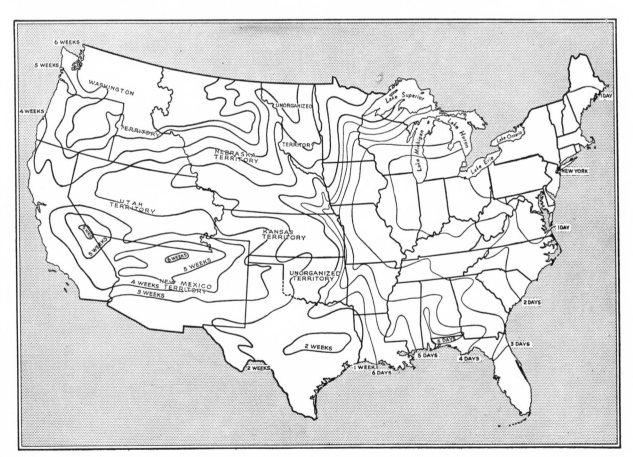

125 Rates of Travel from New York, 1860

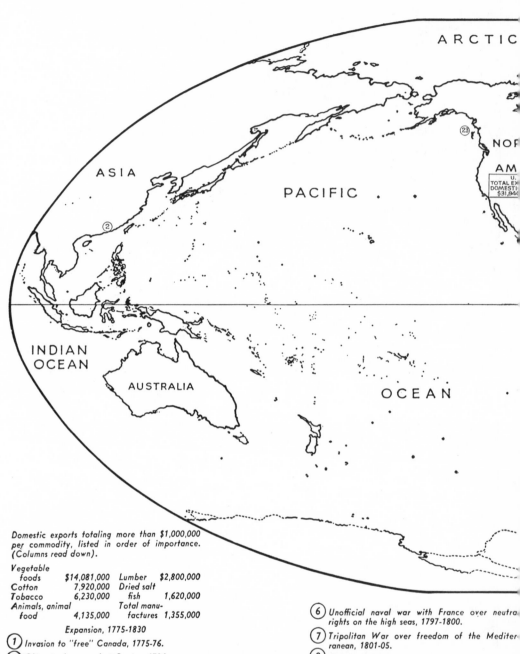

ARCTIC

ASIA

PACIFIC

NOF

AM

U.
TOTAL EX
DOMESTI
$31,84(

②

INDIAN
OCEAN

AUSTRALIA

OCEAN

Domestic exports totaling more than $1,000,000
per commodity, listed in order of importance.
(Columns read down).

Vegetable foods	$14,081,000	Lumber	$2,800,000
Cotton	7,920,000	Dried salt	
Tobacco	6,230,000	fish	1,620,000
Animals, animal food	4,135,000	Total manu- factures	1,355,000

Expansion, 1775-1830

① Invasion to "free" Canada, 1775-76.

② China trade opened at Canton, 1784.

③ Seizure of West Indies shipping by Great Britain, 1794.

④ British agree to evacuate the Northwest fur posts.

⑤ Free navigation of the Mississippi River and rights. of deposit granted by Spain, 1796, for a three year renewable period. British right of navigation (1783) not renewed at Treaty of Ghent.

⑥ Unofficial naval war with France over neutra rights on the high seas, 1797-1800.

⑦ Tripolitan War over freedom of the Mediter- ranean, 1801-05.

⑧ Mobile Act, 1804.

⑨ Carrying trade in European waters at height, yea before Embargo, 1807.

⑩ West Florida (to Pearl River) occupied, 1810.

⑪ Cuba: Jefferson worried lest England or France occupy island during Florida controversy.

126

Expansion, 17

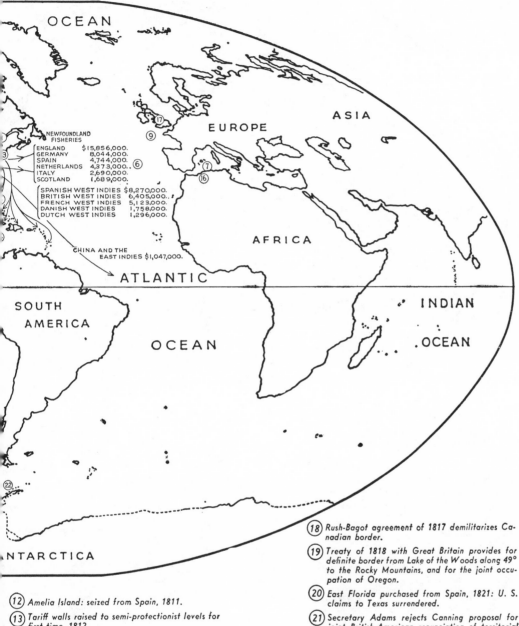

OCEAN

ASIA

EUROPE

⑰

⑨

NEWFOUNDLAND
FISHERIES

ENGLAND	$15,856,000.
GERMANY	8,044,000.
SPAIN	4,744,000.
NETHERLANDS	4,373,000.. ⑥
ITALY	2,690,000.
SCOTLAND	1,689,000.

⑦

⑯

SPANISH WEST INDIES	$8,270,000.
BRITISH WEST INDIES	6,405,000.. ⸸
FRENCH WEST INDIES	5,123,000.
DANISH WEST INDIES	1,758,000.
DUTCH WEST INDIES	1,296,000.

AFRICA

CHINA AND THE
EAST INDIES $1,047,000.

ATLANTIC

SOUTH
AMERICA

INDIAN

OCEAN

.OCEAN

㉒

NTARCTICA

1800

⑫ Amelia Island: seized from Spain, 1811.

⑬ Tariff walls raised to semi-protectionist levels for first time, 1812.

⑭ Canadian invasions, 1812-13.

⑮ West Florida (Pearl River to Perdido River), occupied 1813.

⑯ Decatur Expedition and Barbary pirates, 1815.

⑰ Reciprocal trade relations established with England by commercial convention of 1815, replacing annual grant of restricted trade privileges extended to American bottoms since 1783.

⑱ Rush-Bagot agreement of 1817 demilitarizes Ca-nadian border.

⑲ Treaty of 1818 with Great Britain provides for definite border from Lake of the Woods along 49° to the Rocky Mountains, and for the joint occu-pation of Oregon.

⑳ East Florida purchased from Spain, 1821: U. S. claims to Texas surrendered.

㉑ Secretary Adams rejects Canning proposal for joint British-American renunciation of territorial interests in Latin-America (Cuba).

㉒ Nathaniel Palmer, American whaler, discovers Antarctica, 1821.

㉓ Russian extension of Alaskan claims in Ukase of 1821 helps produce Monroe Doctrine.

㉔ Commercial Treaty of 1830 opens West Indies and Canadian trade to U. S. ships without major re-strictions.

Base Map by Permission of Denoyer-Geppert Company, Chicago

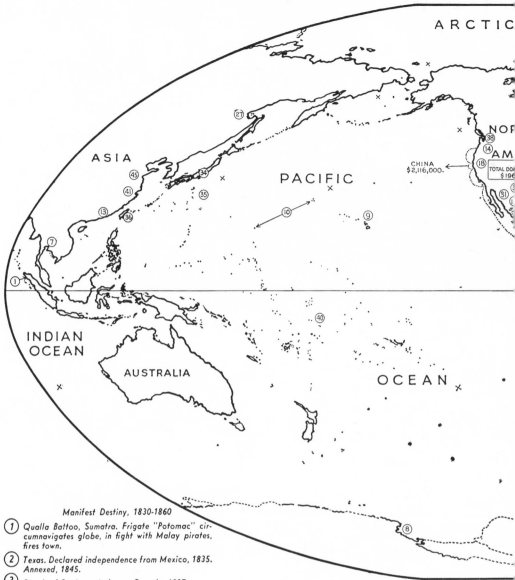

Manifest Destiny, 1830-1860

① Qualla Battoo, Sumatra. Frigate "Potomac" circumnavigates globe, in fight with Malay pirates, fires town.

② Texas. Declared independence from Mexico, 1835. Annexed, 1845.

③ Revolt of Papineau in Lower Canada, 1837.

④ Revolt of Mackenzie in Upper Canada, 1837.

⑤ Caroline Incident, 1837.

⑥ Aroostook War, 1837.

⑦ Siam: trade treaties, 1836, 1856.

⑧ Antarctica: segment discovered by Wilkes, 1840.

⑨ Hawaii. Practical protectorate announced, 1843. Kamehameha offers formal protectorate, 1849; 1852 treaty of annexation not ratified. Important base for Oriental trade and North Pacific whaling fleets.

⑩ Wake Island: claimed by Lt. Wilkes, 1841; Midway Island discovered by Capt. N. C. Brooks, 1859.

⑪ Santo Domingo offers self as protectorate, 1844. American speculators active in the 1850's.

⑫ Greytown, Nicaragua: British seizure produces Polk Corollary to the Monroe Doctrine, 1848.

⑬ Wanghia: treaty with China opens additional ports to U. S. trade, 1844.

⑭ Oregon: border controversy with Great Britain settled, 1846.

⑮ Repeal of British Corn Laws ends Empire preference for Canadian grains, leads to unrest and to Reciprocity Treaty of 1854-64.

⑯ New Granada: 1846 treaty provides for transit rights in Panama.

⑰ Hise treaties with Nicaragua and Honduras, 1848.

⑱ War with Mexico: annexation of New Mexico, Utah and Upper California, 1848.

⑲ Northern Mexico: proposals for further annexations (for details, see map 98).

⑳ Yucatan: asks U. S. protection against native uprising, 1848.

㉑ Panama: scene of ventures of William F. Aspinwall; Pacific Mail Steamship Co. opens line from Panama City to California, 1848; Panama Railroad completed, 1855.

㉒ Isthmus of Tehuantepec: negotiations for transit rights, 1849, 1851; secured by Gadsden Treaty 1854; used by U. S. mails, 1859.

㉓ Cuba: Polk offers $100,000,000, 1848; Lopez filibustering expeditions, 1850, 1851; renunciation of territorial ambitions in Cuba rejected by U. S., 1852; "Black Warrior" incident, Ostend Manifesto, Quitman expedition, 1854; Buchanan proposes purchase, 1858; Ridley expedition, 1858.

㉔ Tigre Island, Gulf of Fonseca: U. S. flag raised abortively, 1849, to thwart British plans.

㉕ Hungary: liberal revolts there and elsewhere, 1848-49; U. S. sentiment expressed in Hulsemann note to Austria and in receptions here to Kossuth.

㉖ Chincha Islands: negotiations with Peru, 1850, over guano deposits.

㉗ Amur River: P. D. Collins plans American steamship line and trading posts.

㉘ Capital export begins to Canadian banks and mines, Mexican railroads and banks.

Expansion and

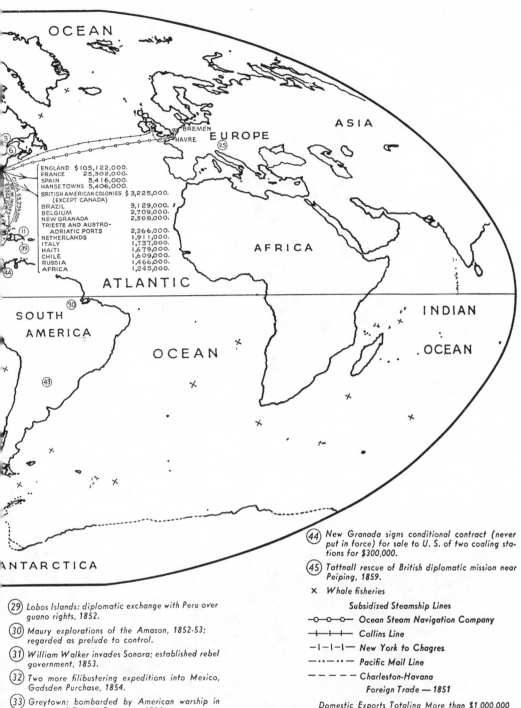

ENGLAND $105,122,000.
FRANCE 25,302,000.
SPAIN 5,416,000.
HANSE TOWNS 5,406,000.
BRITISH AMERICAN COLONIES $3,225,000.
  (EXCEPT CANADA)
BRAZIL 3,129,000.
BELGIUM 2,709,000.
NEW GRANADA 2,508,000.
TRIESTE AND AUSTRO-
  ADRIATIC PORTS 2,266,000.
NETHERLANDS 1,911,000.
ITALY 1,737,000.
HAITI 1,679,000.
CHILE 1,609,000.
RUSSIA 1,466,000.
AFRICA 1,245,000.

(44) New Granada signs conditional contract (never put in force) for sale to U. S. of two coaling stations for $300,000.

(45) Tattnall rescue of British diplomatic mission near Peiping, 1859.

× Whale fisheries

Subsidized Steamship Lines

—o—o—o— Ocean Steam Navigation Company

—+—+—+— Collins Line

—ı—ı—ı— New York to Chagres

—··—··— Pacific Mail Line

— — — — Charleston-Havana

Foreign Trade — 1851

Domestic Exports Totaling More than $1,000,000 per Commodity, Listed in Order of Importance (Columns Read Down):

Cotton	$112,315,000	Iron manufactures	$1,876,000
Gold and silver coin	18,070,000	Indian corn	1,763,000
Flour	10,524,000	Beef, tallow, hides	1,690,000
Tobacco	9,219,000	Wearing apparel	1,212,000
Cotton piece goods	7,241,000	Snuff and tobacco manufactures	1,144,000
Pork, bacon, lard	4,368,000	Butter and cheese	1,125,000
Staves, shingles, boards	2,349,000	Naval stores	1,064,000
Rice	2,171,000	Spermaceti oil	1,045,000
Wood manufactures	2,076,000	Wheat	1,026,000

(29) Lobos Islands: diplomatic exchange with Peru over guano rights, 1852.

(30) Maury explorations of the Amazon, 1852-53; regarded as prelude to control.

(31) William Walker invades Sonora; established rebel government, 1853.

(32) Two more filibustering expeditions into Mexico, Gadsden Purchase, 1854.

(33) Greytown: bombarded by American warship in support of Transit Company, 1854.

(34) Kanagawa: treaty negotiated by Perry, opening Japanese trade to U. S., 1853-54.

(35) Bonin Islands: claimed by Perry, 1853; claimed by Japan, 1861.

(36) Formosa: seizure recommended by Perry, 1854; flag abortively raised.

(37) William Walker filibusters in Nicaragua, 1855, 1857.

(38) Juan de Fuca: U. S. seizes island disputed with England, 1855.

(39) Alta Vela, giving rise to the Guano Act of 1856: basis of claims to guano islands thereafter.

(40) Swains Island occupied by Jennings family.

(41) Tsinan forts, Shanghai, bombarded, 1857.

(42) Navassa: guano island claimed, 1858.

(43) Paraguay: punitive naval expedition avenges 1856 attack on "Water Witch," 1859.

Base Map by Permission of Denoyer-Geppert Company, Chicago

, 1830-1860; Exports, 1850

128   State Public School Legislation, 1790
Additional cities having free school systems not indicated

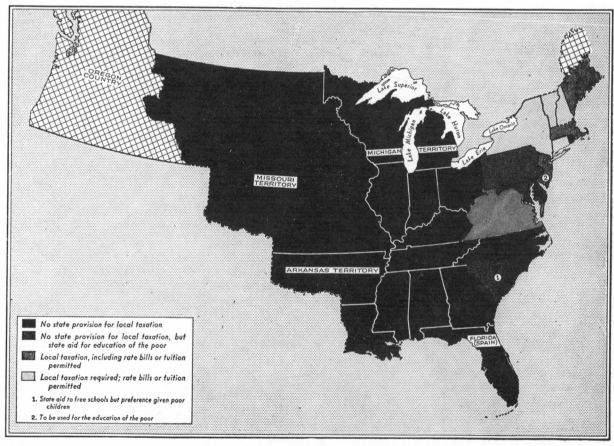

129

State Public School Legislation, 1820
Additional cities having free school systems not indicated

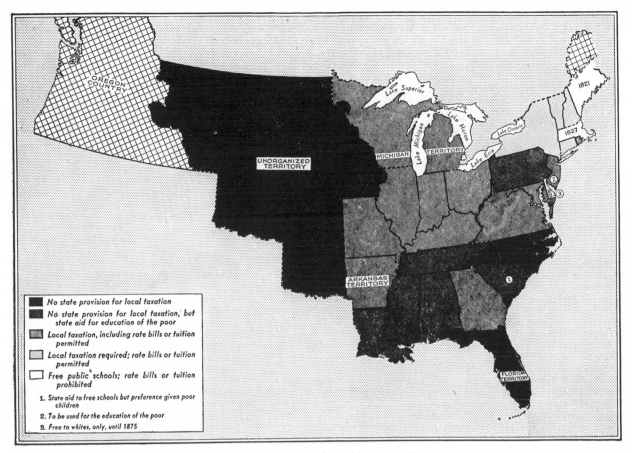

130

State Public School Legislation, 1830
Additional cities having free school systems not indicated

The legend for the 1830 map:

- No state provision for local taxation
- No state provision for local taxation, but state aid for education of the poor
- Local taxation, including rate bills or tuition permitted
- Local taxation required; rate bills or tuition permitted
- Free public schools; rate bills or tuition prohibited

1. State aid to free schools but preference given poor children
2. To be used for the education of the poor
3. Free to whites, only, until 1875

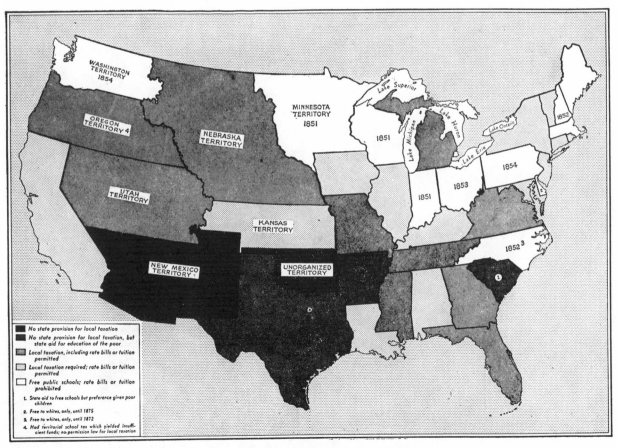

131

State Public School Legislation, 1855
Additional cities having free school systems not indicated

The legend for the 1855 map:

- No state provision for local taxation
- No state provision for local taxation, but state aid for education of the poor
- Local taxation, including rate bills or tuition permitted
- Local taxation required; rate bills or tuition permitted
- Free public schools; rate bills or tuition prohibited

1. State aid to free schools but preference given poor children
2. Free to whites, only, until 1875
3. Free to whites, only, until 1872
4. Had territorial school tax which yielded insufficient funds; no permission law for local taxation

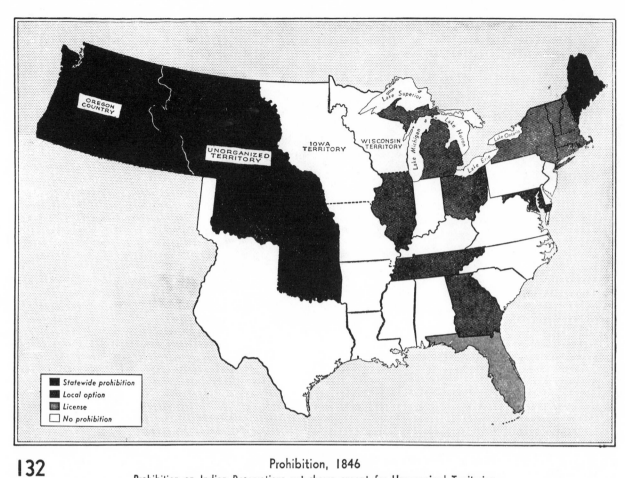

132   Prohibition, 1846

Prohibition on Indian Reservations not shown except for Unorganized Territories

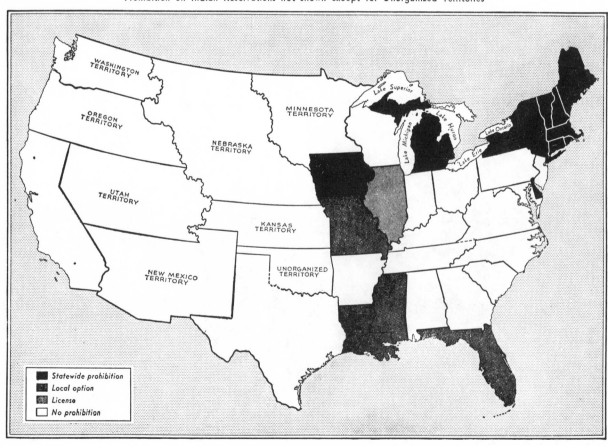

133

Prohibition, 1856

Prohibition on Indian Reservations not shown

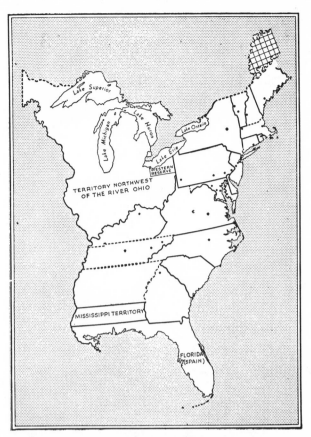

134 Colleges, 1800
Each dot represents one men's college

135 Newspapers, 1800
Each dot represents one paper

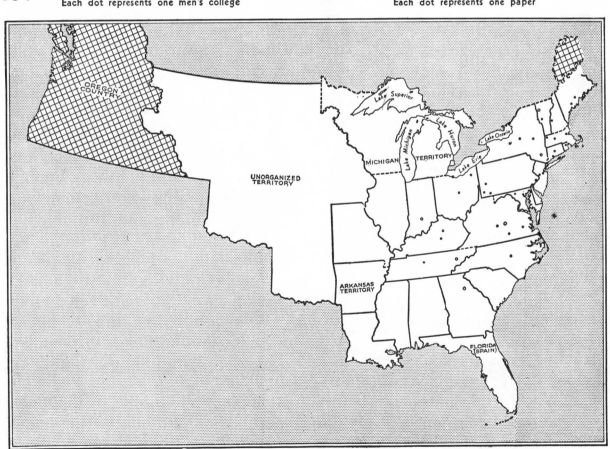

136 Universities, Colleges, and Other Institutions of Higher Learning, 1830
Each dot represents one men's college; each circle represents one public institution

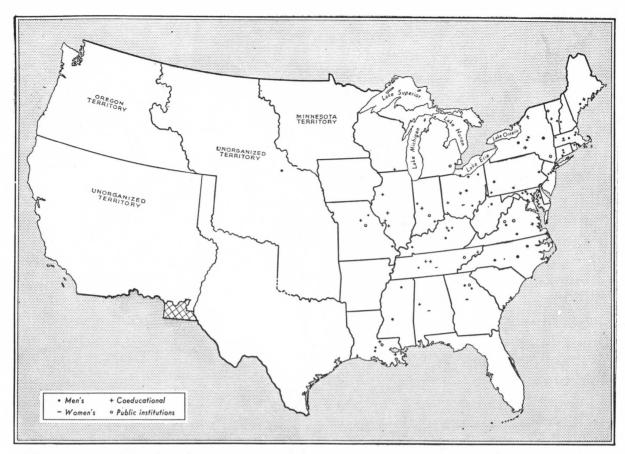

137 Universities, Colleges and Other Institutions of Higher Learning, 1850

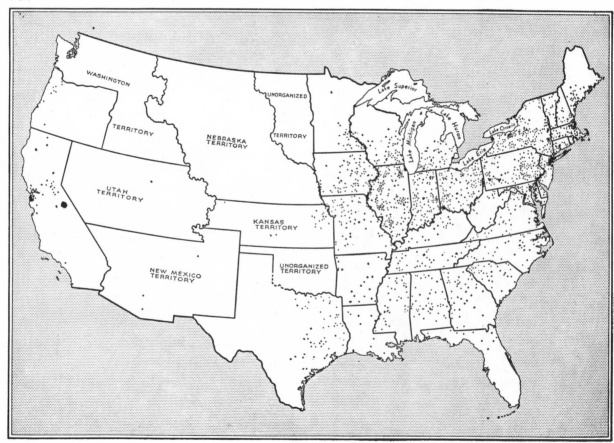

138 Newspapers, 1860
Each dot represents 1-5 papers

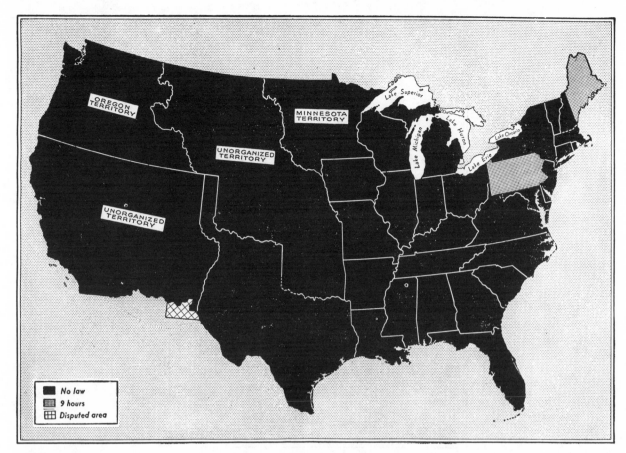

139   Women's Hours of Work, 1850

Legend: No law / 9 hours / Disputed area

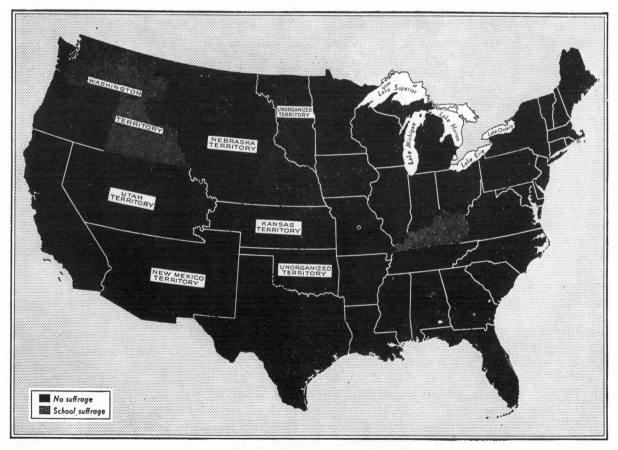

140   Enfranchisement of Women, 1860

Legend: No suffrage / School suffrage

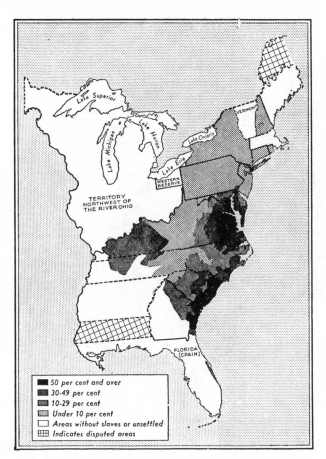

141 Proportion of Slaves to Total Population, 1790

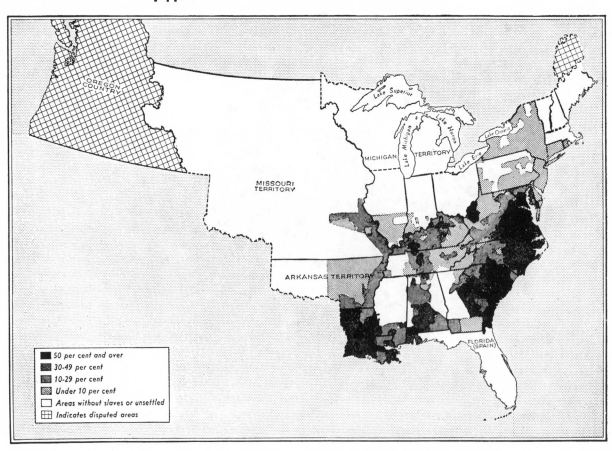

142

Proportion of Slaves to Total Population, 1820

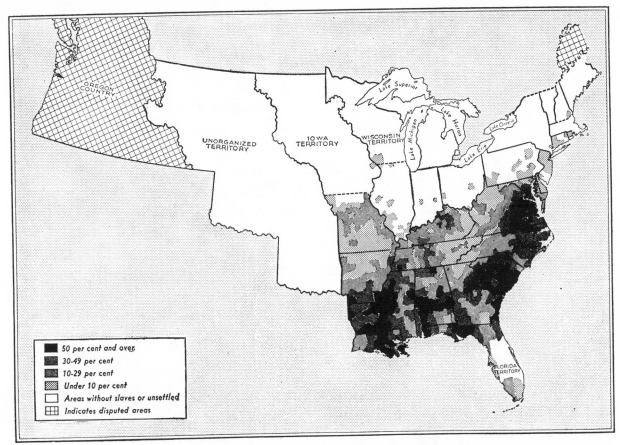

143   Proportion of Slaves to Total Population, by County, 1840

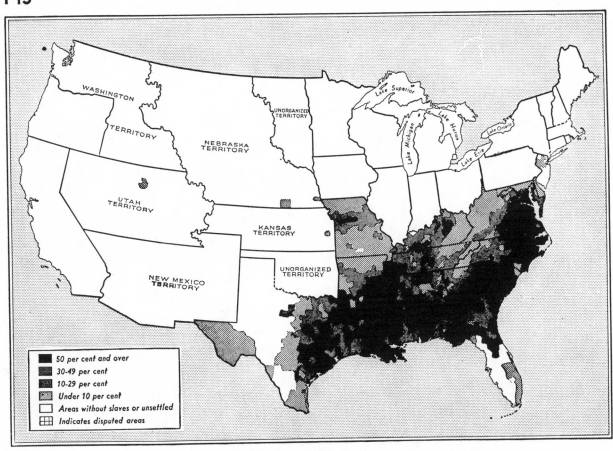

144   Proportion of Slaves to Total Population, by County, 1860

[91]

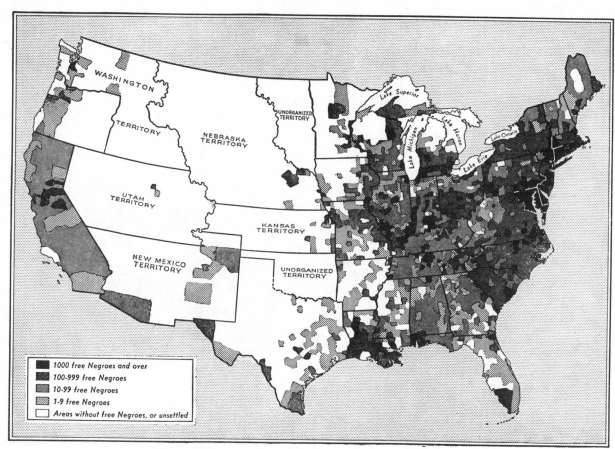

145   Free Negro Population, by County, 1860

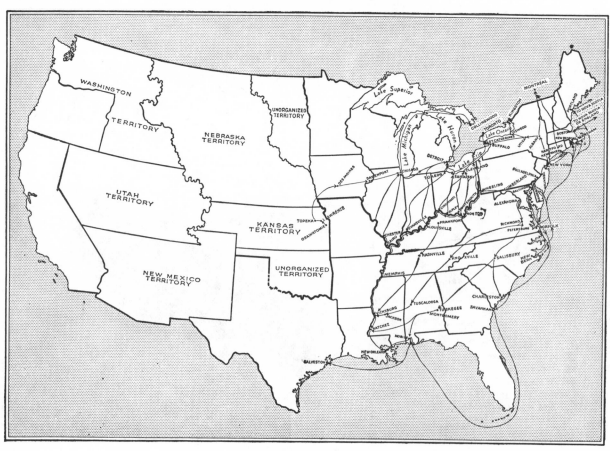

146   Routes of the Underground Railway and of the Domestic Slave Trade

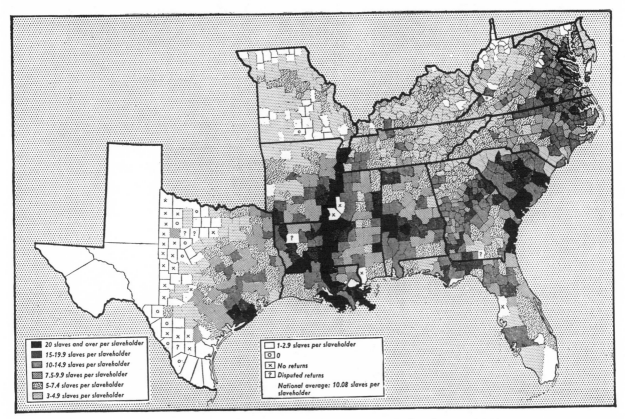

147   Number of Slaves per Slaveholder in the South, by County, 1860

Legend (map 147):
- 20 slaves and over per slaveholder
- 15-19.9 slaves per slaveholder
- 10-14.9 slaves per slaveholder
- 7.5-9.9 slaves per slaveholder
- 5-7.4 slaves per slaveholder
- 3-4.9 slaves per slaveholder
- 1-2.9 slaves per slaveholder
- 0
- No returns
- Disputed returns
- National average: 10.08 slaves per slaveholder

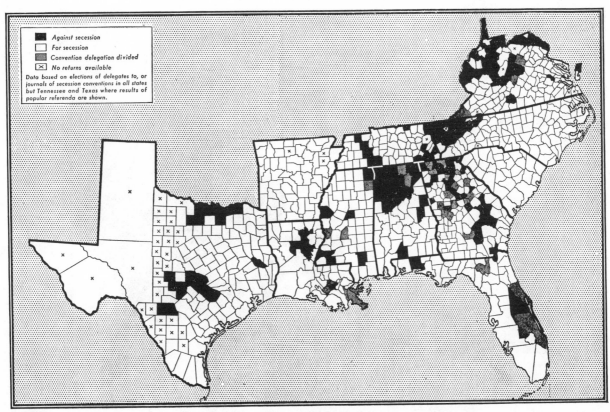

Legend (map 148):
- Against secession
- For secession
- Convention delegation divided
- No returns available

Data based on elections of delegates to, or journals of secession conventions in all states but Tennessee and Texas where results of popular referenda are shown.

148   Opposition to Secession in the South, by County, 1860-1861

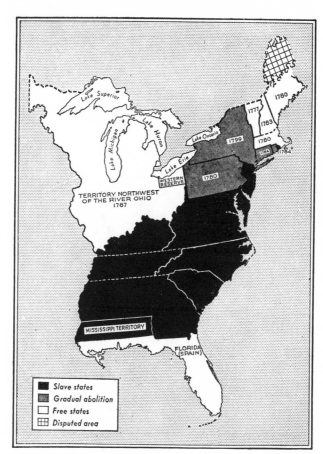

149   Progress of Abolition, 1800
Dates are those of adoption of gradual or
complete abolition

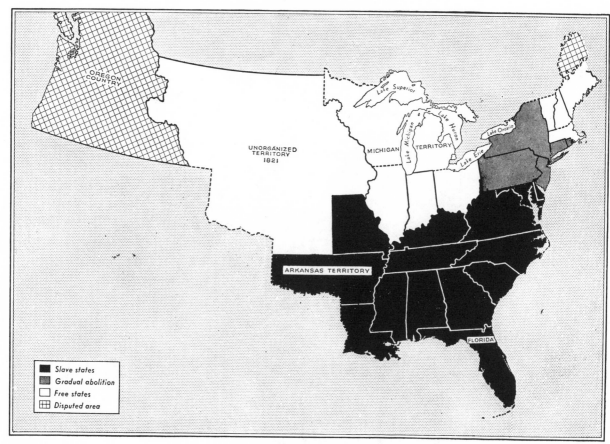

150

Progress of Abolition, 1821
Dates are those of adoption of gradual or complete abolition

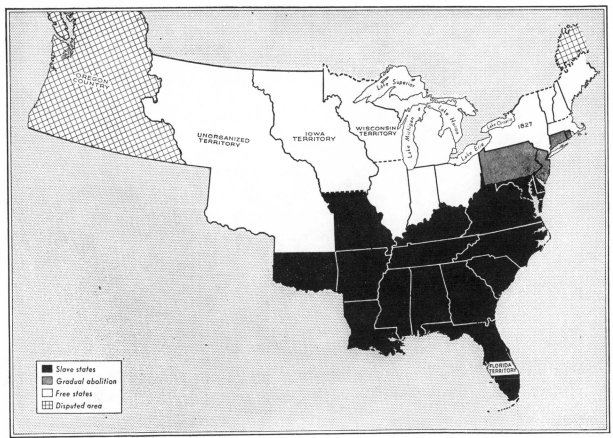

151

Progress of Abolition, 1840
Dates are those of adoption of gradual or complete abolition

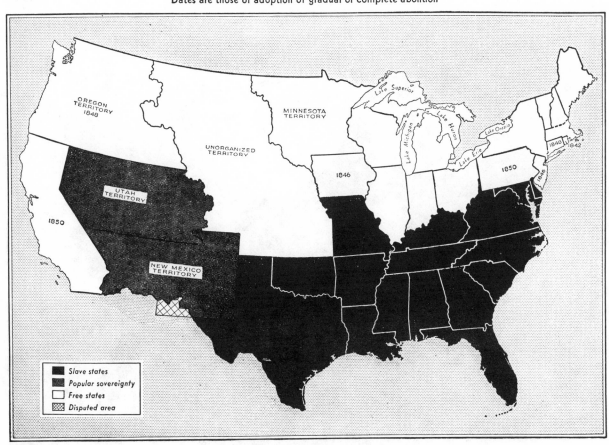

152

Progress of Abolition, 1850
Dates are those of adoption of gradual or complete abolition

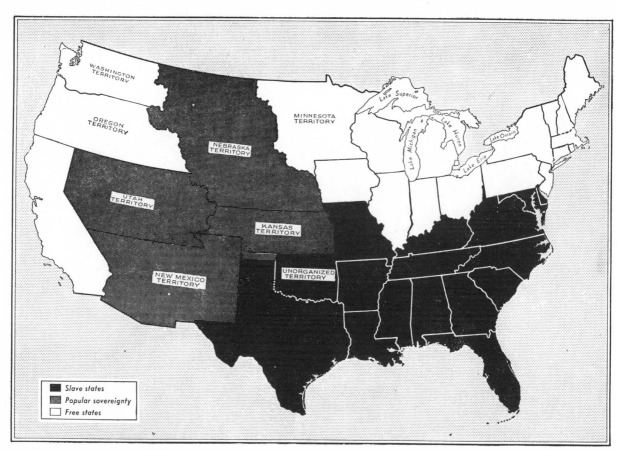

153   Progress of Abolition, 1854

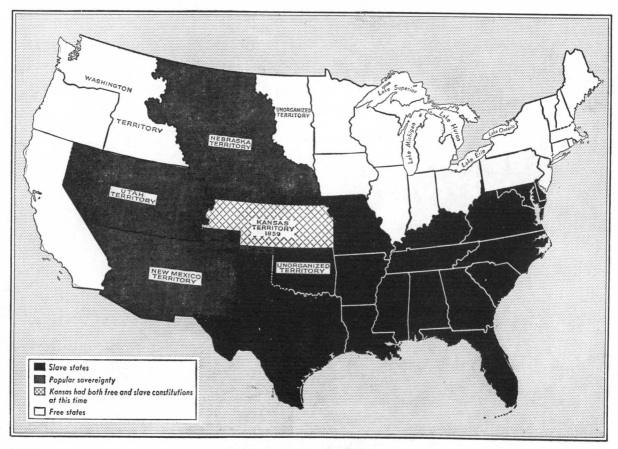

154   Progress of Abolition, 1860

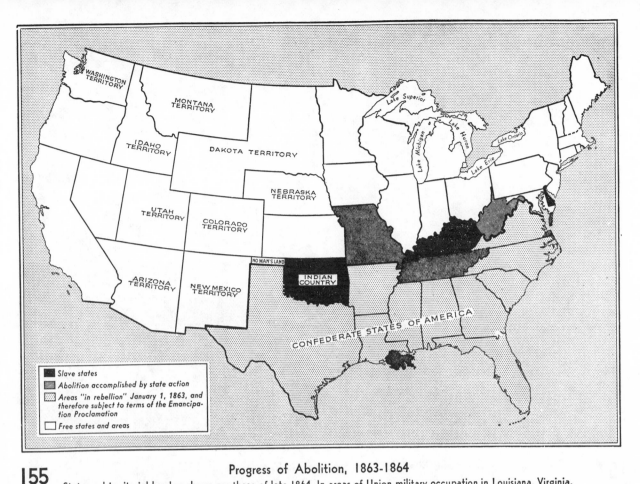

155

Progress of Abolition, 1863-1864

State and territorial borders shown are those of late 1864. In areas of Union military occupation in Louisiana, Virginia,
etc., Emancipation Proclamation had no legal applicability and state action in 1864 effected abolition therein.

Legend:
- Slave states
- Abolition accomplished by state action
- Areas "in rebellion" January 1, 1863, and therefore subject to terms of the Emancipation Proclamation
- Free states and areas

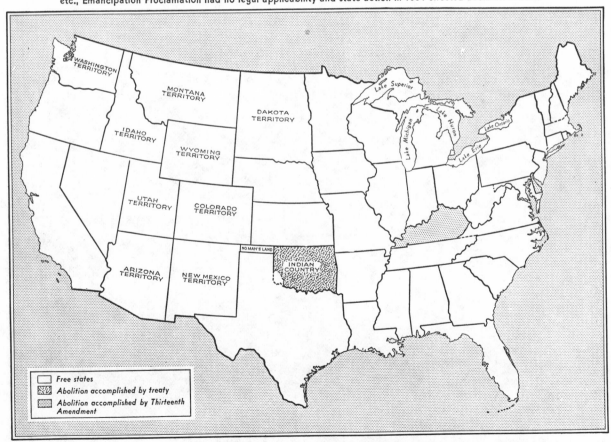

156

Progress of Abolition, 1865-1868

State and territorial borders shown are those of late 1868
(For disputed border between Texas and Indian Country, see map 204)

Legend:
- Free states
- Abolition accomplished by treaty
- Abolition accomplished by Thirteenth Amendment

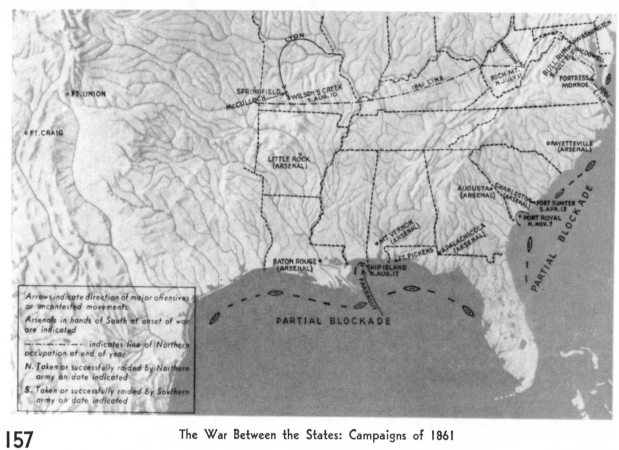

157   The War Between the States: Campaigns of 1861

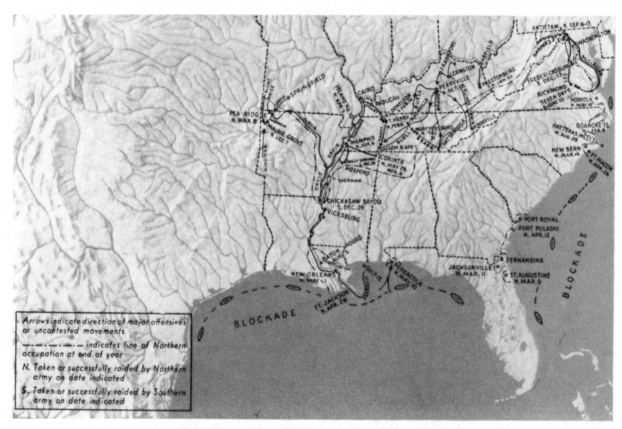

158   The War Between the States: Campaigns of 1862

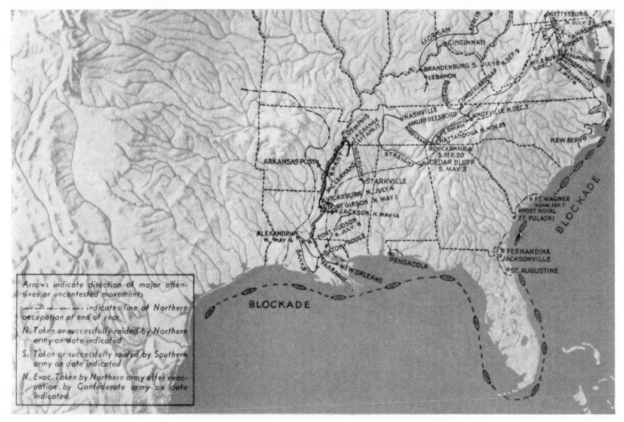

159   The War Between the States: Campaigns of 1863

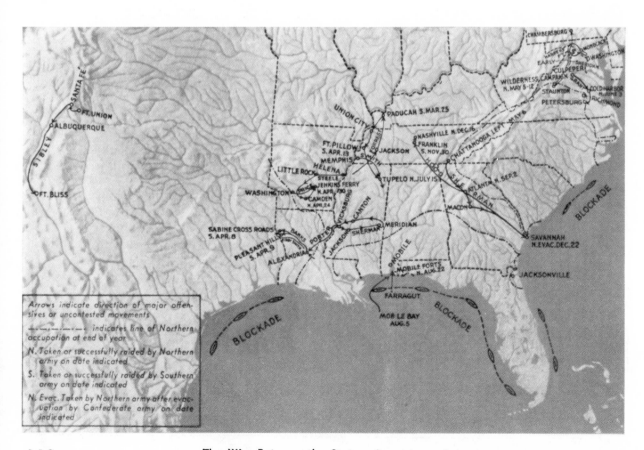

160   The War Between the States: Campaigns of 1864

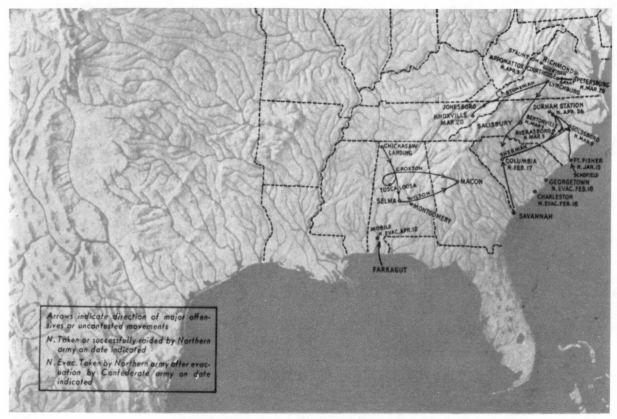

161   The War Between the States: Campaigns of 1865

Kirby Smith, commander in the Trans-Mississippi West, and last Confederate general in the field, after a fruitless trip to Houston to see about continuing the fight, surrendered his forces, including Buckner's men at Shreveport and Price's Missourians, to General Canby at New Orleans, May 26, 1865.

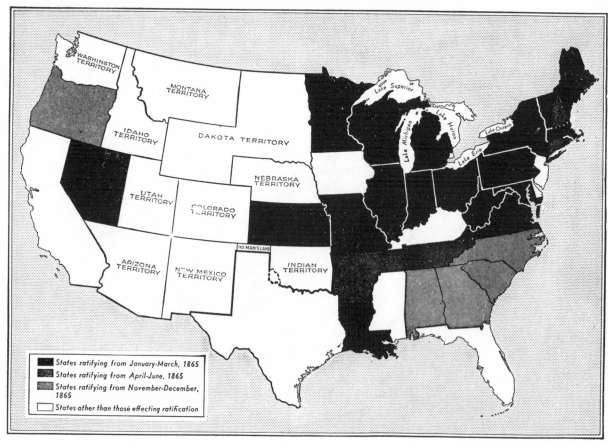

162   States Effecting the Ratification of the Thirteenth Amendment to the Constitution, 1865

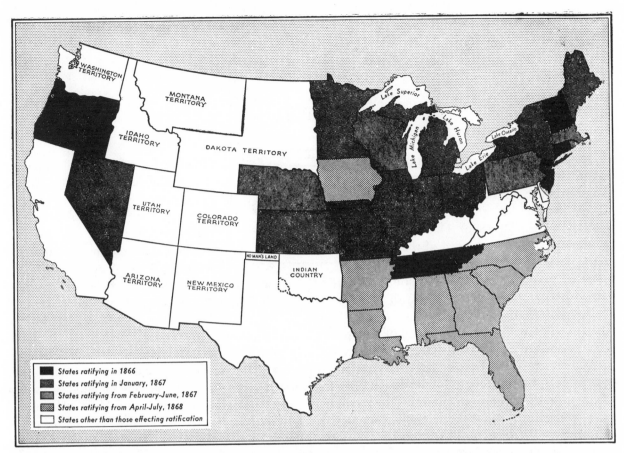

Legend:
- States ratifying in 1866
- States ratifying in January, 1867
- States ratifying from February–June, 1867
- States ratifying from April–July, 1868
- States other than those effecting ratification

163   States Effecting the Ratification of the Fourteenth Amendment to the Constitution, 1868

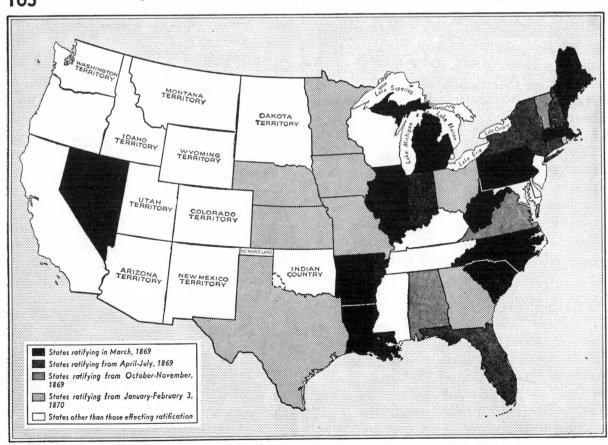

Legend:
- States ratifying in March, 1869
- States ratifying from April–July, 1869
- States ratifying from October–November, 1869
- States ratifying from January–February 3, 1870
- States other than those effecting ratification

164   States Effecting the Ratification of the Fifteenth Amendment to the Constitution, 1870

The continued movement of population westward after the war produced the miscalled "disappearance" of the frontier, as shown on the population map of 1890. This development signalized the end of the cattle kingdom (already seriously crippled by disease and particularistic state-restrictive legislation) and the evolution of the age-old Indian problem from a military to a civil and social status, far more than it did the end of free public homesteads. Actually, more lands were patented in the decade of the 1890's than ever before in a comparable period of time. In this period also, for the first time in our history, accurate census figures were taken of the national origin of our immigrant residents and citizens, making it possible to show their geographical distribution.

Suffrage, extended by some states to aliens taking out their first papers or declaring their intention of seeking citizenship, underwent three important developments: the establishment in the South of various legal devices designed to curb the newly won franchise of the Negro; the extension, slowly but surely, of woman suffrage; and in an increasing number of states, the requirement of literacy as a qualification of the voter.

The economic growth of the country continued at a phenomenal rate. It brought great benefits in the form of an enormously improved and generally improving, standard of living, with a tremendously increased national income. It also brought grave abuses, which Grangers, Populists, Progressives, and New Dealers were to attack successively. The farming picture saw the slow but steady recovery of the South from the chaos of 1865. Disruption of the old slave labor system and the almost total lack of fluid capital speeded the evolution of sharecropping farm tenancy. Over-enthusiasm about western farming led to the development of share and cash tenancy there, most dramatically on unsuccessful irrigation projects like that in the Uncompahgre Valley. Such overexpansion, encouraged in the early part of this period by the railroads and the states and territories, and directly and indirectly fostered by the government during World War I, intensified the farm problem during the prolonged period of falling prices from 1871 to 1897, and again from 1920 to the establishment of parity price supports.

The manufacturing and business world saw the evolution of pools, trusts, combines, mergers, trade associations, branch factories abroad, and finally the centripetal development of cartelization and the centrifugal movement toward geographic decentralization. Domestically, the introduction of oil, the establishment in the twentieth century of a vast power network over the country, the creation of the so-called "second mill zone" in the Middle West, and latterly the "third mill zone" in the industrial South, have been of outstanding importance, together with the completion of the railroad, telegraph and telephone networks—the former greatly assisted by grants-in-aid from the federal, state, county and town governments. The automobile and the truck brought with them tremendous social and economic changes, as our present great highway systems evolved, first haphazardly and then, beginning in New Jersey, under state supervision. Still later, since 1921, federal funds have been allotted to construction on arterial highways designated by the states, and since 1941 the construction of great traffic routes has been influenced by considerations of national defense.

The Federal Reserve System, inaugurated in 1914, brought a much needed elasticity and uniformity to the currency of the country. It gave added stability to member banks through the pooling of reserves, and constituted a marked improvement over the system established by the National Banking Acts of 1863 and 1864, which, in their turn, had brought an appreciable improvement over the chaotic conditions of earlier days.

Integration of the country, well begun by the roads, canals and particularly the railroads of the previous period, continued, and indeed was accelerated. The length of time required to move from one place to another rapidly decreased, until, with the advent of the modern airplane, the entire country lay within the compass of a single day's trip, and the continent could be crossed in approximately half a day. This development not only made drastic changes in business and social habits, but obviously introduced fundamental innovations in the strategy of national defense.

Just before the turn of the century, our aggressively expanding business economy turned enthusiastically to a search for increased foreign markets. Simultaneously, America began for the first time to export capital in really significant quantities and to shift gradually from the position of a debtor nation to that of creditor—an evolution which reached its climax with dramatic swiftness during World War I. This export of capital came after a long series of post-Civil War leaders, like Seward and Grant, had urged further acquisitions of trade and defense bases, and after others, such as Blaine, had tried unsuccessfully to build up our economic relations with Latin America. Through capital export, America achieved true status as a world power. This development, flanked by the revival of ship subsidies for the languishing American merchant marine, the tardy rebuilding of American naval power, and the doctrines of the influential A. T. Mahan, coincided neatly and logically with the acquisition of empire through the Spanish-American War. It led to the establishment of the Republic of Panama and the building of the Panama Canal. It was essential background for the Portsmouth Conference, and for the participation of the United States in the Algeciras Conference. It took the interesting form of dollar diplomacy both in the Caribbean, with resulting strain on our relations with the rest of Latin America, and in the Orient, where, reinforcing the slightly earlier but closely related Open Door policy, it laid for thirty-seven years the bases for an inevitable conflict with Japan. It also brought increasing collisions with the recently industrialized new naval power, Germany, and had obvious connections with our entrance into World War I and subsequently into World War II.

After the prodigal waste of resources which more or less inevitably characterized much of the early expansion of American enterprise, a marked conservation drive began about the turn of the century, when for the first time the conservation movement entered the field of national rather than state action. This departure resulted in the creation of the national parks, national monuments, and national forests, the beginnings of the reclamation movement under the Newlands Act of 1902, and the very important report of the Inland Waterways Commission which foreshadowed in 1907 the general line of watershed development and land-use policy to be followed years later by the Franklin Roosevelt administrations.

The development of the public school system was also forwarded by the beginning of effective compulsory school attendance laws, which were in part an oblique attack on the problem of child labor. Colleges, particularly coeducational institutions, spread rapidly with the enormous increase of free public high school education and with the increasing emancipation of women. Social legislation included limitations on the hours of labor of both men and women, a reform which was based on the long crusade of organized labor dating back to the 1820's and including Ira Steward's campaign for the eight-hour day, the Knights of Labor, the ill-fated general strike of 1886, and the early opposition of the American Federation of Labor. This legislation progressed first in dangerous occupations and public works, then in mercantile and manufacturing occupations, and finally in blanket regulations governing work of all types in the states. Federal action, beginning with regulations on the hours of labor of federal employees, workers on government contracts, and interstate carriers, became general only with the passage of the Wages and Hours Act in 1937.

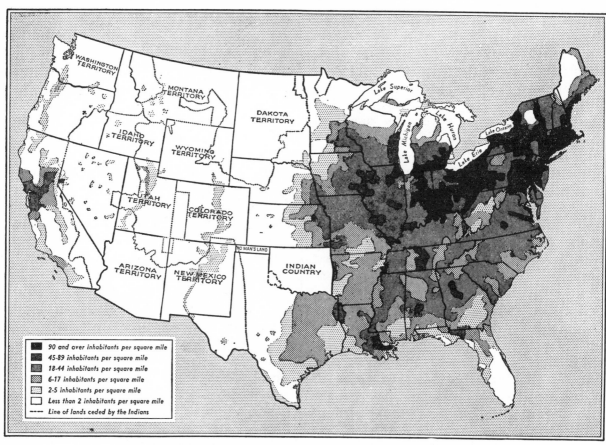

165   Population Density, Line of Indian Cessions, 1870

Legend:
- 90 and over inhabitants per square mile
- 45-89 inhabitants per square mile
- 18-44 inhabitants per square mile
- 6-17 inhabitants per square mile
- 2-5 inhabitants per square mile
- Less than 2 inhabitants per square mile
- Line of lands ceded by the Indians

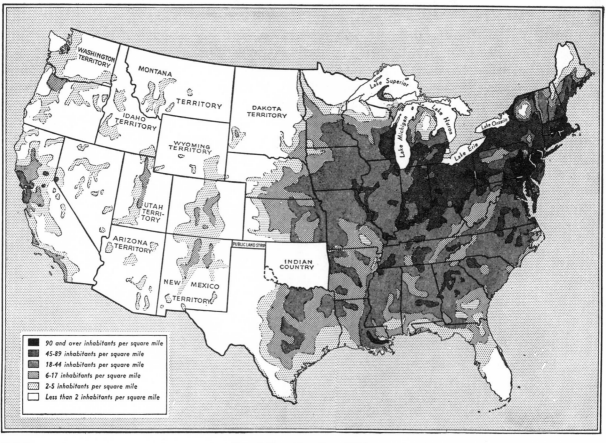

166   Population Density, 1880

Legend:
- 90 and over inhabitants per square mile
- 45-89 inhabitants per square mile
- 18-44 inhabitants per square mile
- 6-17 inhabitants per square mile
- 2-5 inhabitants per square mile
- Less than 2 inhabitants per square mile

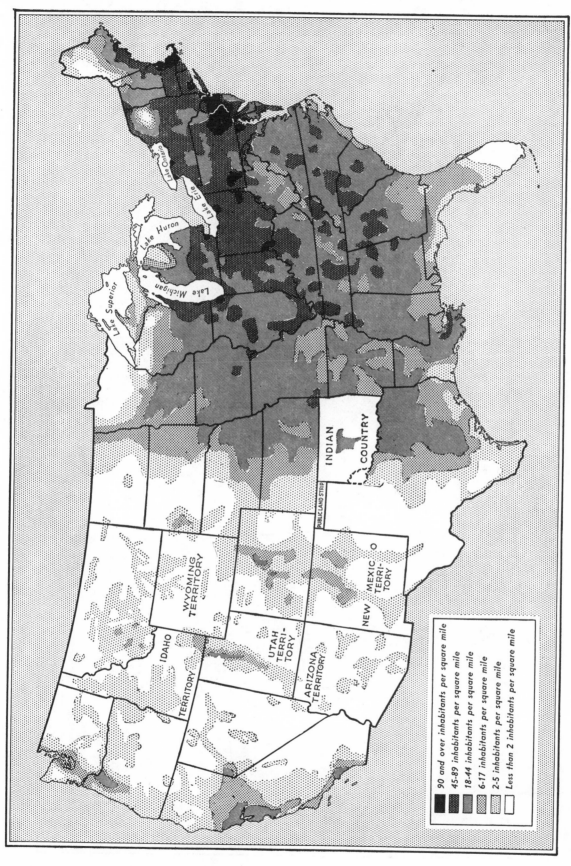

Population Density, 1890

167

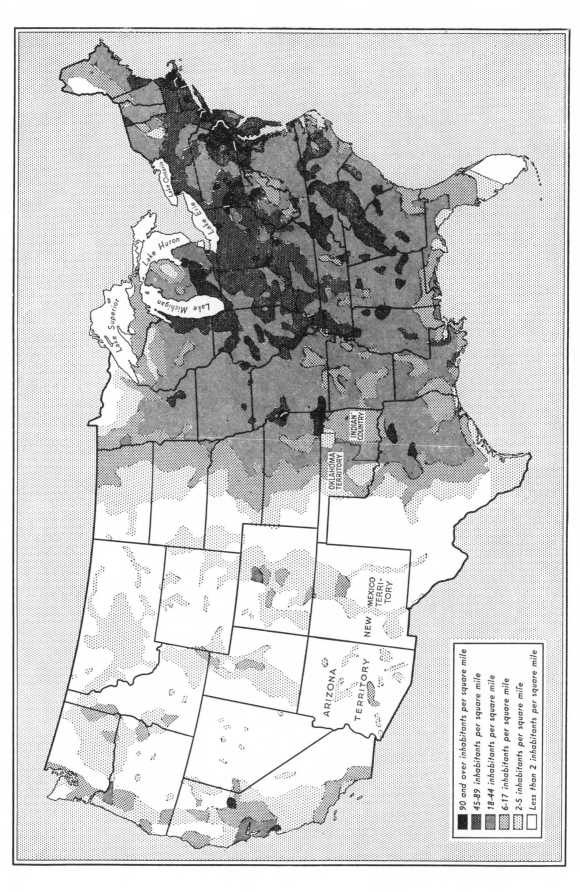

Population Density, 1900

90 and over inhabitants per square mile
45-89 inhabitants per square mile
18-44 inhabitants per square mile
6-17 inhabitants per square mile
2-5 inhabitants per square mile
Less than 2 inhabitants per square mile

168

[106]

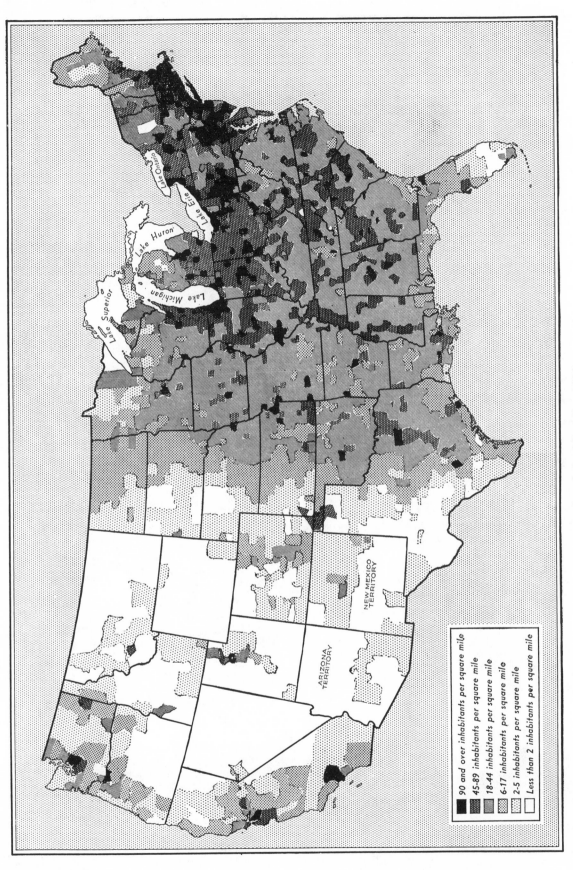

Population Density, 1910

■	90 and over inhabitants per square mile
	45-89 inhabitants per square mile
	18-44 inhabitants per square mile
	6-17 inhabitants per square mile
	2-5 inhabitants per square mile
□	Less than 2 inhabitants per square mile

169

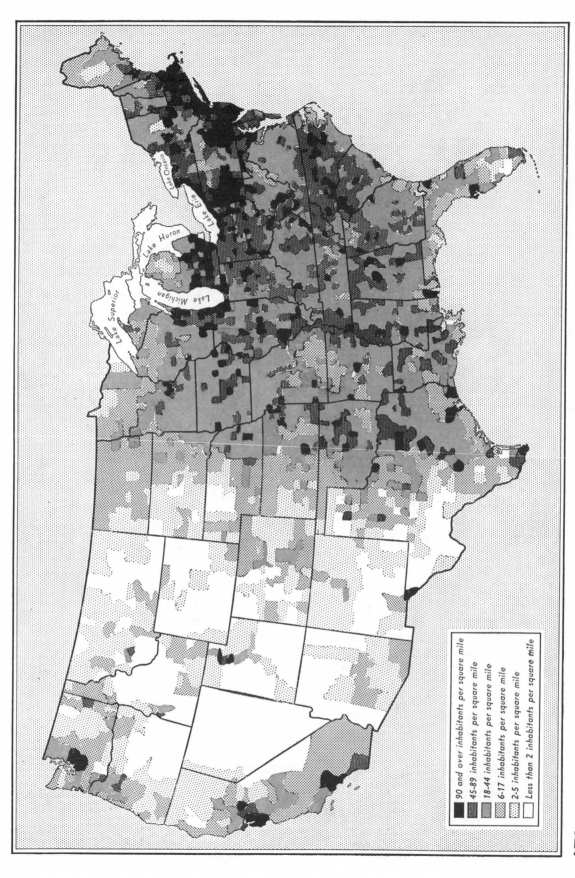

Population Density, 1930

90 and over inhabitants per square mile
45-89 inhabitants per square mile
18-44 inhabitants per square mile
6-17 inhabitants per square mile
2-5 inhabitants per square mile
Less than 2 inhabitants per square mile

Lake Ontario
Lake Erie
Lake Huron
Lake Michigan
Lake Superior

170

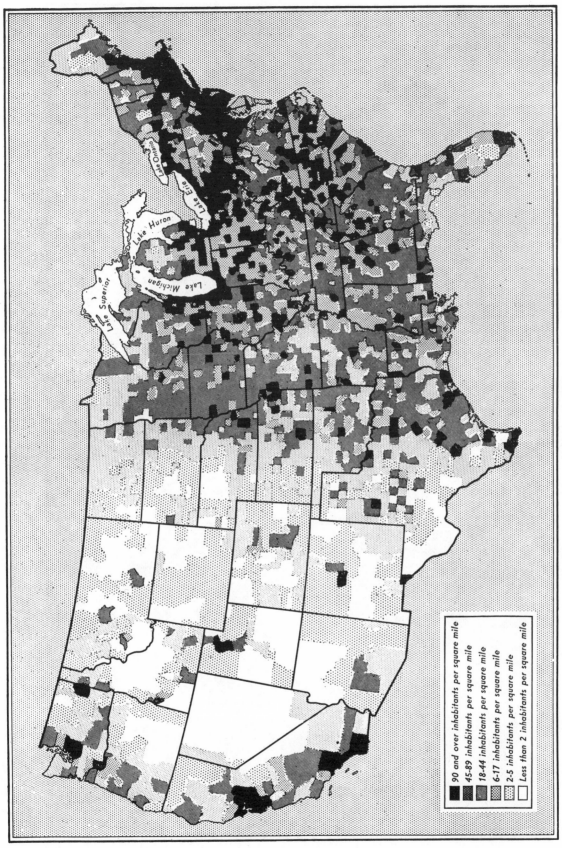

Population Density, 1950

171

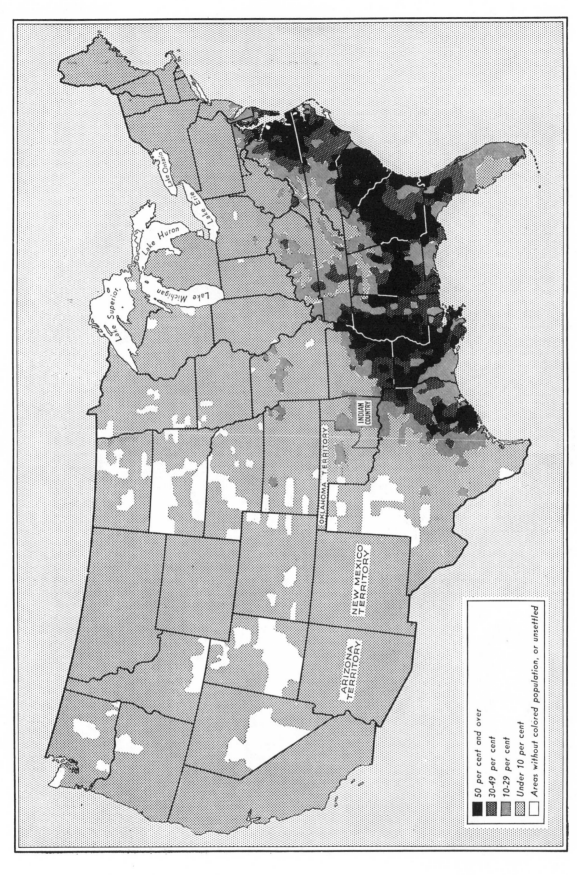

Negro Population, 1900

50 per cent and over
30-49 per cent
10-29 per cent
Under 10 per cent
Areas without colored population, or unsettled

172

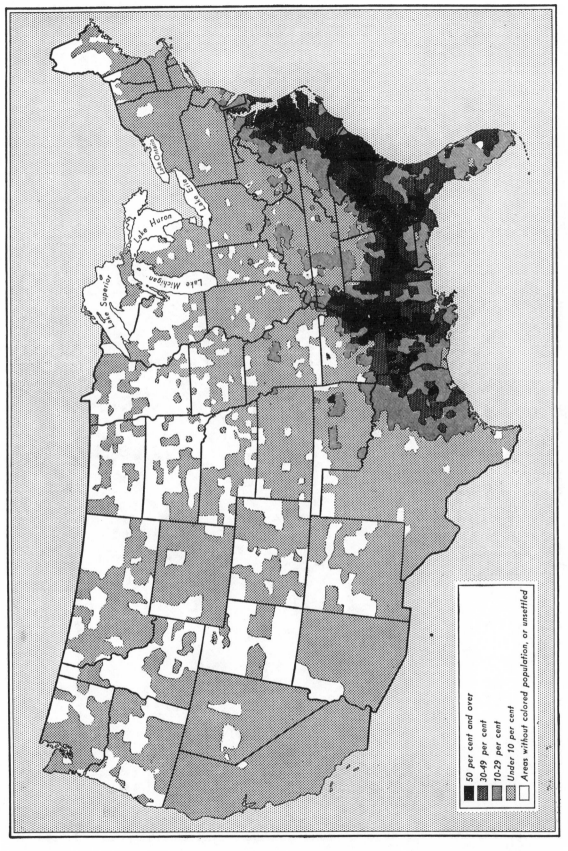

Negro Population, 1930

■	50 per cent and over
▓	30-49 per cent
▒	10-29 per cent
░	Under 10 per cent
□	Areas without colored population, or unsettled

173

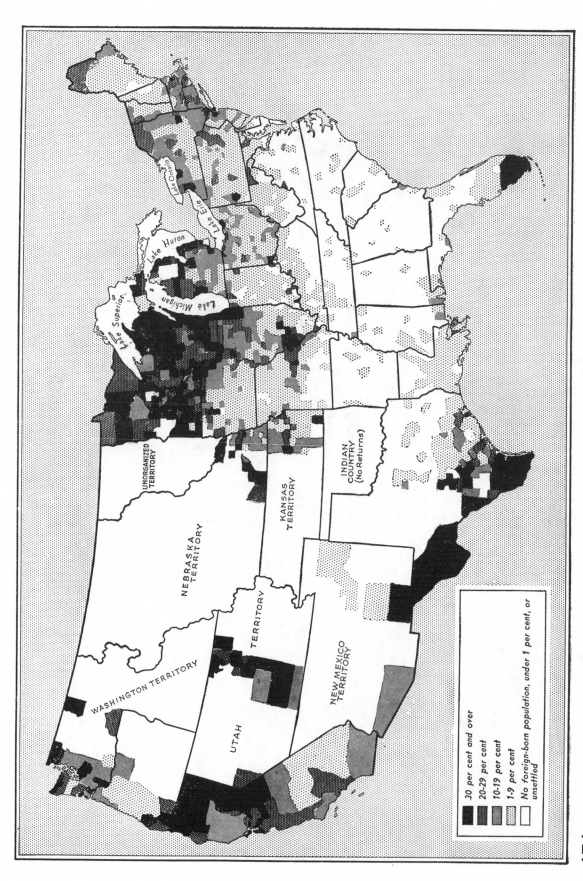

Population of Foreign Birth, 1860

30 per cent and over
20-29 per cent
10-19 per cent
1-9 per cent
No foreign-born population, under 1 per cent, or unsettled

174

[112]

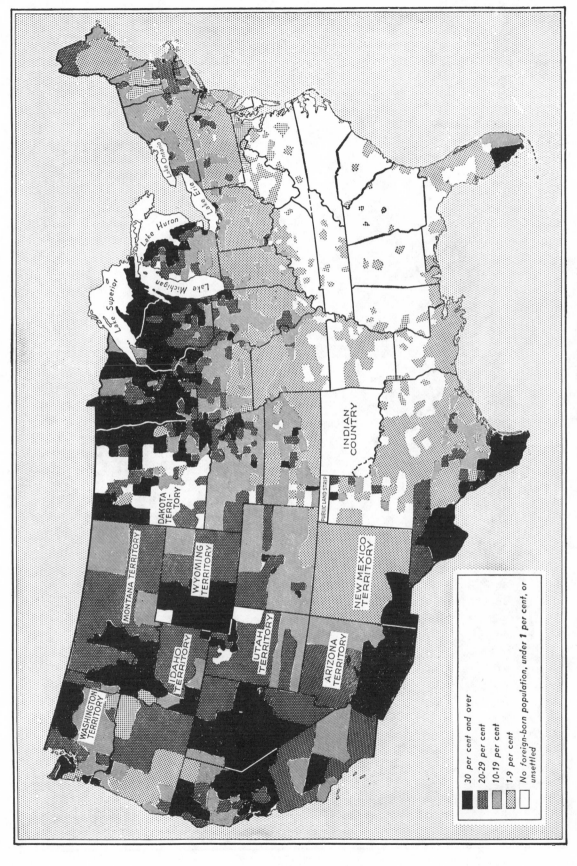

Population of Foreign Birth, 1880

Legend:
- 30 per cent and over
- 20-29 per cent
- 10-19 per cent
- 1-9 per cent
- No foreign-born population, under 1 per cent, or unsettled

175

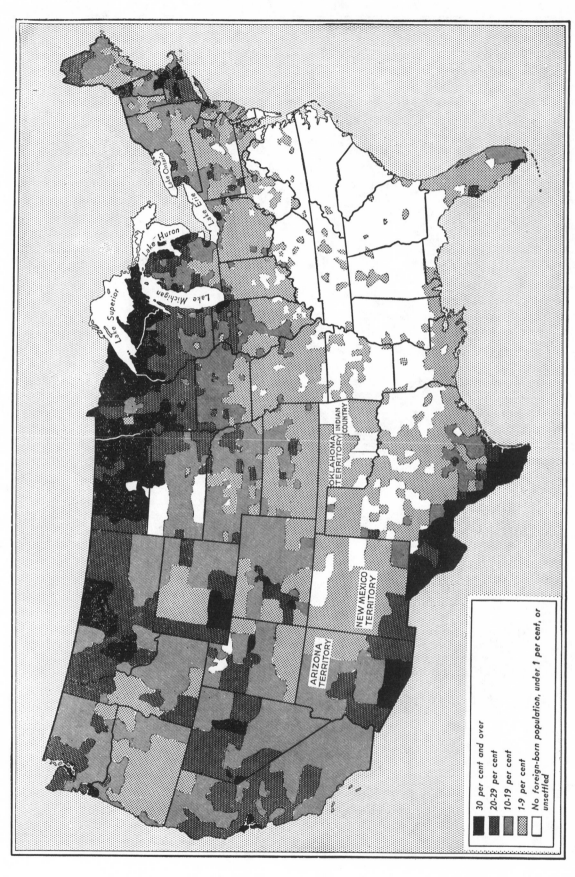

Population of Foreign Birth, 1900

Legend:
- 30 per cent and over
- 20-29 per cent
- 10-19 per cent
- 1-9 per cent
- No foreign-born population, under 1 per cent, or unsettled

176

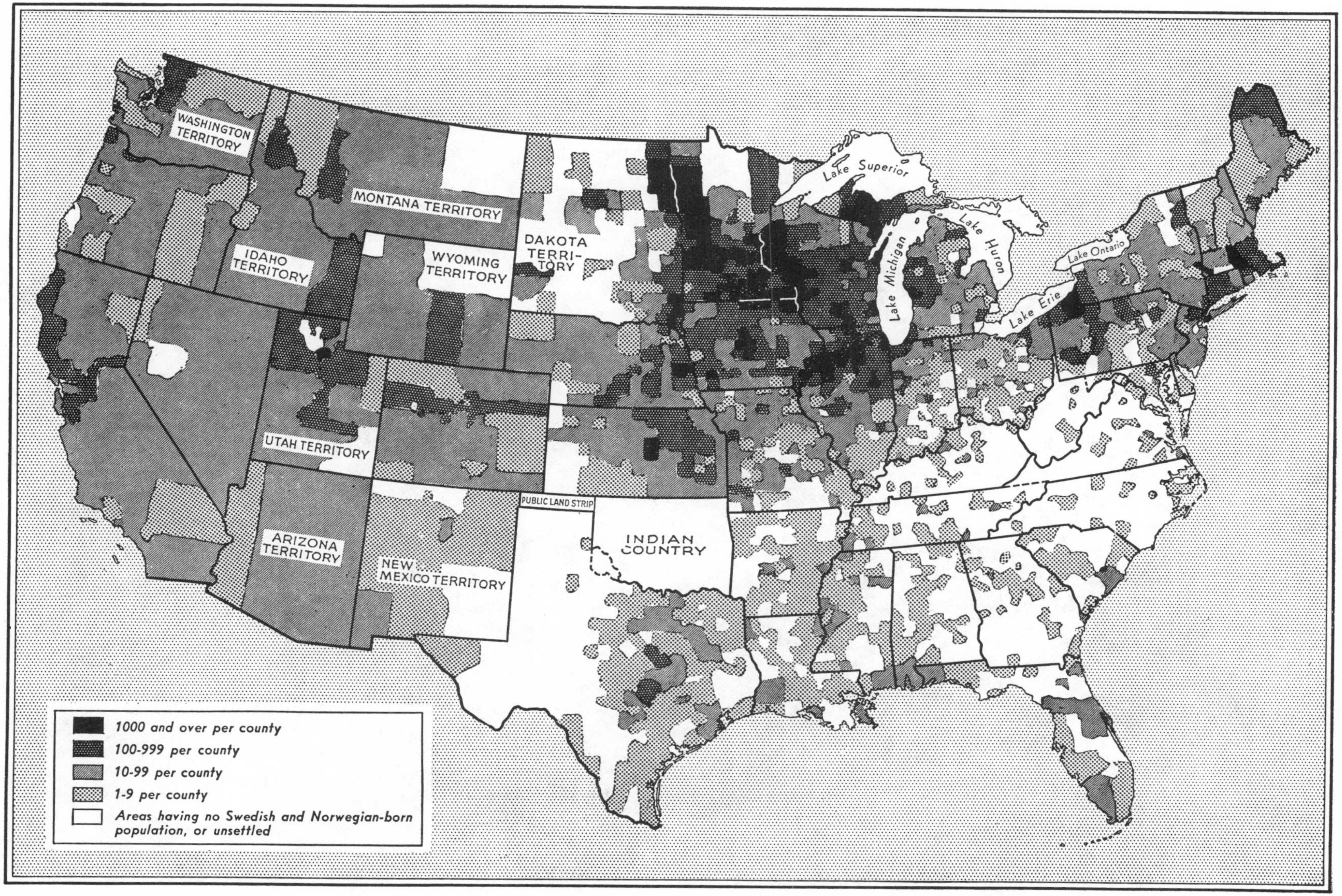
WASHINGTON TERRITORY
MONTANA TERRITORY
IDAHO TERRITORY
WYOMING TERRITORY
DAKOTA TERRI-TORY
UTAH TERRITORY
ARIZONA TERRITORY
NEW MEXICO TERRITORY
PUBLIC LAND STRIP
INDIAN COUNTRY
Lake Superior
Lake Michigan
Lake Huron
Lake Erie
Lake Ontario
1000 and over per county
100-999 per county
10-99 per county
1-9 per county
Areas having no Swedish and Norwegian-born population, or unsettled

177

Swedish- and Norwegian-born Population, 1880

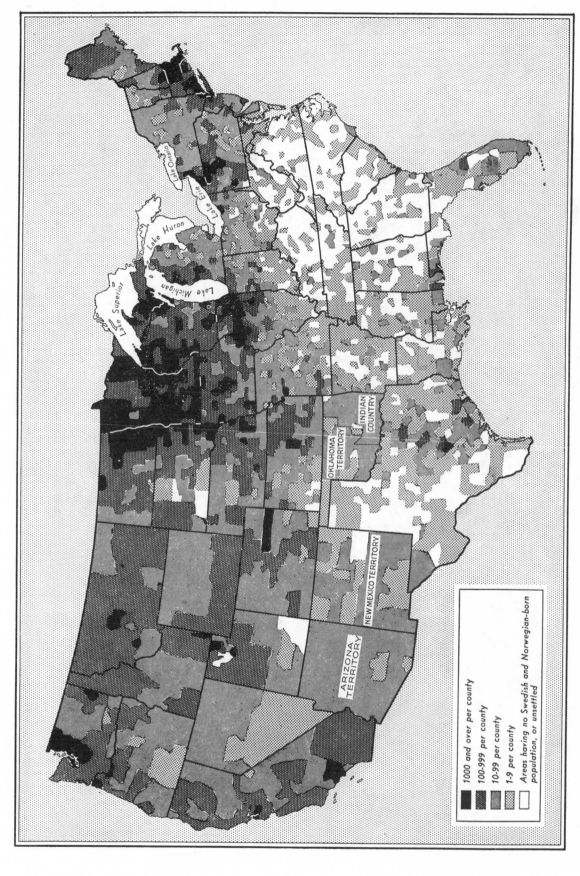

Swedish- and Norwegian-born Population, 1900

1000 and over per county
100-999 per county
10-99 per county
1-9 per county
Areas having no Swedish and Norwegian-born population, or unsettled

178

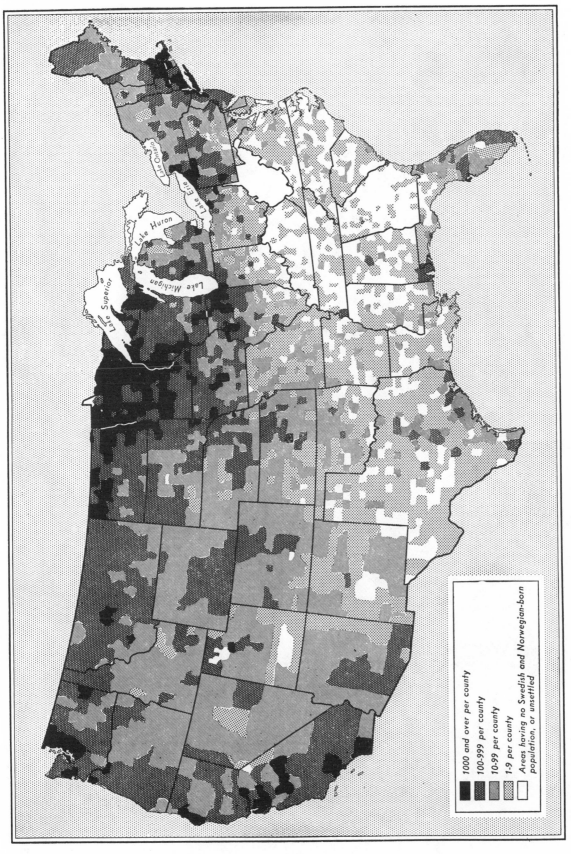

Swedish- and Norwegian-born Population, 1930

179

Lake Ontario
Lake Erie
Lake Huron
Lake Michigan
Lake Superior

1000 and over per county
100-999 per county
10-99 per county
1-9 per county
Areas having no Swedish and Norwegian-born population, or unsettled

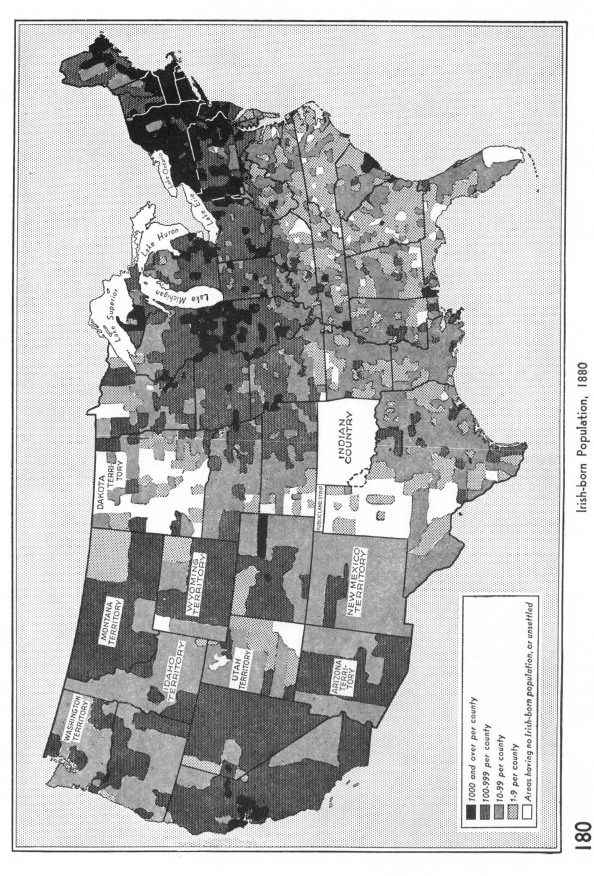

Irish-born Population, 1880

180

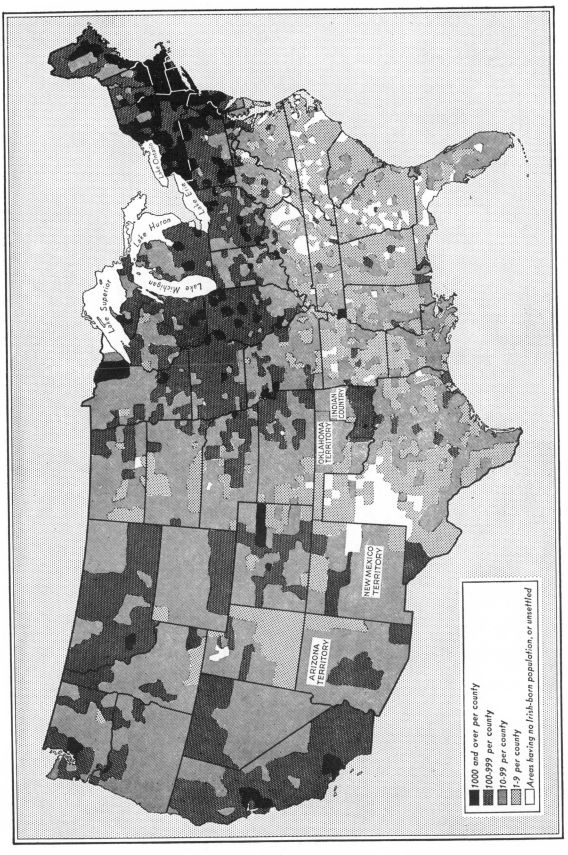

Irish-born Population, 1900

1000 and over per county
100-999 per county
10-99 per county
1-9 per county
Areas having no Irish-born population, or unsettled

181

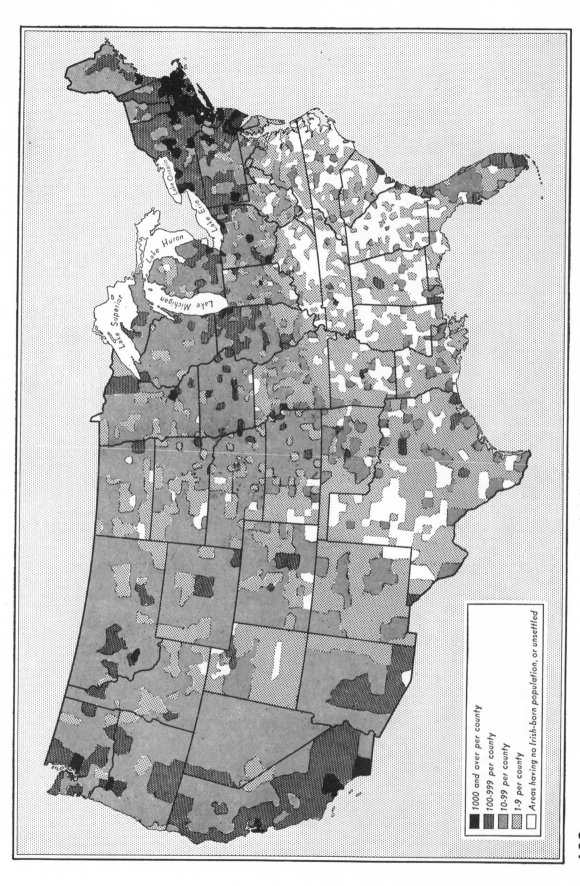

Irish-born Population, 1930

182

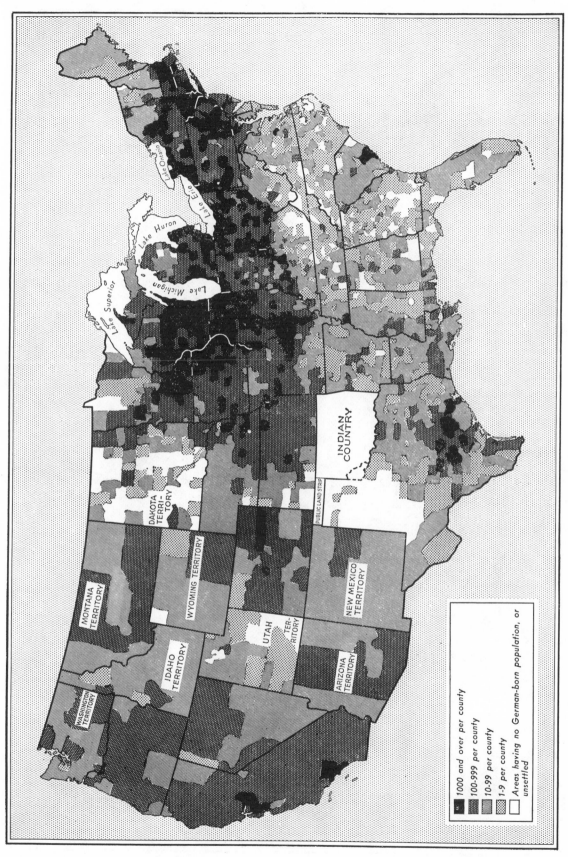

German-born Population, 1880

Lake Ontario
Lake Erie
Lake Huron
Lake Superior
Lake Michigan

WASHINGTON TERRITORY

MONTANA TERRITORY

IDAHO TERRITORY

WYOMING TERRITORY

DAKOTA TERRI- TORY

UTAH TERRITORY

ARIZONA TERRITORY

NEW MEXICO TERRITORY

PUBLIC LAND STRIP

INDIAN COUNTRY

1000 and over per county
100-999 per county
10-99 per county
1-9 per county
Areas having no German-born population, or unsettled

183

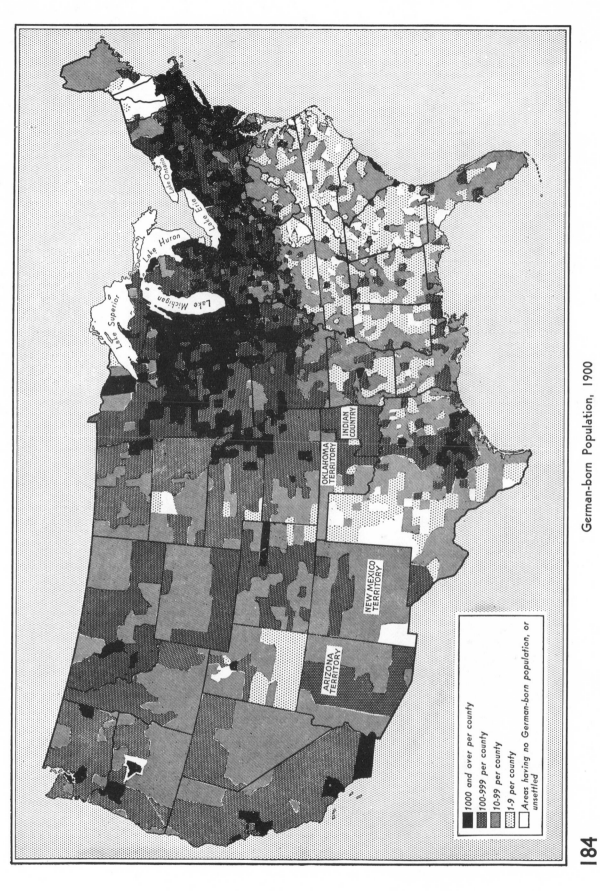

German-born Population, 1900

1000 and over per county
100-999 per county
10-99 per county
1-9 per county
Areas having no German-born population, or unsettled

184

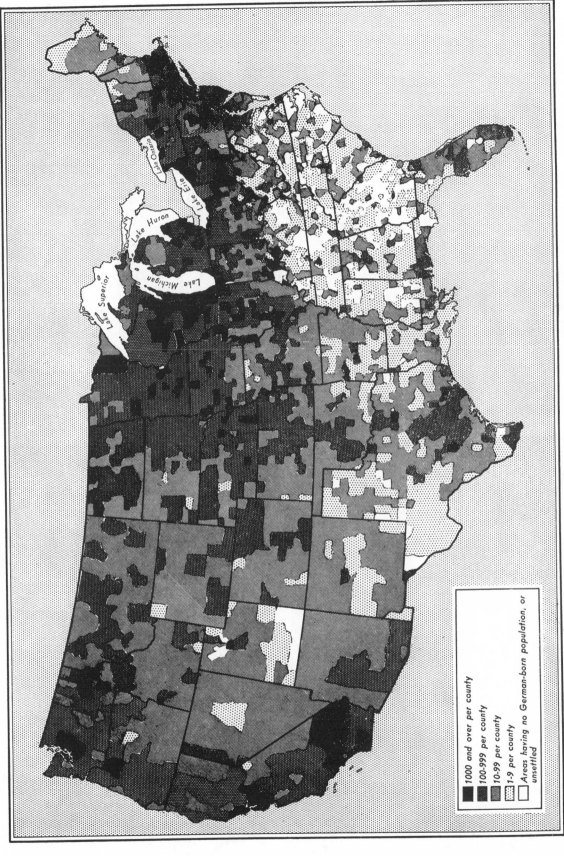

German-born Population, 1930

1000 and over per county
100-999 per county
10-99 per county
1-9 per county
Areas having no German-born population, or unsettled

Lake Ontario
Lake Erie
Lake Huron
Lake Michigan
Lake Superior

185

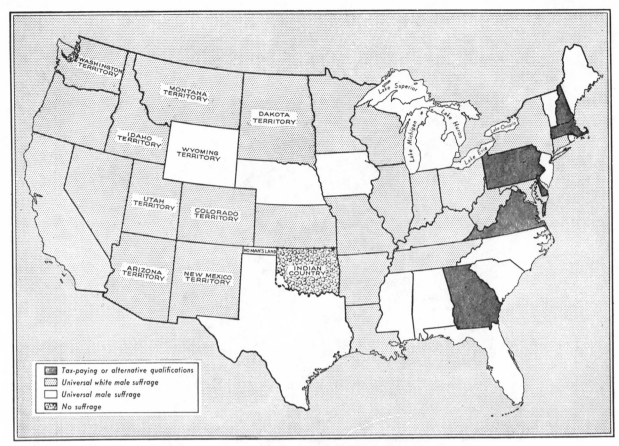

186

Male Suffrage, 1870

Legend:
- Tax-paying or alternative qualifications
- Universal white male suffrage
- Universal male suffrage
- No suffrage

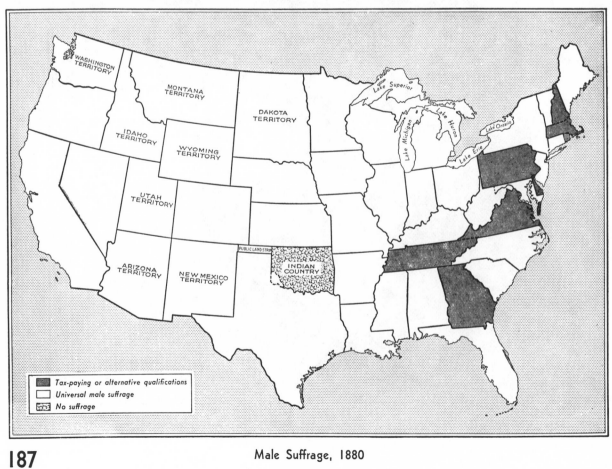

187

Male Suffrage, 1880

Legend:
- Tax-paying or alternative qualifications
- Universal male suffrage
- No suffrage

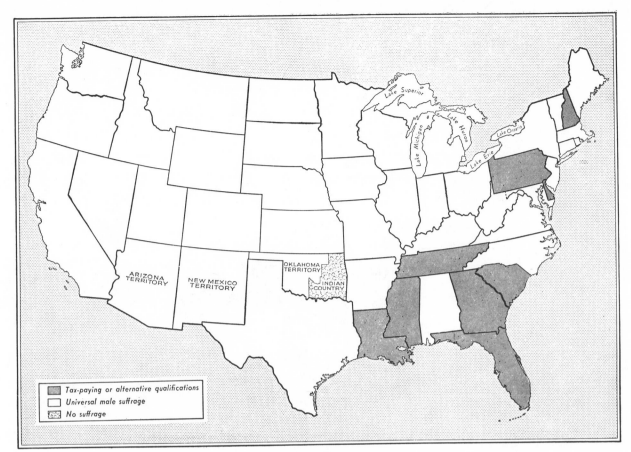

Tax-paying or alternative qualifications
Universal male suffrage
No suffrage

Male Suffrage, 1900

188

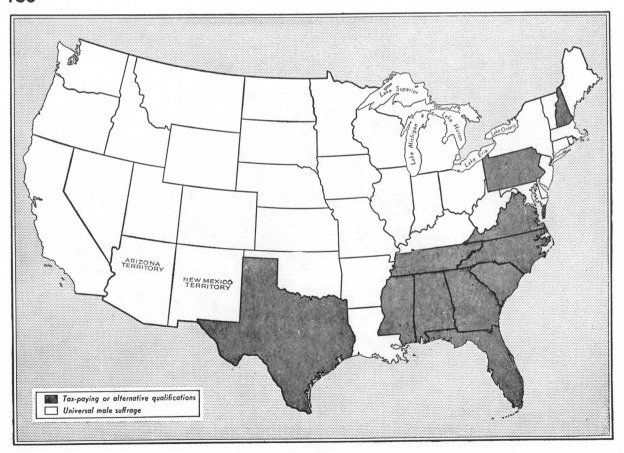

Tax-paying or alternative qualifications
Universal male suffrage

Male Suffrage, 1910

189

[125]

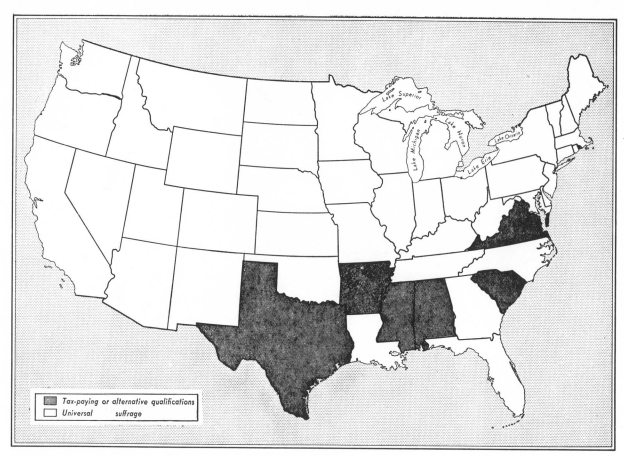

190   Suffrage, 1950

Legend:
- Tax-paying or alternative qualifications
- Universal suffrage

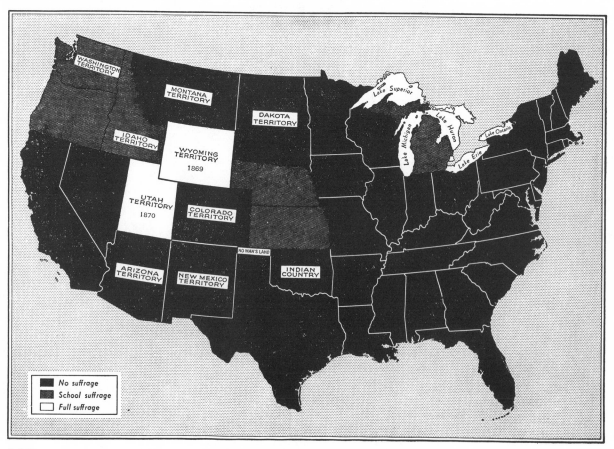

191   Enfranchisement of Women, 1870

Legend:
- No suffrage
- School suffrage
- Full suffrage

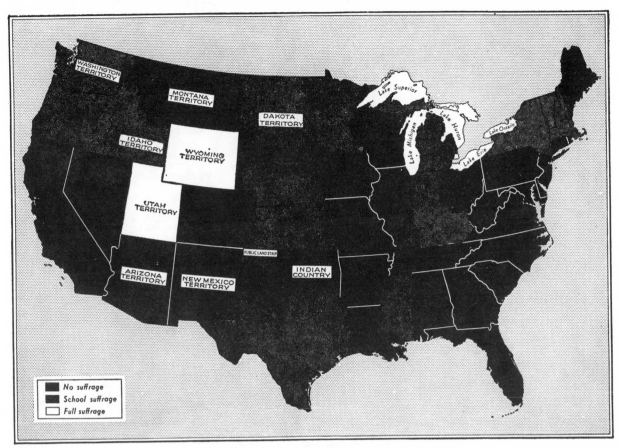

192
Enfranchisement of Women, 1880

- ■ No suffrage
- ■ School suffrage
- □ Full suffrage

WASHINGTON TERRITORY
MONTANA TERRITORY
DAKOTA TERRITORY
IDAHO TERRITORY
WYOMING TERRITORY
UTAH TERRITORY
ARIZONA TERRITORY
NEW MEXICO TERRITORY
PUBLIC LAND STRIP
INDIAN COUNTRY

Lake Superior
Lake Michigan
Lake Huron
Lake Ontario
Lake Erie

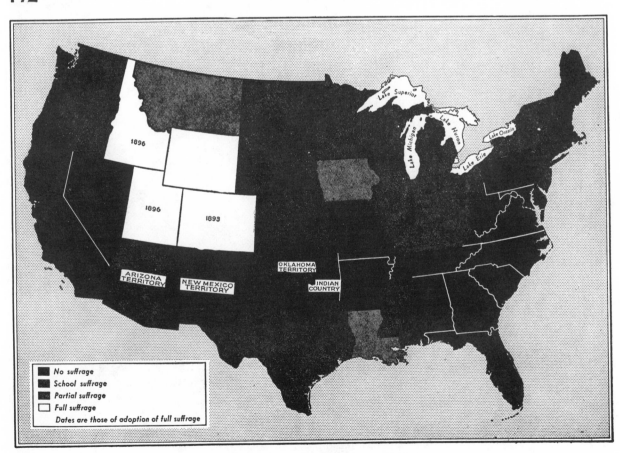

193
Enfranchisement of Women, 1900

- ■ No suffrage
- ■ School suffrage
- ▨ Partial suffrage
- □ Full suffrage
- *Dates are those of adoption of full suffrage*

1896
1896
1893
ARIZONA TERRITORY
NEW MEXICO TERRITORY
OKLAHOMA TERRITORY
INDIAN COUNTRY

Lake Superior
Lake Michigan
Lake Huron
Lake Ontario
Lake Erie

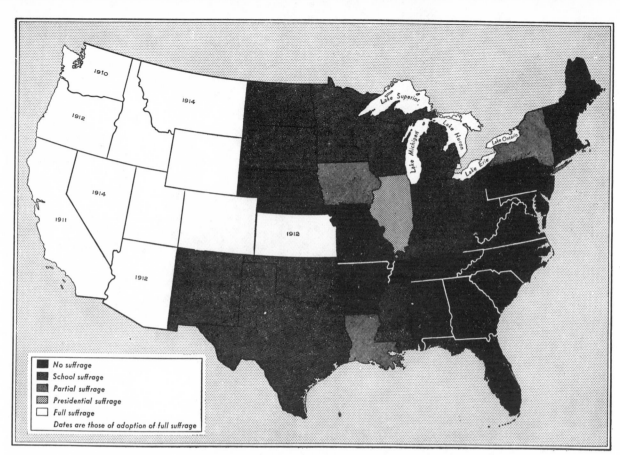

194   Enfranchisement of Women, 1915

Legend (map 194):
- No suffrage
- School suffrage
- Partial suffrage
- Presidential suffrage
- Full suffrage
- *Dates are those of adoption of full suffrage*

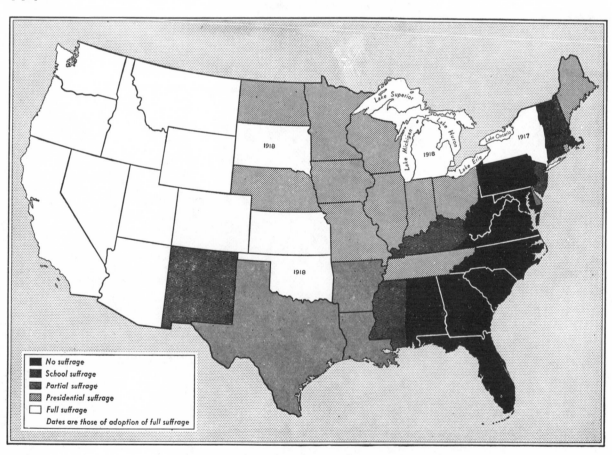

195   Enfranchisement of Women, 1919
The Nineteenth Amendment in 1920 extended suffrage to women in all states
(See maps 190 and 196 for suffrage qualifications)

Legend (map 195):
- No suffrage
- School suffrage
- Partial suffrage
- Presidential suffrage
- Full suffrage
- *Dates are those of adoption of full suffrage*

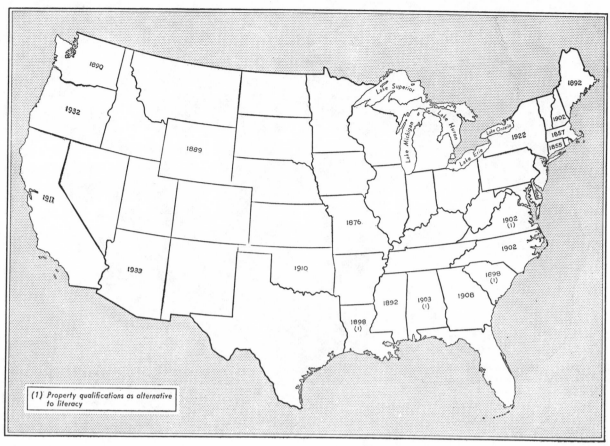

196   Dates of the Establishment of Literacy Qualifications for the Franchise

(Map labels:) 1890, 1932, 1911, 1889, 1933, 1876, 1910, 1892, 1898 (1), 1903 (1), 1908, 1898 (1), 1902 (1), 1902, 1892, 1902, 1922, 1857, 1855

(1) Property qualifications as alternative to literacy

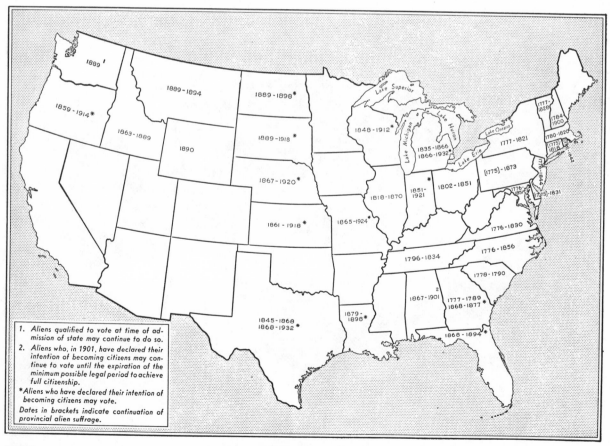

1. Aliens qualified to vote at time of admission of state may continue to do so.
2. Aliens who, in 1901, have declared their intention of becoming citizens may continue to vote until the expiration of the minimum possible legal period to achieve full citizenship.
*Aliens who have declared their intention of becoming citizens may vote.
Dates in brackets indicate continuation of provincial alien suffrage.

(Map labels:) 1889, 1859–1914*, 1863–1889, 1889–1894, 1890, 1889–1898*, 1889–1918*, 1867–1920*, 1861–1918*, 1865–1924*, 1848–1912*, 1835–1866 1866–1932*, 1818–1870, 1851–1921*, 1802–1851, 1796–1834, 1867–1901, 1777–1789* 1868–1877*, 1878–1790, 1868–1894*, 1845–1868 1868–1932*, 1879–1898*, (1775)–1873, 1777–1821, 1776–1830, 1776–1856, 1777–1828, 1784–1900, 1780–1820, (1775) 1816, 1776–1844, (1775)–1831

197   Alien Enfranchisement, 1775-1942

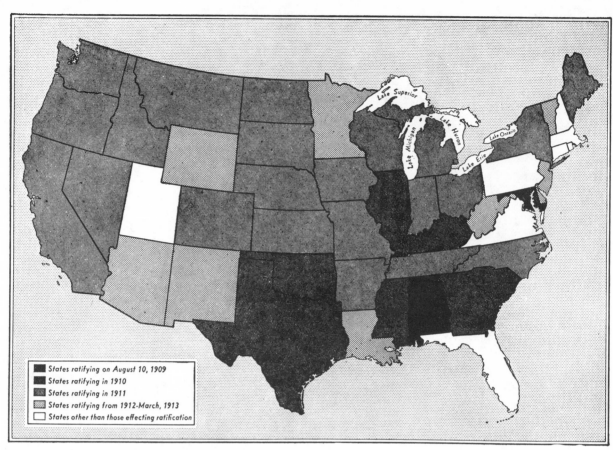

198 States Effecting the Ratification of the Sixteenth Amendment to the Constitution, 1913

Legend:
- States ratifying on August 10, 1909
- States ratifying in 1910
- States ratifying in 1911
- States ratifying from 1912–March, 1913
- States other than those effecting ratification

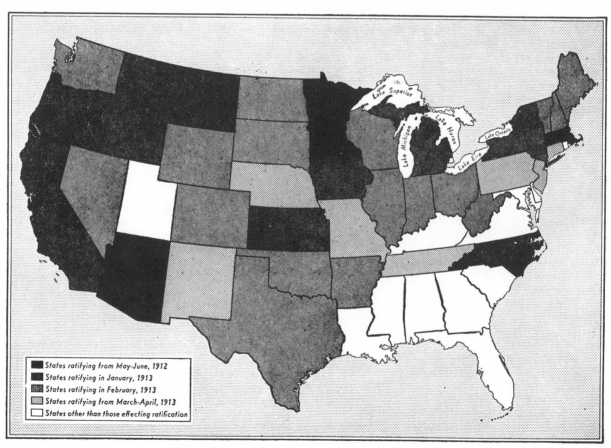

199 States Effecting the Ratification of the Seventeenth Amendment to the Constitution, 1913

Legend:
- States ratifying from May–June, 1912
- States ratifying in January, 1913
- States ratifying in February, 1913
- States ratifying from March–April, 1913
- States other than those effecting ratification

[130]

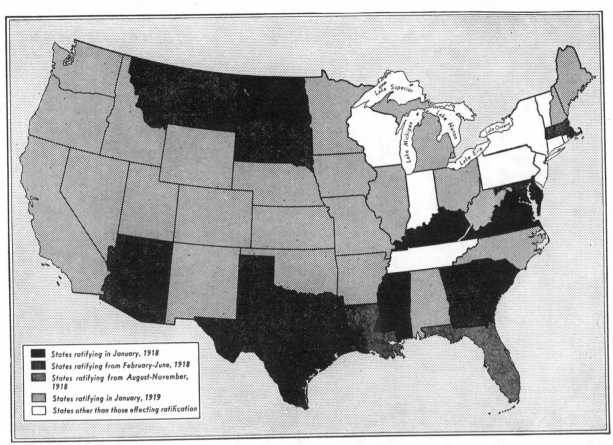

200   States Effecting the Ratification of the Eighteenth Amendment to the Constitution, 1919

Legend (top map):
- States ratifying in January, 1918
- States ratifying from February-June, 1918
- States ratifying from August-November, 1918
- States ratifying in January, 1919
- States other than those effecting ratification

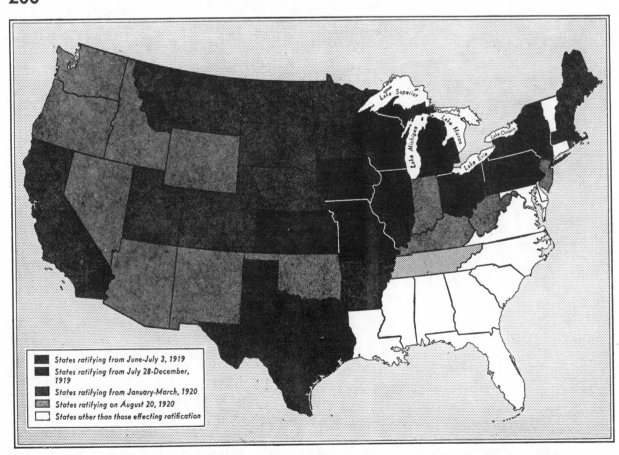

201   States Effecting the Ratification of the Nineteenth Amendment to the Constitution, 1920

Legend (bottom map):
- States ratifying from June-July 3, 1919
- States ratifying from July 28-December, 1919
- States ratifying from January-March, 1920
- States ratifying on August 20, 1920
- States other than those effecting ratification

[131]

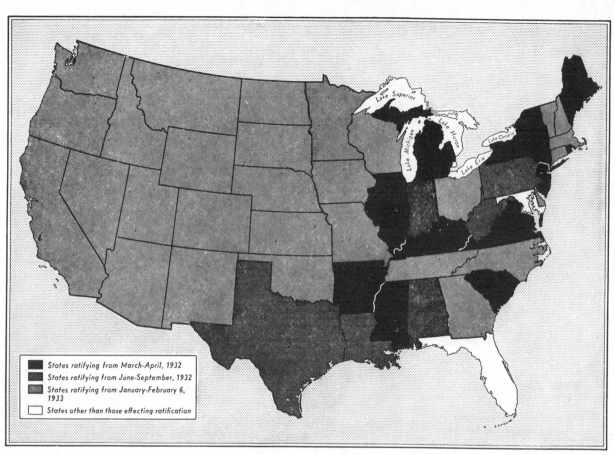

202   States Effecting the Ratification of the Twentieth Amendment to the Constitution, 1933

Legend (map 202):
- States ratifying from March-April, 1932
- States ratifying from June-September, 1932
- States ratifying from January-February 6, 1933
- States other than those effecting ratification

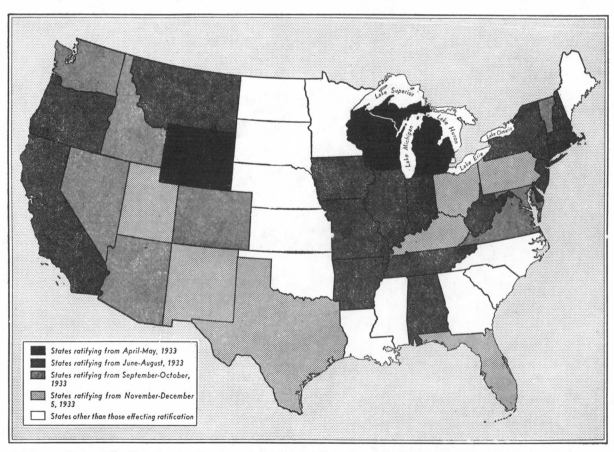

203   States Effecting the Ratification of the Twenty-first Amendment to the Constitution, 1933

(For proposed child labor amendment, see map 303)

Legend (map 203):
- States ratifying from April-May, 1933
- States ratifying from June-August, 1933
- States ratifying from September-October, 1933
- States ratifying from November-December 5, 1933
- States other than those effecting ratification

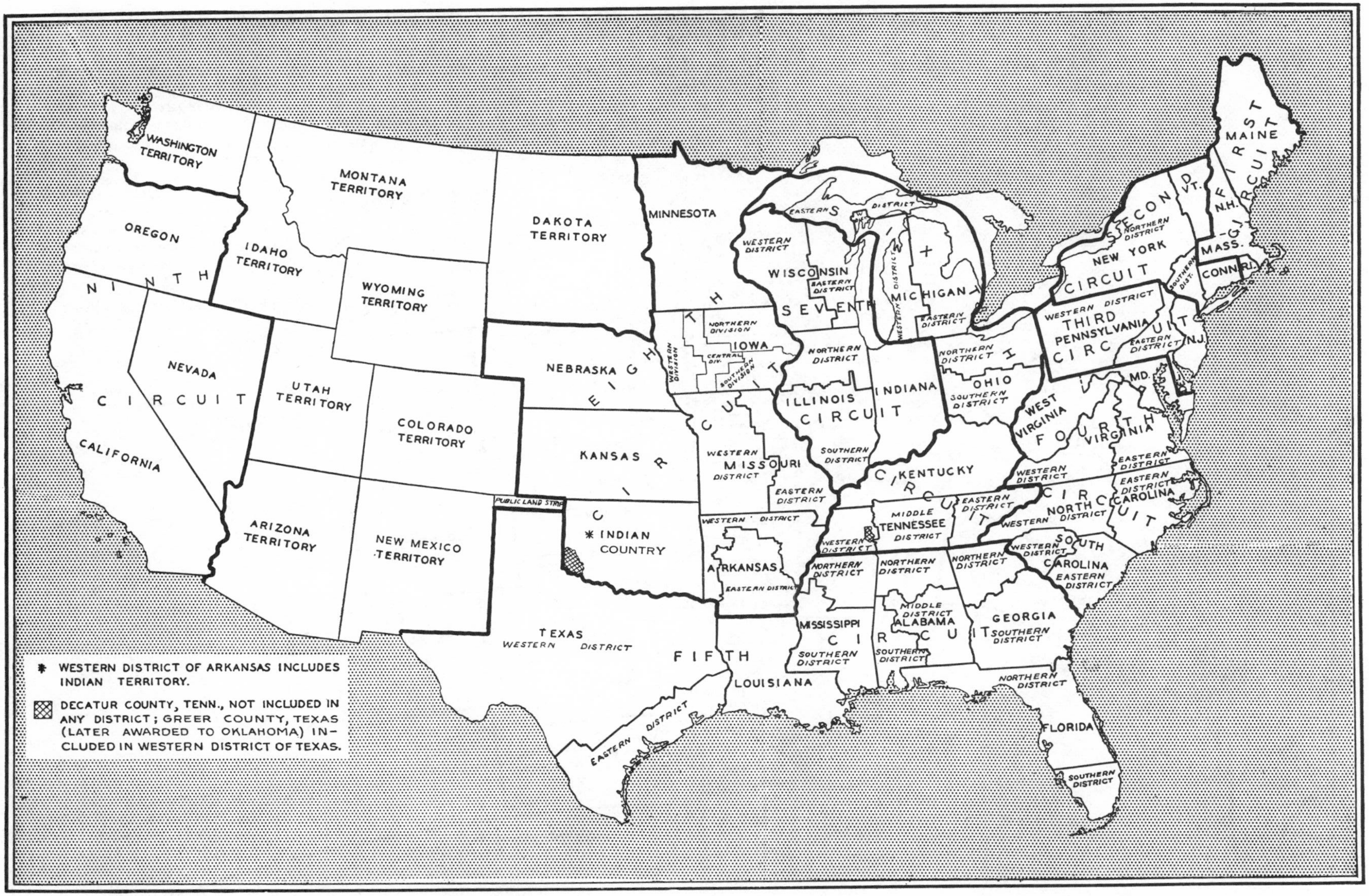

Federal Circuit and District Courts, 1873

Circuit court borders are marked by heavy lines; district court borders by medium lines; division borders by light lines

204

Federal Circuit and District Courts, 1911

Circuit court borders are marked by heavy lines; district court borders by medium lines; division borders by light lines

205

NOTE
1 EASTERN DIV. OF SOUTHERN DIST OF IOWA
2 DAVENPORT DIV. OF SOUTHERN DIST. OF IOWA
3 JEFFERSON DIV. OF EASTERN DIST. OF TEXAS
4 PARIS DIV OF EASTERN DIST. OF TEXAS
5 TEXARKANA OF EASTERN DIST. OF TEXAS

DISTRICT OF HAWAII IS PART OF NINTH CIRCUIT
PORTO RICO ADDED TO FIRST CIRCUIT BY AMENDMENT
OF JANUARY 28, 1915.

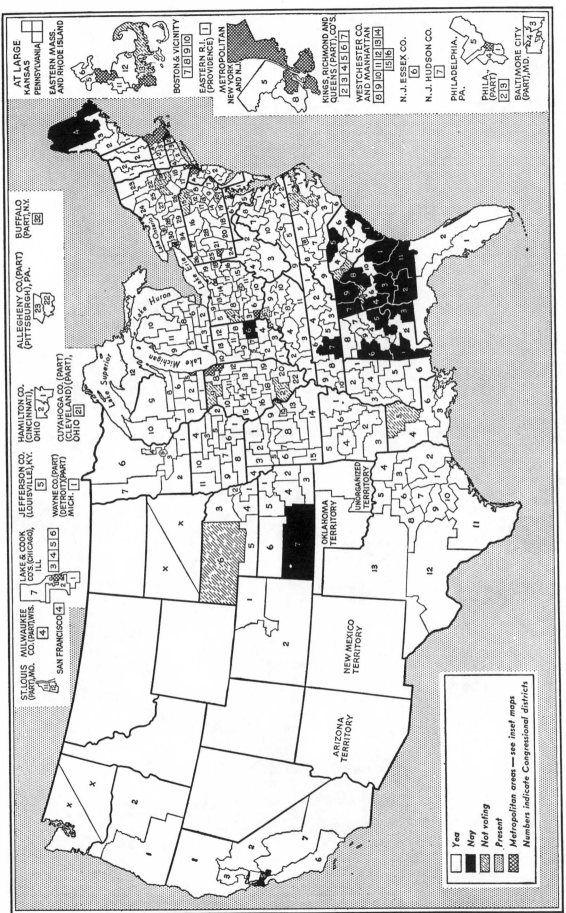

AT LARGE
KANSAS
PENNSYLVANIA

EASTERN MASS.
AND RHODE ISLAND

BOSTON & VICINITY
7 8 9 10

EASTERN R.I.
(PROVIDENCE) 1

METROPOLITAN
NEW YORK
AND N.J.

KINGS, RICHMOND AND
QUEENS (PART), CO'S. 2 3 4 5 6 7

WESTCHESTER CO.
AND MANHATTAN 8 9 10 11 12 13 14
15 16

N.J. ESSEX CO. 6

N.J. HUDSON CO. 7

PHILADELPHIA,
PA. 5

PHILA.
(PART) 2 3

BALTIMORE CITY
(PART),MD. 24 5 3

BUFFALO
(PART),N.Y. 32

ALLEGHENY CO.(PART)
(PITTSBURGH), PA. 23 22

HAMILTON CO.
(CINCINNATI),
OHIO 2 1

CUYAHOGA CO. (PART)
(CLEVELAND)(PART),
OHIO 21

JEFFERSON CO.
(LOUISVILLE), KY. 5

WAYNE CO.(PART)
(DETROIT)(PART)
MICH. 1

ST.LOUIS
(PART),MO.

MILWAUKEE
CO.(PART),WIS. 4

LAKE & COOK
CO'S.(CHICAGO),
ILL. 3 4 5 6
2 1
7

SAN FRANCISCO 4

206 House Vote of April 13, 1898, on Resolution Declaring War on Spain, Taken Prior to and Lacking Unanimity of Final
Action Agreeing to Conference Report

In cases where a number is repeated in the same state, it indicates two geographically separated parts of the same district.

Yea
Nay
Not voting
Present
Metropolitan areas — see inset maps
Numbers indicate Congressional districts

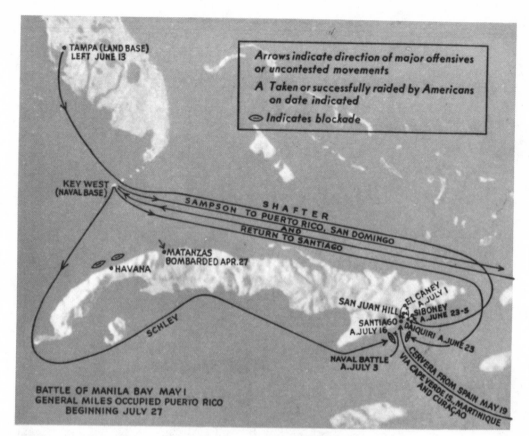

207   The Spanish-American War: Caribbean Campaign

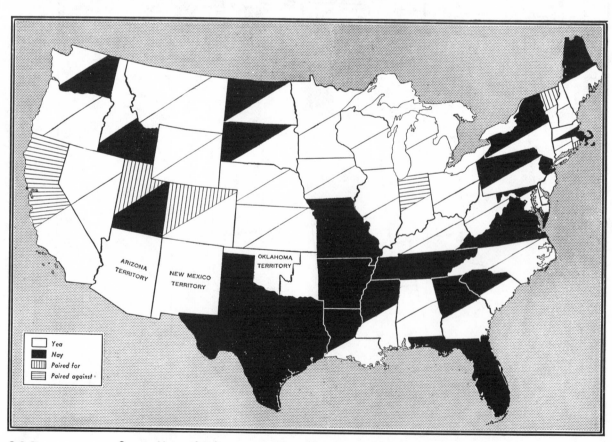

208   Senate Vote of February 6, 1899, on Ratification of the Treaty of Paris

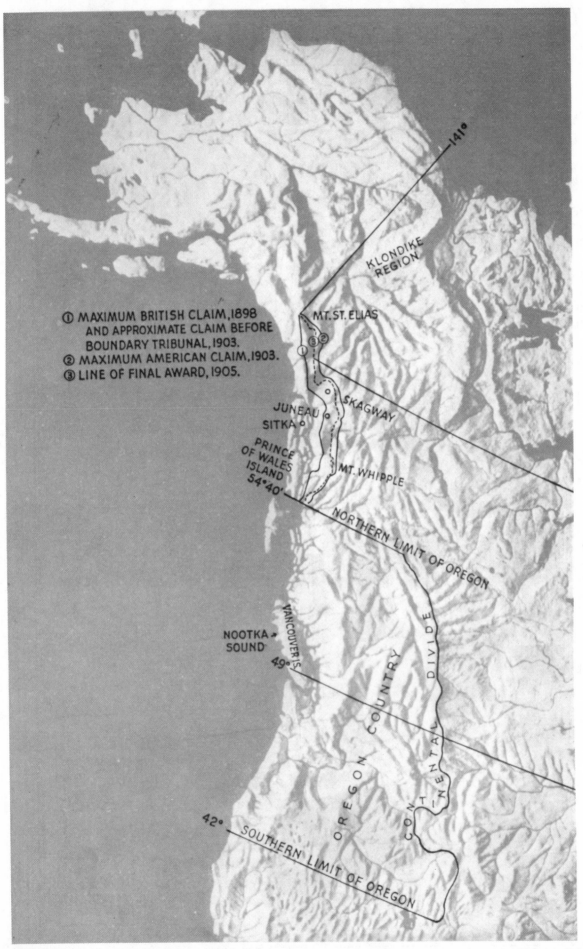

Alaska Border Dispute, 1878-1905

Within the map:

① MAXIMUM BRITISH CLAIM,1898 AND APPROXIMATE CLAIM BEFORE BOUNDARY TRIBUNAL,1903.
② MAXIMUM AMERICAN CLAIM,1903.
③ LINE OF FINAL AWARD,1905.

141°

KLONDIKE REGION

MT.ST.ELIAS

JUNEAU
SITKA

SKAGWAY

PRINCE OF WALES ISLAND
54°40'

MT.WHIPPLE

NORTHERN LIMIT OF OREGON

VANCOUVER IS.

NOOTKA SOUND

49°

OREGON COUNTRY

CONTINENTAL DIVIDE

42°

SOUTHERN LIMIT OF OREGON

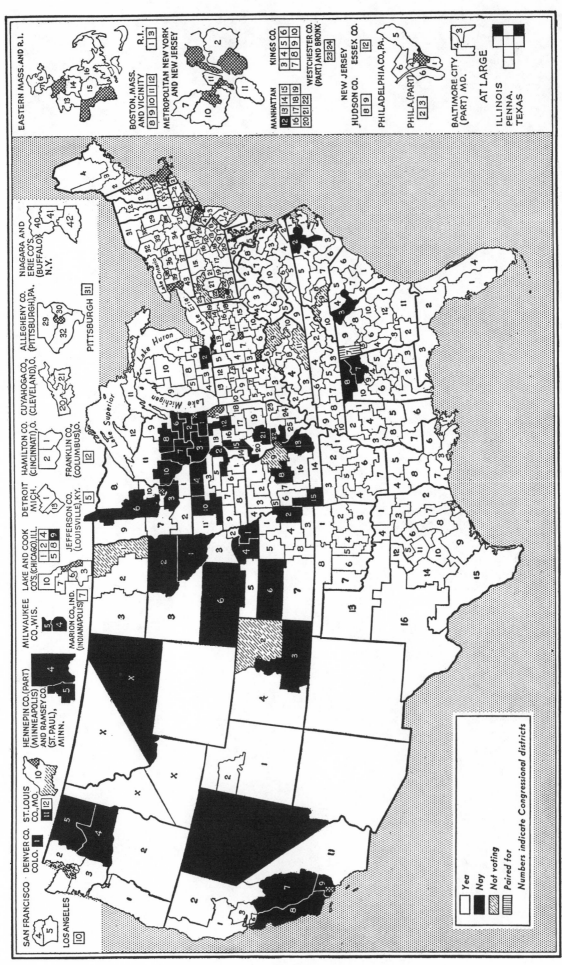

House Vote of April 5, 1917, on Resolution Declaring War on Germany

In cases where a number is repeated in the same state, it indicates two parts of the same district

Legend:

☐	Yea
■	Nay
▨	Not voting
▤	Paired for

Numbers indicate Congressional districts

210

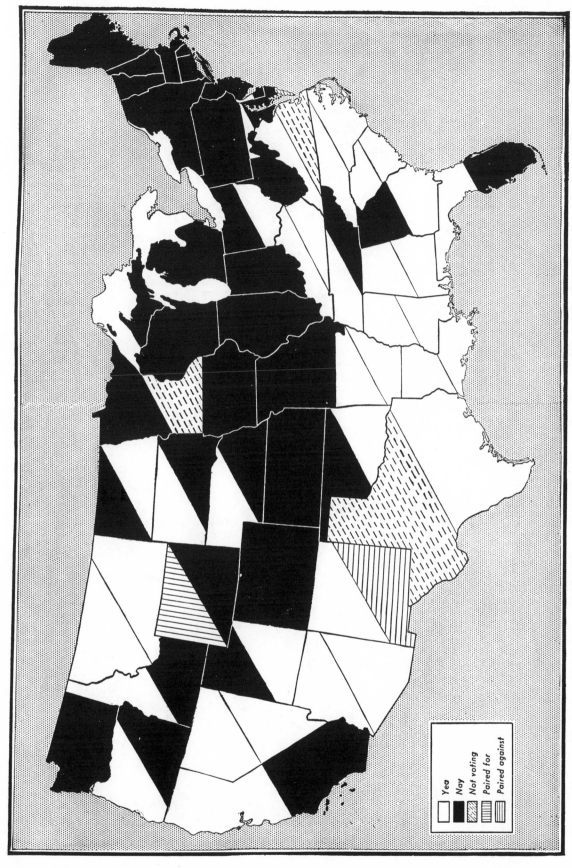

Senate Vote of November 19, 1919, on Unconditional Ratification of the Versailles Treaty

Yea
Nay
Not voting
Paired for
Paired against

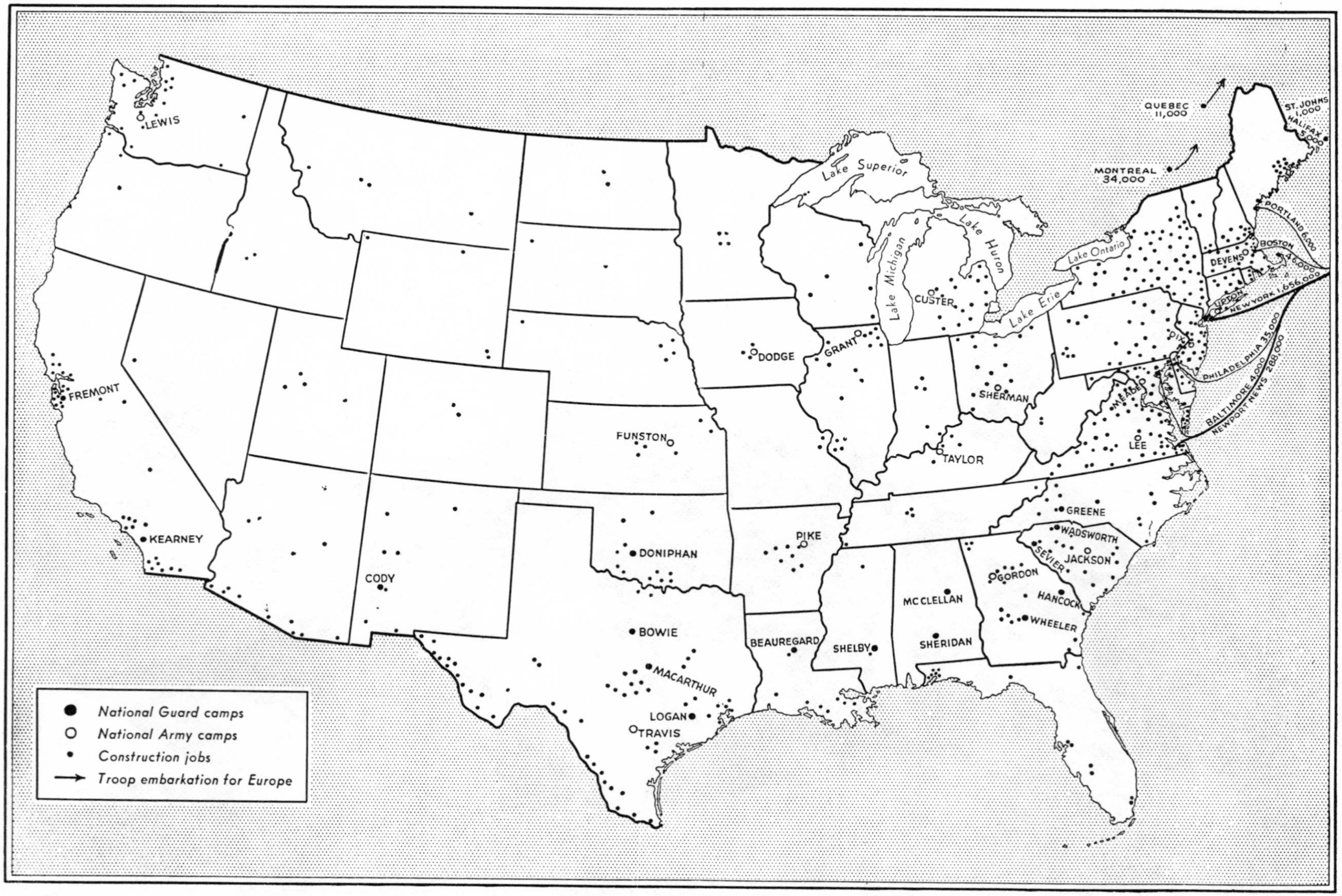

America in the First World War: Training Camps, Embarkation Ports, and Construction Projects

National Guard camps ●
National Army camps ○
Construction jobs ·
Troop embarkation for Europe →

212

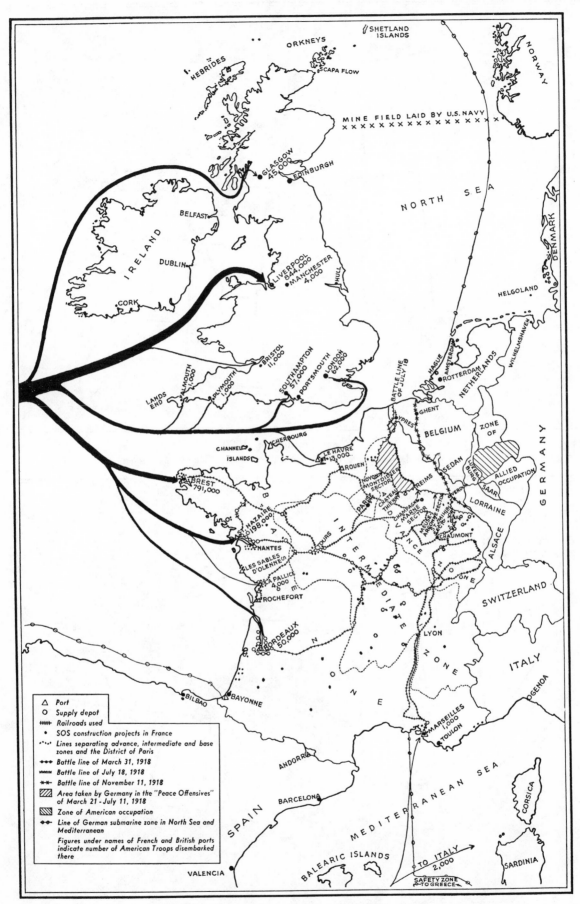

HEBRIDES
ORKNEYS
SHETLAND ISLANDS
NORWAY
CAPA FLOW
MINE FIELD LAID BY U.S. NAVY
× × × × × × × × × × × × × × × × ×
NORTH SEA
GLASGOW 45,000
EDINBURGH
BELFAST
IRELAND
DUBLIN
HELGOLAND
DENMARK
WILHELMSHAVEN
CORK
LIVERPOOL 644,000
MANCHESTER 4,000
HULL
BRISTOL 11,000
HAGUE
AMSTERDAM
ROTTERDAM
SOUTHAMPTON 57,000
FALMOUTH 1,000
PLYMOUTH 1,000
PORTSMOUTH
LONDON 62,000
NETHERLANDS
BATTLE LINE OF JULY 18
GHENT
LANDS END
BELGIUM
ZONE OF
CHANNEL ISLANDS
CHERBOURG
YPRES
ALLIED OCCUPATION
LE HAVRE 13,000
ROUEN
SEDAN
GERMANY
BREST 791,000
NOYON
MONTDIDIER SECTOR
REIMS
PARIS
CHATEAU THIERRY
SAAR
ST. NAZAIRE 198,000
CHAMPAGNE MARNE SECTOR
LORRAINE
NANTES
AISNE SECTOR
CHAUMONT
ALSACE
LES SABLES D'OLENNE
A
I
ADVANCE
LA PALLICE 4,000
INTERMEDIATE ZONE
ROCHEFORT
TOURS
ZONE
SWITZERLAND
BORDEAUX 50,000
LYON
ITALY
GENOA
BILBAO
BAYONNE
MARSEILLES 1,000
TOULON
ANDORRA
M
E
D
I
T
E
R
R
A
N
E
A
N
S
E
A
CORSICA
BARCELONA
SPAIN
BALEARIC ISLANDS
TO ITALY 2,000
SARDINIA
VALENCIA
SAFETY ZONE TO GREECE

△ Port
○ Supply depot
╫╫╫ Railroads used
• SOS construction projects in France
‒‥‒‥ Lines separating advance, intermediate and base zones and the District of Paris
+‒+‒+ Battle line of March 31, 1918
××× Battle line of July 18, 1918
+×+× Battle line of November 11, 1918
▨ Area taken by Germany in the "Peace Offensives" of March 21 - July 11, 1918
▩ Zone of American occupation
•◆•◆ Line of German submarine zone in North Sea and Mediterranean
    Figures under names of French and British ports indicate number of American Troops disembarked there

213

America in the First World War: The European Front

Sea routes indicated are those of American troop transports

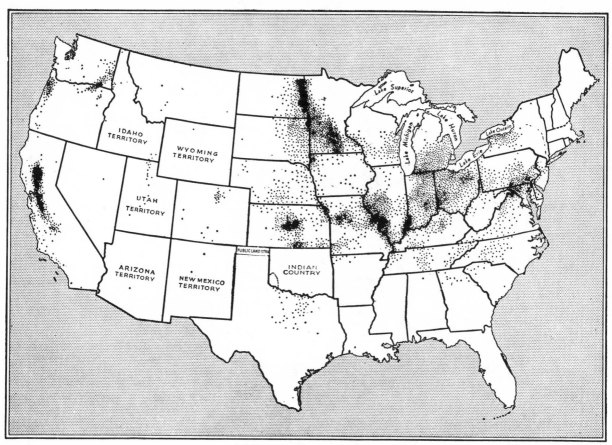

214

Wheat Production, 1890
Each dot represents 100,000 bushels; total crop, 468,373,986 bushels

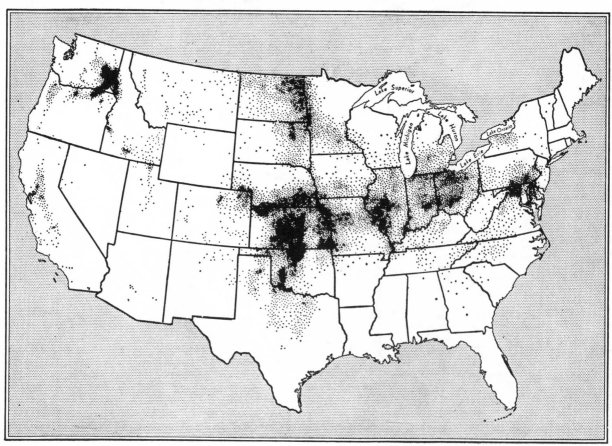

215

Wheat Production, 1920
Each dot represents 100,000 bushels; total crop, 945,403,215 bushels

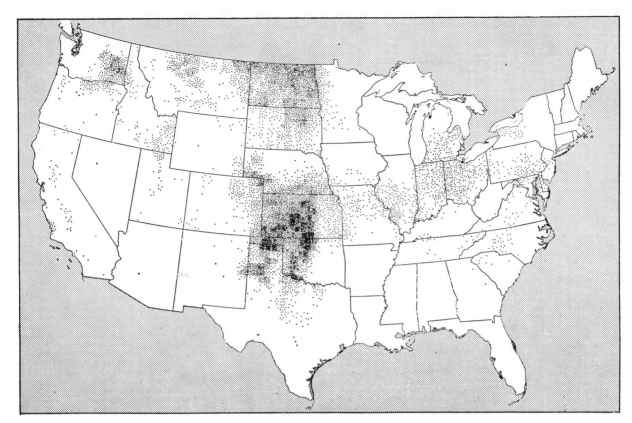

216
Wheat Production, 1950
Each dot represents 10,000 acres; total, 72,825,893 acres

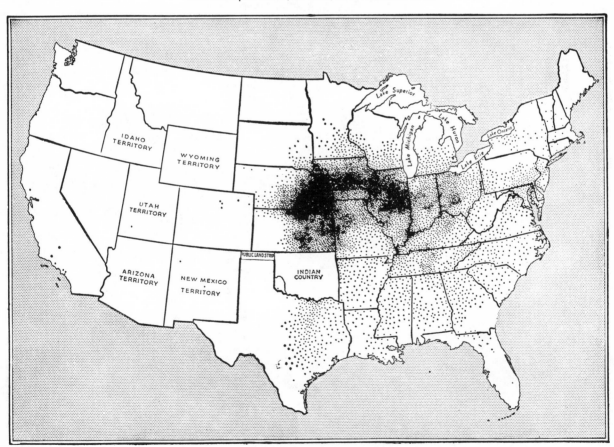

217
Corn Production, 1890
Each dot represents 300,000 bushels; total crop, 2,122,327,547 bushels

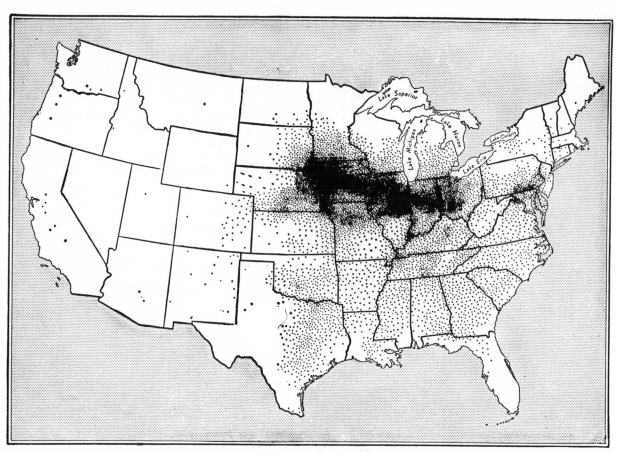

218 Corn Production, 1920
Each dot represents 300,000 bushels; total crop, 2,345,832,507 bushels

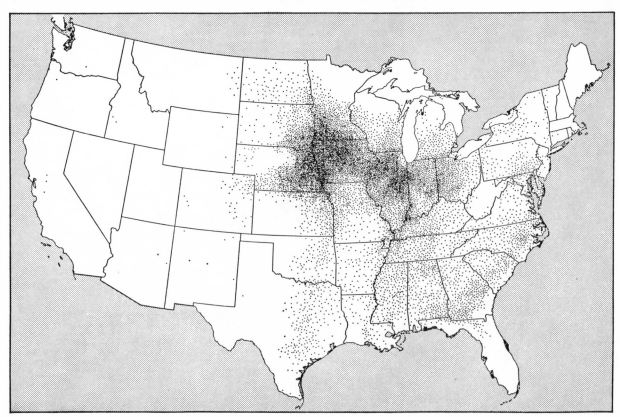

219 Corn Production, 1950
Each dot represents 10,000 acres; total, 83,336,045 acres

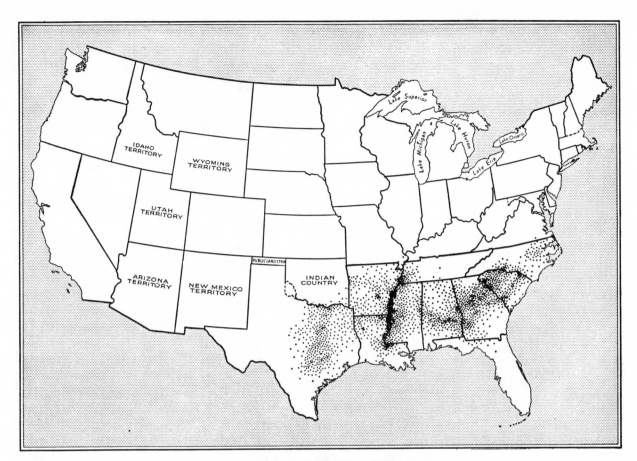

220
Cotton Production, 1890
Each dot represents 4,000 500-lb. bales; total crop, 7,472,511 500-lb. bales

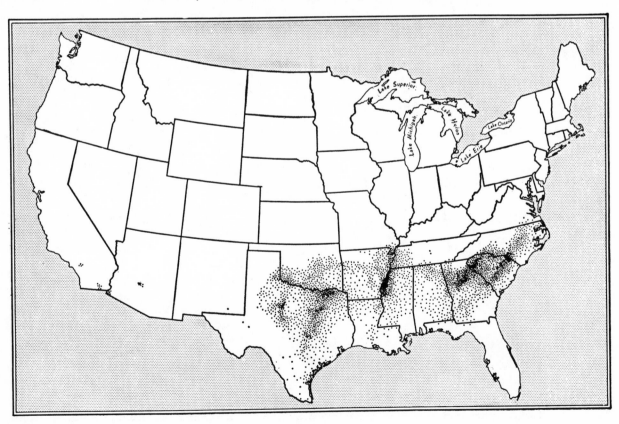

221
Cotton Production, 1920
Each dot represents 4,000 500-lb. bales; total crop, 11,376,130 500-lb. bales

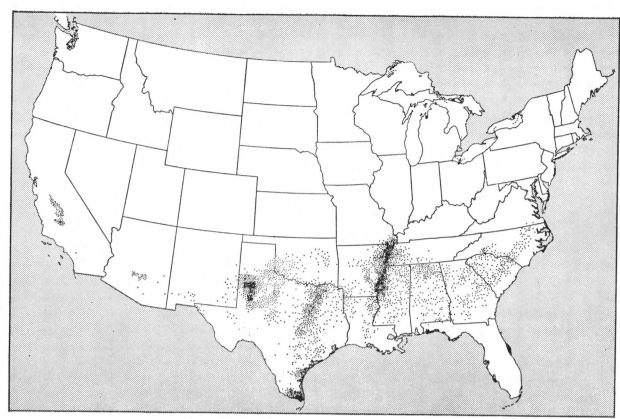

222

Cotton Production, 1950
Each dot represents 10,000 acres; total, 26,599,263 acres

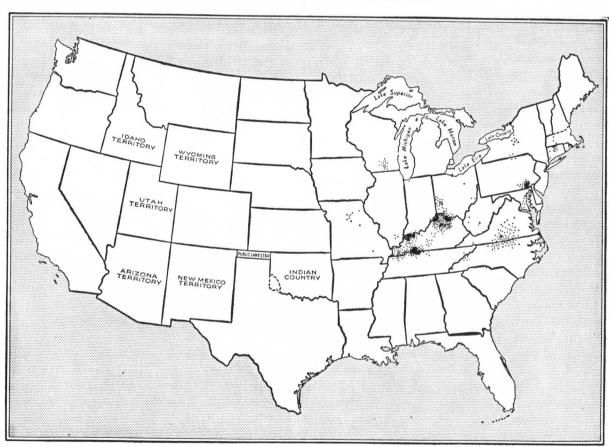

223

Tobacco Production, 1890
Each dot represents 1,000,000 lbs.; total crop, 488,256,646 lbs.

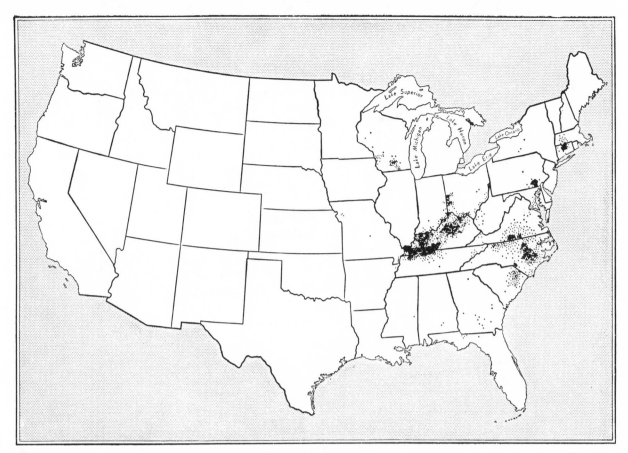

224   Tobacco Production, 1920
Each dot represents 1,000,000 lbs.; total crop, 1,371,504,261 lbs.

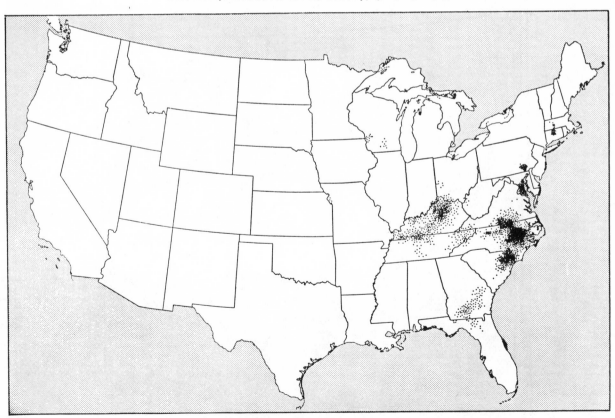

225   Tobacco Production, 1950
Each dot represents 1,000 acres; total 1,532,373 acres

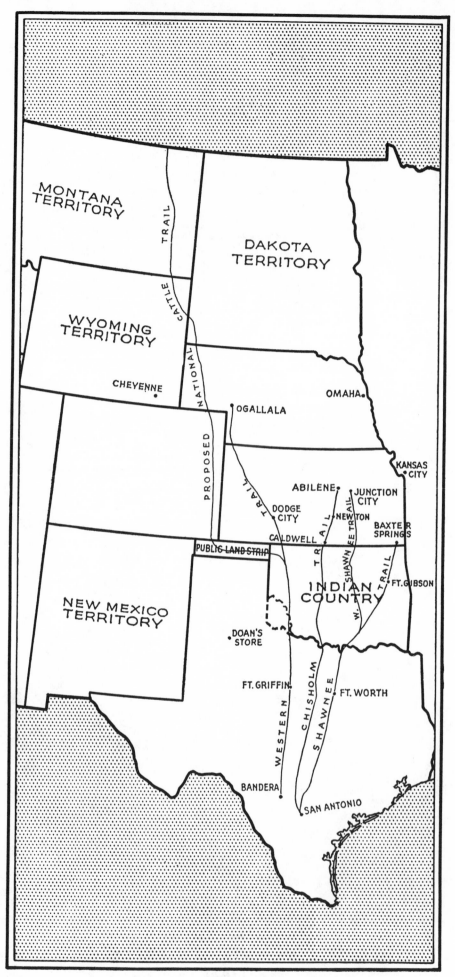

MONTANA
TERRITORY

DAKOTA
TERRITORY

WYOMING
TERRITORY

TRAIL

NATIONAL CATTLE

PROPOSED

TRAIL

CHEYENNE

OGALLALA

OMAHA

KANSAS
CITY

ABILENE

JUNCTION
CITY

DODGE
CITY

NEWTON

CALDWELL

BAXTER
SPRINGS

TRAIL

SHAWNEE TRAIL

W. TRAIL

FT. GIBSON

PUBLIC LAND STRIP

INDIAN
COUNTRY

NEW MEXICO
TERRITORY

DOAN'S
STORE

FT. GRIFFIN

WESTERN

CHISHOLM

SHAWNEE

FT. WORTH

BANDERA

SAN ANTONIO

Cattle Trails and Cow Towns, 1880

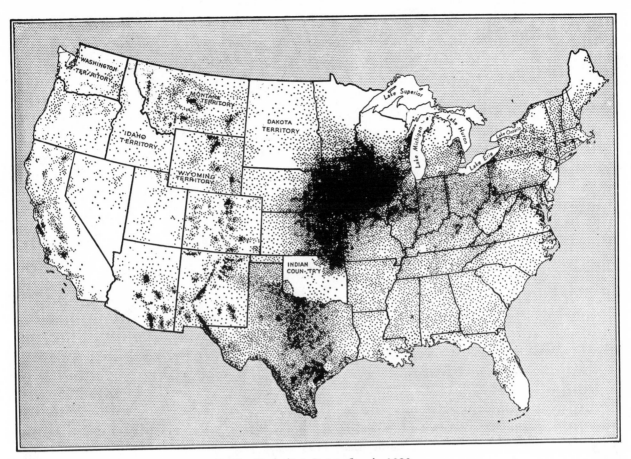

227

Cattle (Excluding Dairy Cows), 1890
Each dot represents 2,000 head; total, 34,851,622 head

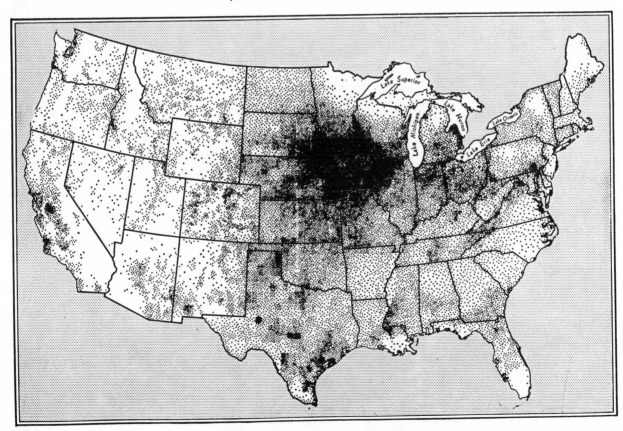

228

Cattle (Excluding Dairy Cows), 1920
Each dot represents 2,000 head; total, 46,977,000 head

[149]

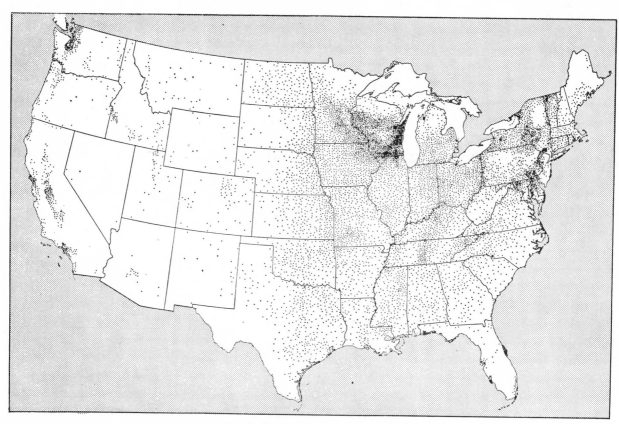

229   Cattle (Dairy Cows Only), 1950
Each dot represents 2,500 head; total, 21,232,213 head

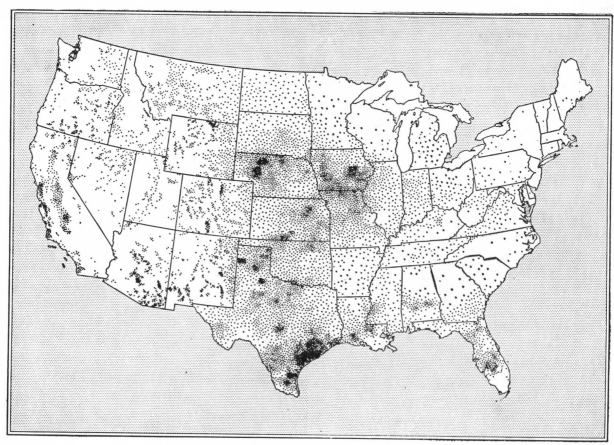

230   Cattle (Excluding Dairy Cows), 1940
Each dot represents 1,000 head; total, 9,448,671 head

[150]

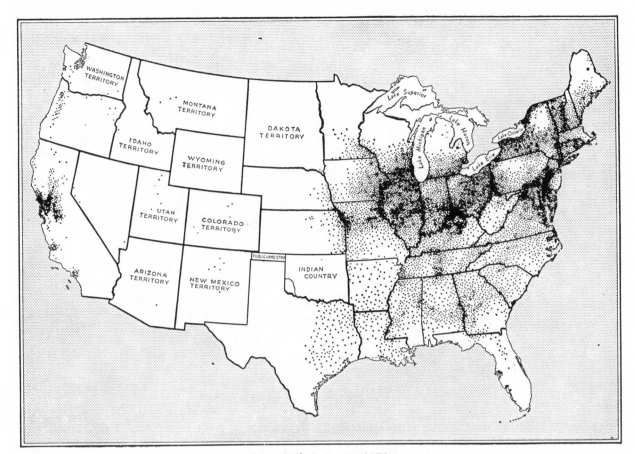

231   Improved Acreage, 1870

Each dot represents 25,000 acres; total, 188,921,099 acres

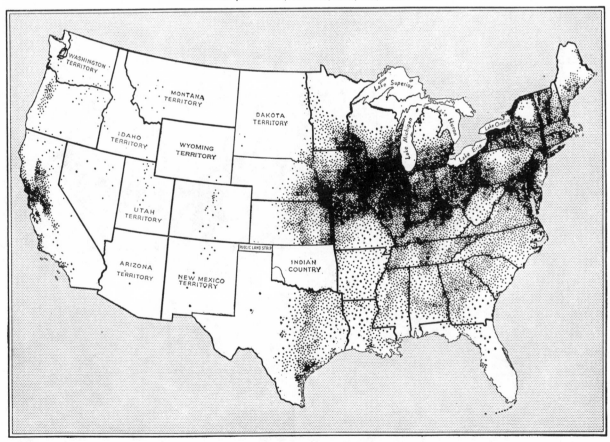

232   Improved Acreage, 1880

Each dot represents 25,000 acres; total, 284,771,042 acres

[151]

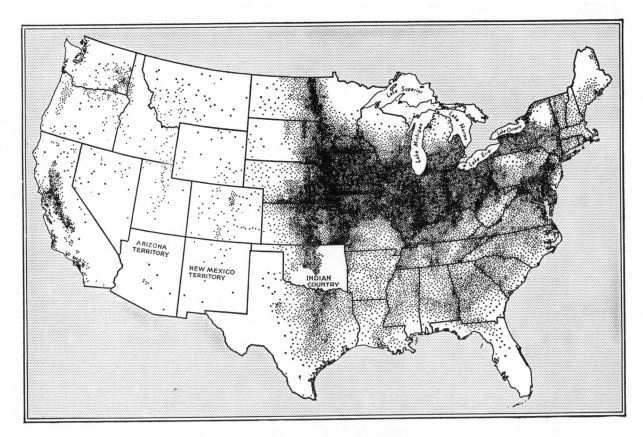

233

Improved Acreage, 1900

Each dot represents 25,000 acres; total, 414,498,487 acres

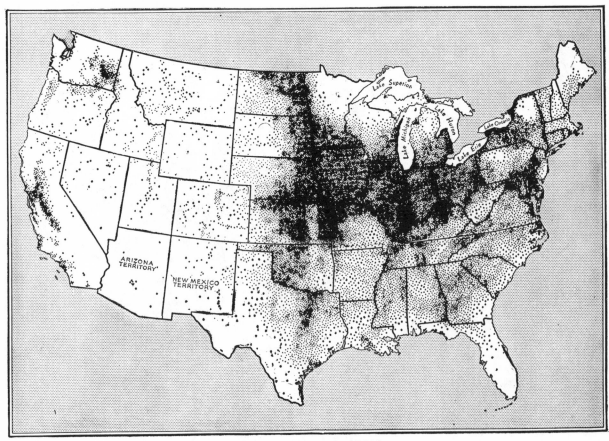

234

Improved Acreage, 1910

Each dot represents 25,000 acres; total, 478,451,756 acres

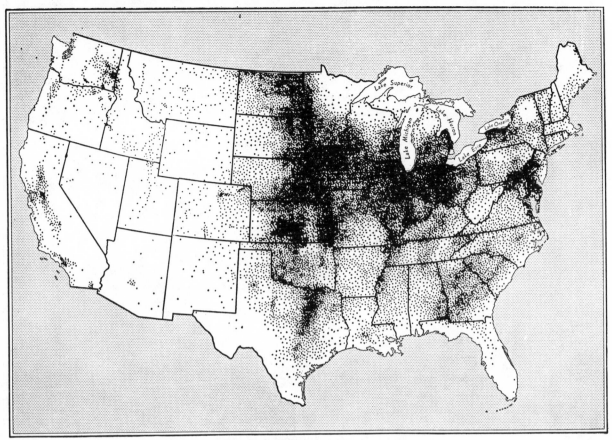

235
Acreage in Harvested Crops, 1920
Each dot represents 25,000 acres; total, 503,073,007 acres

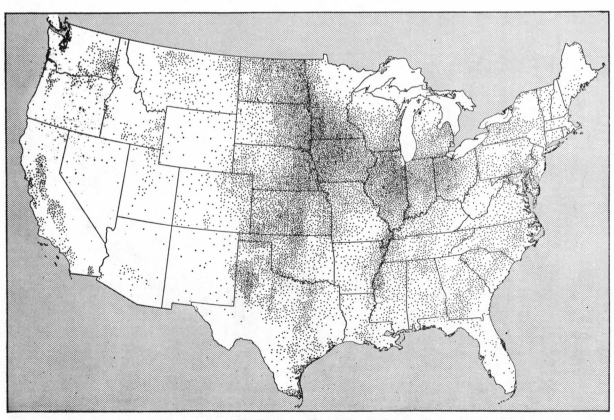

236
Acreage in Harvested Crops, 1950
Each dot represents 25,000 acres; total, 344,398,550 acres

[153]

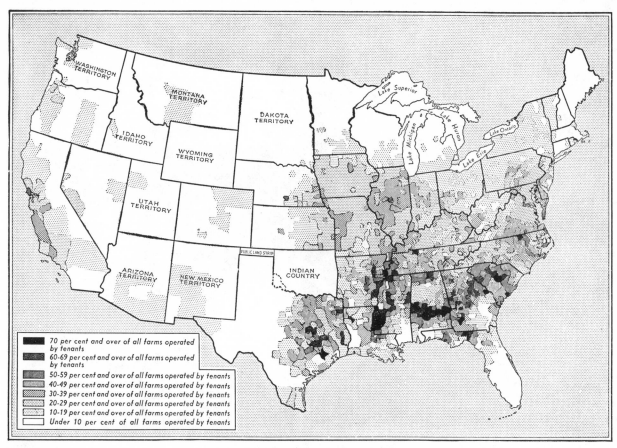

237

Farm Tenancy, by Counties, 1880

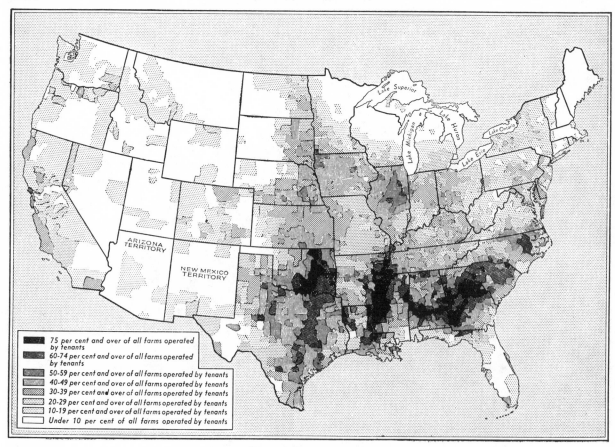

238

Farm Tenancy, by Counties, 1910

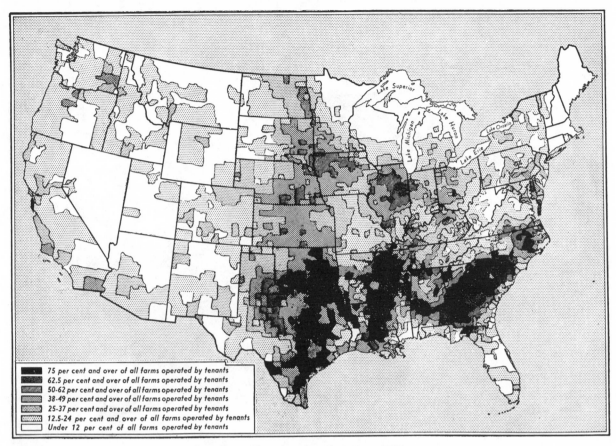

239

■	75 per cent and over of all farms operated by tenants
■	62.5 per cent and over of all farms operated by tenants
▨	50-62 per cent and over of all farms operated by tenants
▦	38-49 per cent and over of all farms operated by tenants
▧	25-37 per cent and over of all farms operated by tenants
░	12.5-24 per cent and over of all farms operated by tenants
□	Under 12 per cent of all farms operated by tenants

Farm Tenancy, by Counties, 1920

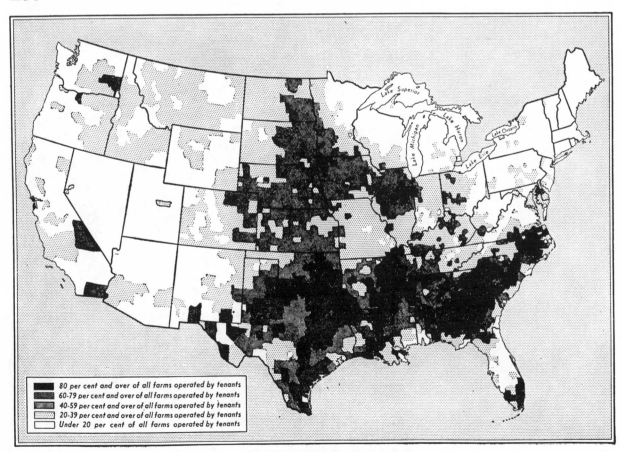

240

■	80 per cent and over of all farms operated by tenants
■	60-79 per cent and over of all farms operated by tenants
▨	40-59 per cent and over of all farms operated by tenants
░	20-39 per cent and over of all farms operated by tenants
□	Under 20 per cent of all farms operated by tenants

Farm Tenancy, by Counties, 1930

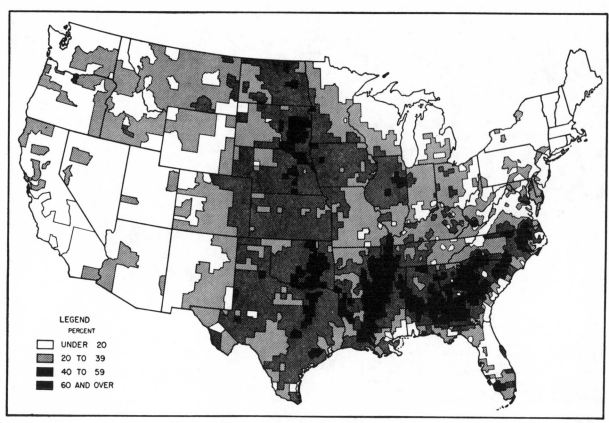

241

Farm Tenancy, by Counties, 1940

LEGEND

PERCENT

- UNDER 20
- 20 TO 39
- 40 TO 59
- 60 AND OVER

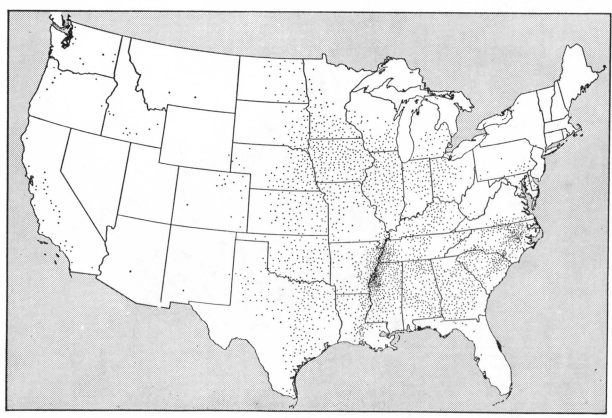

242

Farm Tenancy, 1950

Each dot represents 500 farms; total, 1,444,129 farms

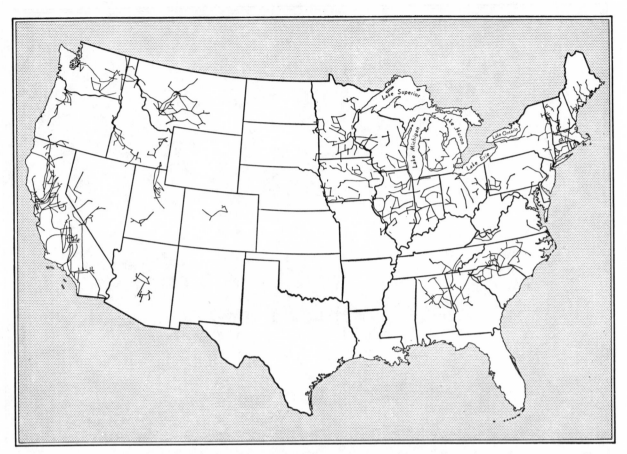

243   Power Transmission Lines Carrying a Potential of 55,000 or More Volts, 1923

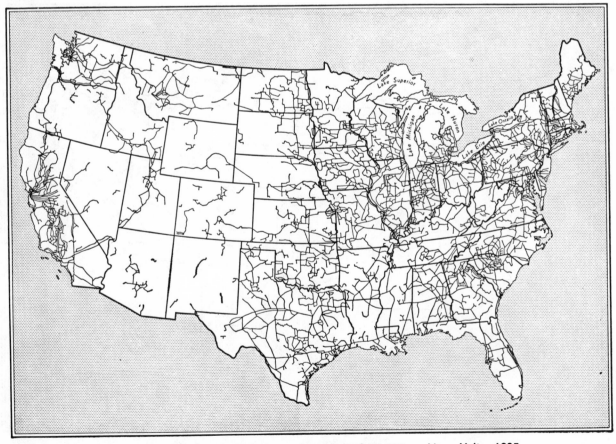

244   Power Transmission Lines Carrying a Potential of 55,000 or More Volts, 1935

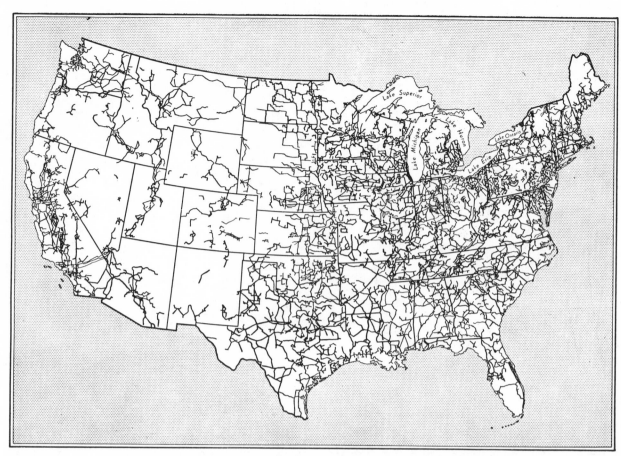

245   Power Transmission Lines Carrying a Potential of 33 Kilowatts or More, 1950

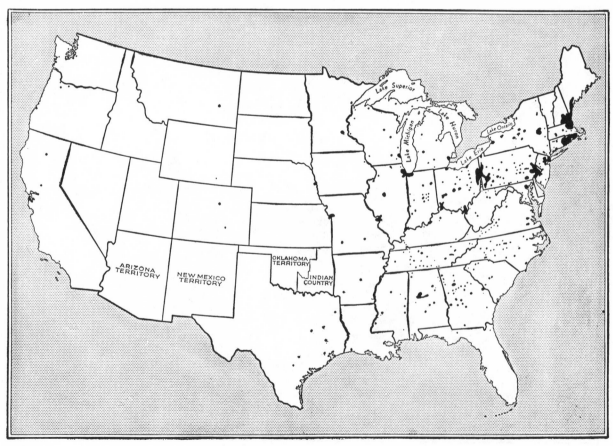

246   Manufacturing Areas, 1900

Based on iron, steel and textiles, together with cities having more than 5,000 industrial employees

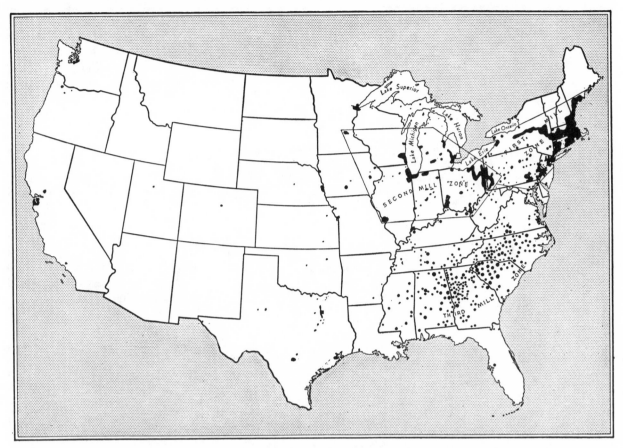

247
Manufacturing Areas, 1940
Based on iron, steel and textiles, together with cities having more than 5,000 industrial employees

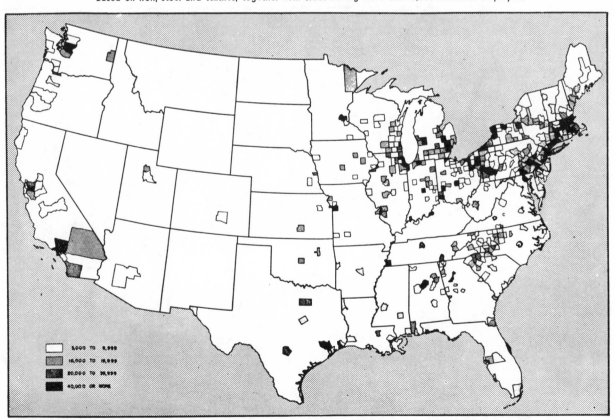

5,000 TO 9,999
10,000 TO 19,999
20,000 TO 39,999
40,000 OR MORE

248
Manufacturing Areas, 1947
Selected Industrial Counties with 5,000 or more manufacturing employees

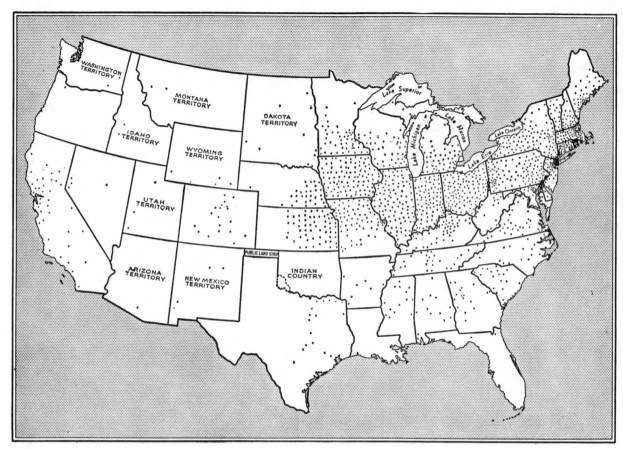

249
Banks of 1880
Each dot represents 1-5 banks

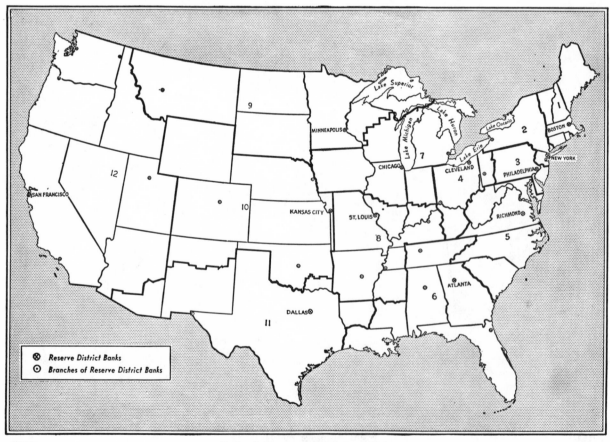

- ⊗ *Reserve District Banks*
- ⊙ *Branches of Reserve District Banks*

250
Federal Reserve Districts, 1914

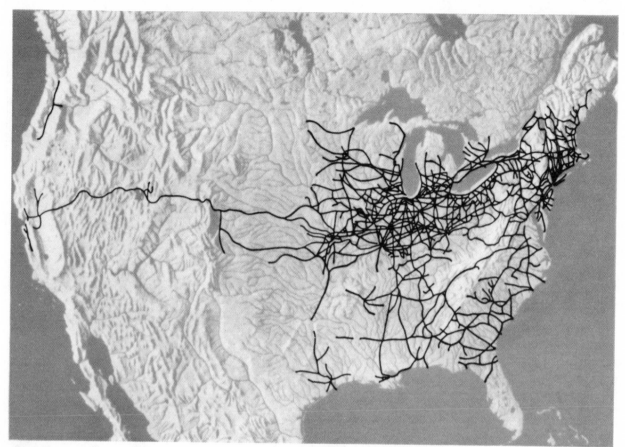

251   Railroads in Operation, 1870

For railroad mileage statistics, see Appendix V

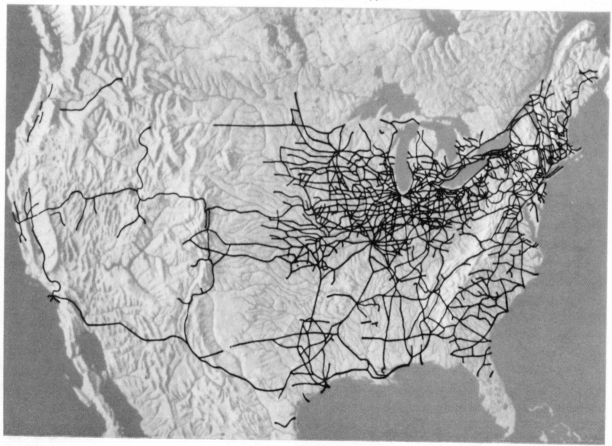

252   Railroads in Operation, 1882

For railroad mileage statistics, see Appendix V

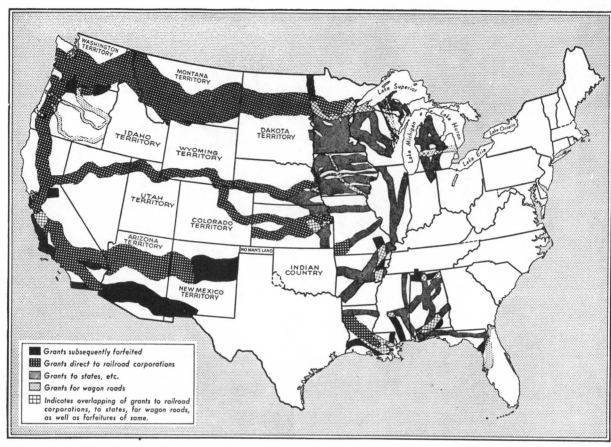

253   Federal Land Grants in Aid of Railroad and Wagon-Road Construction, 1828-1871

Legend (inset on map 253):

- Grants subsequently forfeited
- Grants direct to railroad corporations
- Grants to states, etc.
- Grants for wagon roads
- Indicates overlapping of grants to railroad corporations, to states, for wagon roads, as well as forfeitures of same.

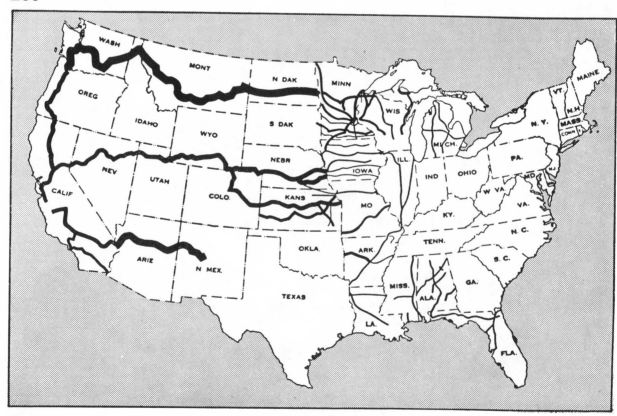

254   Federal Land Grants to Railroads, 1828-1871
Showing Actual Amounts of Land Granted

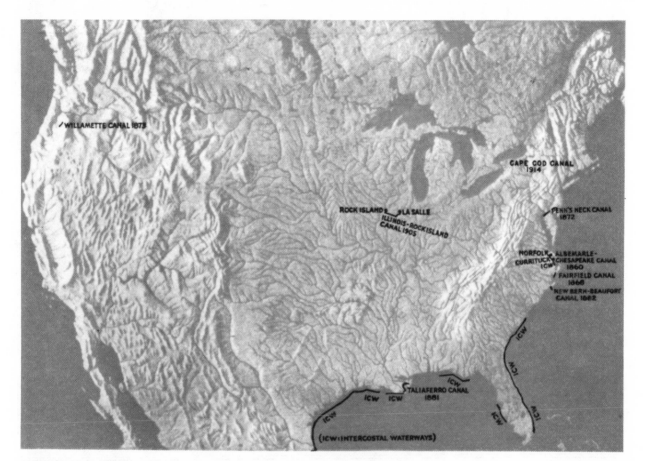

255   Canals Constructed Since 1860

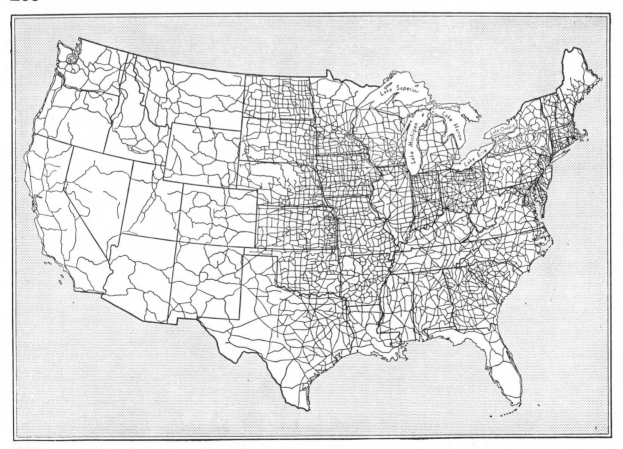

256   Federal Highways System, 1925

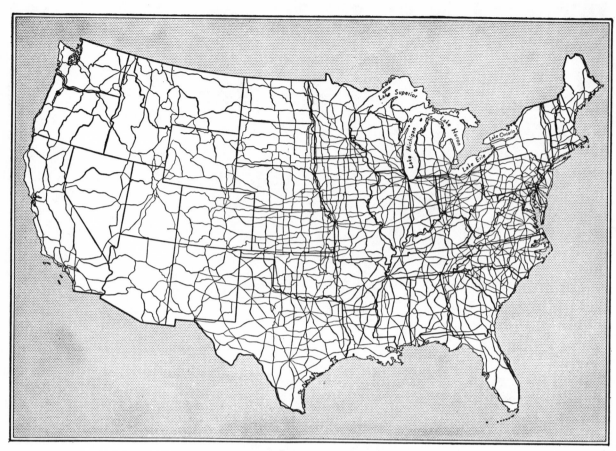

257 Revised Federal Highways System, 1940

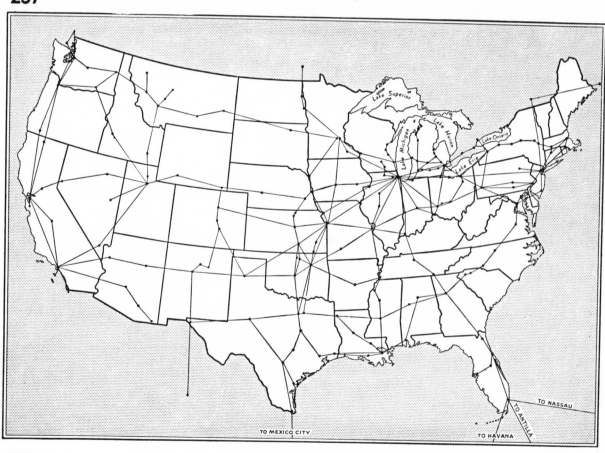

258 Commercial Air Lines, 1930

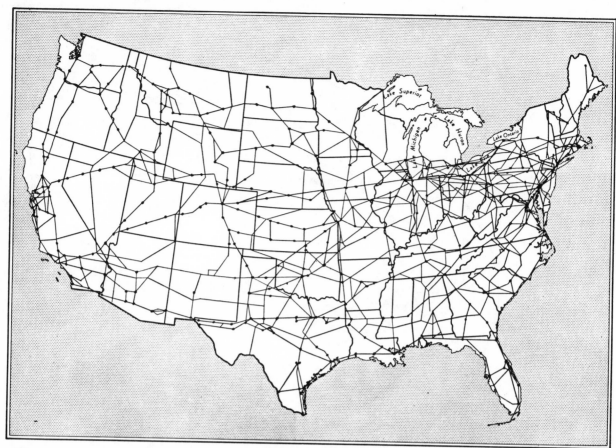

259   Commercial Air Lines, 1950

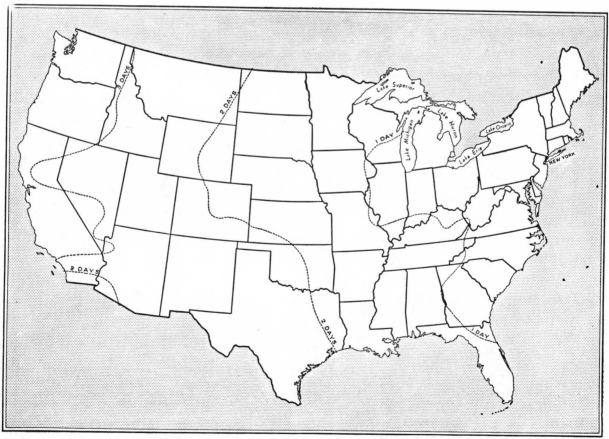

260   Rates of Travel: Railroad Time from New York, 1930

Commercial flying time Coast to Coast, 1930, 36 hours; 1940, 16 hours

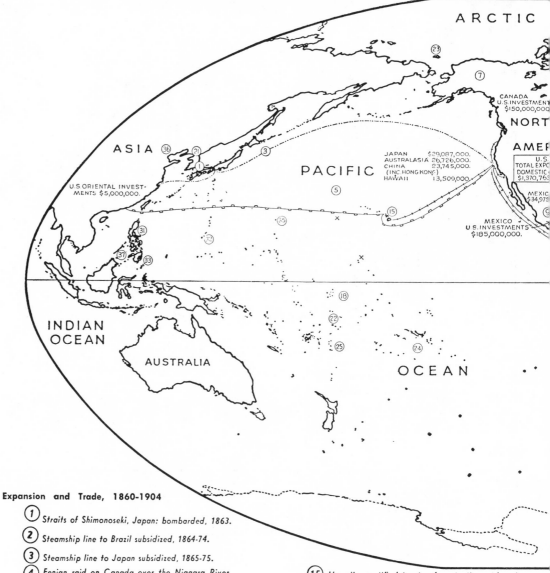

ASIA

U.S.ORIENTAL INVEST-
MENTS $5,000,000.

PACIFIC

JAPAN $29,087,000.
AUSTRALASIA 26,726,000.
CHINA   23,745,000.
(INC.HONG KONG)
HAWAII   13,509,000.

CANADA
U.S.INVESTMENT
$150,000,000

U.S.
TOTAL EXPO
DOMESTIC
$1,370,763

MEXIC
$34,979

MEXICO
U.S.INVESTMENTS
$185,000,000.

INDIAN
OCEAN

AUSTRALIA

OCEAN

Expansion and Trade, 1860-1904

(1) Straits of Shimonoseki, Japan: bombarded, 1863.

(2) Steamship line to Brazil subsidized, 1864-74.

(3) Steamship line to Japan subsidized, 1865-75.

(4) Fenian raid on Canada over the Niagara River, 1866.

(5) Midway Island, seized by U.S.S. Lackawanna, 1867.

(6) Nicaragua: unratified treaty for exclusive canal rights, 1867.

(7) Annexation of Alaska, 1867.

(8) Haiti offers Mole of St. Nicholas for assumption by U. S. of Haiti's debt to France, 1867. President Johnson announces it may be necessary to take over all Haiti, 1867. House resolution declaring protectorate defeated, 1869.

(9) French forces leave Mexico, 1867. General Sheridan sent to border to point up American protests.

(10) Santo Domingo offers Samaná Bay naval base to the United States, 1867. President Johnson announces it may be necessary to take over all Santo Domingo, 1867. House resolution establishing protectorate defeated, 1869. Babcock Treaties, 1869, 1870. Warships sent to keep Baez regime in power, 1870.

(11) Purchase of Culebra and Culebrita discussed by Seward, 1867.

(12) Cuba. President Johnson announces it may be necessary to take over the island, 1867. Ten Years War, 1868-78. Virginius incident, 1873. Spanish-American War, 1898. Platt Amendment, 1901-34.

(13) Danish West Indies: unratified treaty of cession to the United States for $7,500,000, signed, 1867; unratified treaty of cession for $5,000,000, signed, 1902; ceded for $25,000,000, 1917.

(14) St. Bartholomew: purchase contemplated by Seward from Sweden, 1867.

(15) Hawaii: unratified treaty of protection and reciprocity signed, 1867. Similar treaty ratified, 1875. Pearl Harbor naval base acquired, 1884. Native monarchy overthrown, 1891. Unratified treaty of annexation signed, 1892. Annexed, 1898.

(16) Disturbances in Red River valley led by Louis Riel revive Canadian annexation hopes, 1869, 1885.

(17) House resolution to declare all West Indies islands under American protection defeated, 1869.

(18) House resolution to declare all Pacific islands under American protection defeated, 1869.

(19) Fenian "invasions" of Canada halted at St. Albans, Vt., and Malone, N. Y., 1870.

(20) United States secures perpetual right of free navigation of the St. Lawrence in the Treaty of Washington, 1871.

(21) Ping-Yang forts, Korea, bombarded, 1871.

(22) Samoa: unratified treaty giving the United States exclusive rights at Pago Pago signed, 1872. Similar treaty ratified, 1878. Crisis with England and Germany, 1889. Tripartite condominion, 1889-99. Annexation arranged, 1899; formally accepted by Congress, 1929.

(23) Possession claimed to Wrangell, Bennett, Henrietta and Jeanette Islands, 1881.

(24) Approximately 70 guano islands, mostly in the South Pacific, bonded and claimed under the Guano Act of 1867 by 1884, including Swain's, Johnston's*, Palmyra*, Baker, Howland, Kingman Reef, Navassa (1858); [Also Swan (1863), Quito Sueño, Serrana and Seranilla Banks, Roncador Cay, in Caribbean].

Subsidized Trade Routes Under Acts of 1864 and

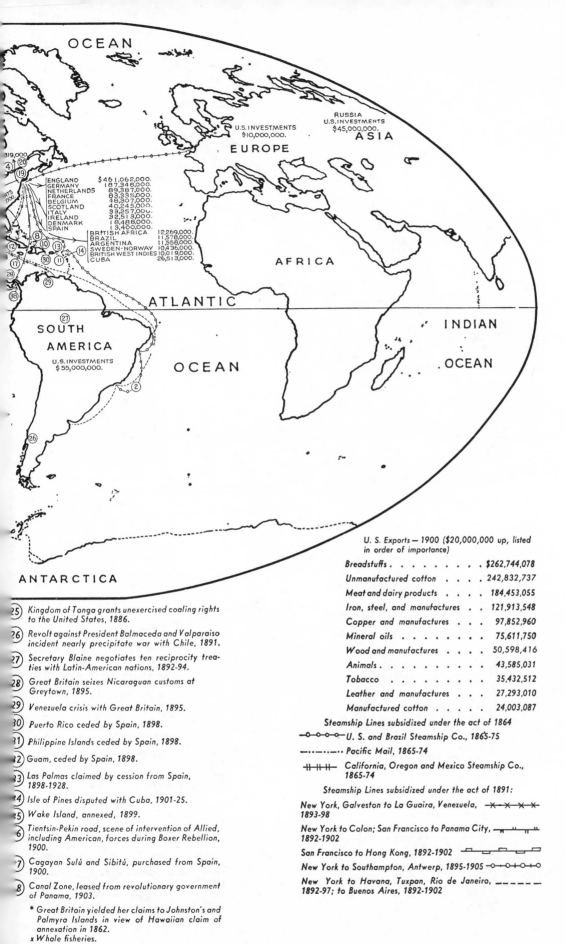

OCEAN

RUSSIA
U.S.INVESTMENTS
$45,000,000.

ASIA

U.S. INVESTMENTS
$10,000,000.

EUROPE

ENGLAND	$461,062,000.
GERMANY	187,348,000.
NETHERLANDS	89,387,000.
FRANCE	83,335,000.
BELGIUM	48,307,000.
SCOTLAND	40,245,000.
ITALY	33,257,000.
IRELAND	32,513,000.
DENMARK	18,488,000.
SPAIN	13,400,000.
BRITISH AFRICA	12,269,000.
BRAZIL	11,578,000.
ARGENTINA	11,558,000.
SWEDEN–NORWAY	10,436,000.
BRITISH WEST INDIES	10,019,000.
CUBA	26,513,000.

AFRICA

ATLANTIC

SOUTH
AMERICA
U.S. INVESTMENTS
$55,000,000.

OCEAN

INDIAN

OCEAN

ANTARCTICA

25) Kingdom of Tonga grants unexercised coaling rights to the United States, 1886.

26) Revolt against President Balmaceda and Valparaiso incident nearly precipitate war with Chile, 1891.

27) Secretary Blaine negotiates ten reciprocity treaties with Latin-American nations, 1892-94.

28) Great Britain seizes Nicaraguan customs at Greytown, 1895.

29) Venezuela crisis with Great Britain, 1895.

30) Puerto Rico ceded by Spain, 1898.

31) Philippine Islands ceded by Spain, 1898.

32) Guam, ceded by Spain, 1898.

33) Las Palmas claimed by cession from Spain, 1898-1928.

34) Isle of Pines disputed with Cuba, 1901-25.

35) Wake Island, annexed, 1899.

6) Tientsin-Pekin road, scene of intervention of Allied, including American, forces during Boxer Rebellion, 1900.

7) Cagayan Sulú and Sibitú, purchased from Spain, 1900.

8) Canal Zone, leased from revolutionary government of Panama, 1903.

* Great Britain yielded her claims to Johnston's and Palmyra Islands in view of Hawaiian claim of annexation in 1862.
x Whale fisheries.

U. S. Exports — 1900 ($20,000,000 up, listed in order of importance)

Breadstuffs	$262,744,078
Unmanufactured cotton	242,832,737
Meat and dairy products	184,453,055
Iron, steel, and manufactures	121,913,548
Copper and manufactures	97,852,960
Mineral oils	75,611,750
Wood and manufactures	50,598,416
Animals	43,585,031
Tobacco	35,432,512
Leather and manufactures	27,293,010
Manufactured cotton	24,003,087

Steamship Lines subsidized under the act of 1864

–o–o–o–o– U. S. and Brazil Steamship Co., 1865-75

–··–··–··– Pacific Mail, 1865-74

–II–II–II– California, Oregon and Mexico Steamship Co., 1865-74

Steamship Lines subsidized under the act of 1891:

New York, Galveston to La Guaira, Venezuela, –x–x–x–x– 1893-98

New York to Colon; San Francisco to Panama City, 1892-1902

San Francisco to Hong Kong, 1892-1902

New York to Southampton, Antwerp, 1895-1905 –o–+–o–+–o–

New York to Havana, Tuxpan, Rio de Janeiro, – – – – – – 1892-97; to Buenos Aires, 1892-1902

Base Map by Permission of Denoyer-Geppert Company, Chicago

...ion, 1865-1904; Exports and Foreign Investments, 1900

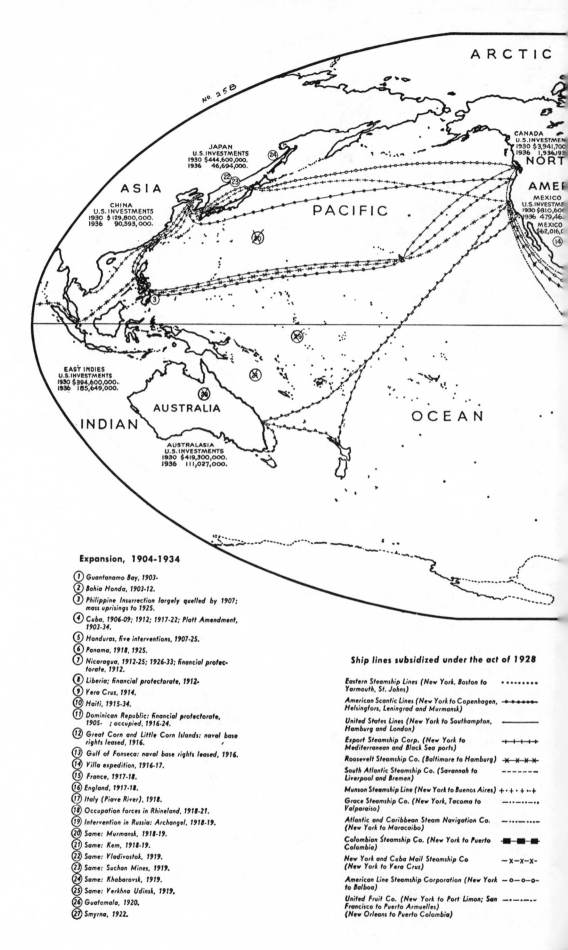

ARCTIC

NO. 258

JAPAN
U.S. INVESTMENTS
1930 $444,600,000.
1936   46,694,000.

ASIA

CHINA
U.S. INVESTMENTS
1930 $129,800,000.
1936   90,593,000.

PACIFIC

CANADA
U.S. INVESTMEN
1930 $3,941,700
1936   1,936,19

NORT

AME

MEXICO
U.S. INVESTME
1930 $810,60
1936 479,46.

MEXICO
$62,016,0

EAST INDIES
U.S. INVESTMENTS
1930 $394,600,000.
1936 185,649,000.

AUSTRALIA

INDIAN

AUSTRALASIA
U.S. INVESTMENTS
1930 $419,300,000.
1936 111,027,000.

OCEAN

Expansion, 1904-1934

① Guantanamo Bay, 1903-
② Bahia Honda, 1903-12.
③ Philippine Insurrection largely quelled by 1907;
   mass uprisings to 1925.
④ Cuba, 1906-09; 1912; 1917-22; Platt Amendment,
   1903-34.
⑤ Honduras, five interventions, 1907-25.
⑥ Panama, 1918, 1925.
⑦ Nicaragua, 1912-25; 1926-33; financial protectorate, 1912.
⑧ Liberia; financial protectorate, 1912.
⑨ Vera Cruz, 1914.
⑩ Haiti, 1915-34.
⑪ Dominican Republic: financial protectorate,
   1905- ; occupied, 1916-24.
⑫ Great Corn and Little Corn Islands: naval base
   rights leased, 1916.
⑬ Gulf of Fonseca: naval base rights leased, 1916.
⑭ Villa expedition, 1916-17.
⑮ France, 1917-18.
⑯ England, 1917-18.
⑰ Italy (Piave River), 1918.
⑱ Occupation forces in Rhineland, 1918-21.
⑲ Intervention in Russia: Archangel, 1918-19.
⑳ Same: Murmansk, 1918-19.
㉑ Same: Kem, 1918-19.
㉒ Same: Vladivostok, 1919.
㉓ Same: Suchan Mines, 1919.
㉔ Same: Khabarovsk, 1919.
㉕ Same: Verkhna Udinsk, 1919.
㉖ Guatemala, 1920.
㉗ Smyrna, 1922.

Ship lines subsidized under the act of 1928

Eastern Steamship Lines (New York, Boston to Yarmouth, St. Johns)	• • • • • • • •
American Scantic Lines (New York to Copenhagen, Helsingfors, Leningrad and Murmansk)	-•-•-•-•-
United States Lines (New York to Southampton, Hamburg and London)	—————
Export Steamship Corp. (New York to Mediterranean and Black Sea ports)	+++++
Roosevelt Steamship Co. (Baltimore to Hamburg)	×-×-××
South Atlantic Steamship Co. (Savannah to Liverpool and Bremen)	- - - - - - -
Munson Steamship Line (New York to Buenos Aires)	+·+·+··+
Grace Steamship Co. (New York, Tacoma to Valparaiso)	—··—··—··
Atlantic and Caribbean Steam Navigation Co. (New York to Maracaibo)	—···—····
Colombian Steamship Co. (New York to Puerto Colombia)	■-■-■-
New York and Cuba Mail Steamship Co (New York to Vera Cruz)	—×—×—×—
American Line Steamship Corporation (New York to Balboa)	—o—o—o—
United Fruit Co. (New York to Port Limon; San Francisco to Puerto Armuelles) (New Orleans to Puerto Colombia)	—·—·—·—

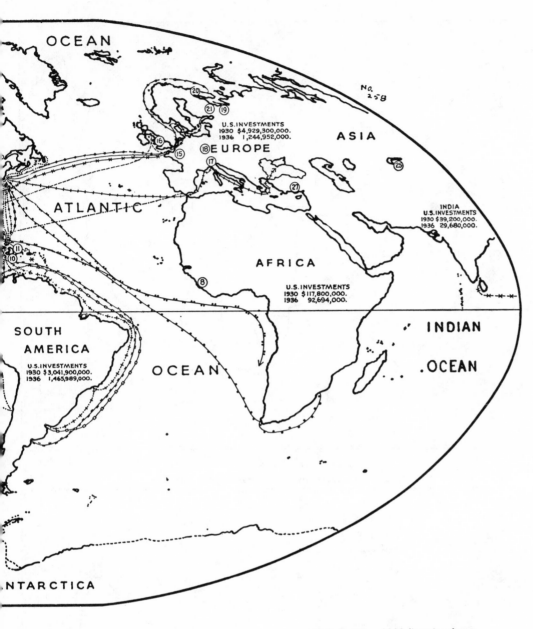

OCEAN

ASIA

No. 258

U.S. INVESTMENTS
1930 $4,929,300,000.
1936   1,244,952,000.

EUROPE

ATLANTIC

INDIA
U.S. INVESTMENTS
1930 $39,200,000.
1936   29,680,000.

AFRICA

U.S. INVESTMENTS
1930 $117,800,000.
1936   92,694,000.

SOUTH
AMERICA

INDIAN

U.S. INVESTMENTS
1930 $3,041,900,000.
1936   1,465,989,000.

OCEAN

.OCEAN

NTARCTICA

American South African Line (New York to
Capetown and Berea)

American West African Line (New York, New
Orleans to West African ports)

Gulf Mail Steamship Co. (Galveston to Santo
Domingo)

Mississippi Shipping Co. (New Orleans to Bahia
Blanca)

Tampa Inter-Ocean Steamship Co. (New Orleans
to Spain)

Tacoma Oriental Steamship Co. (Tacoma to
Darien, Manila)

American Mail Line (Seattle to Manila)

States Steamship Co. (Portland to Manila, Darien)

Dollar Steamship Co. (San Francisco to Manila,
Colombo)

Oceanic and Oriental Navigation Co.
(San Francisco to Darien, Saigon)

Oceanic Steamship Co.; Oceanic and Oriental
Navigation Co. (San Francisco to Sydney)
(Los Angeles to Auckland, Melbourne)

Panama Mail Steamship Co. (San Francisco to
Puerto Colombia)

Pacific Argentine Brazil Line (San Francisco to
Buenos Aires)

New York and Puerto Rico Steamship Co.
(San Juan and Santo Domingo)

**U. S. Exports—1938 (in units of over
$20,000,000, listed in order of importance)**

Machinery*	$476,161,000
Petroleum and products	388,606,000
Industrial machinery	269,908,000
Iron and steel manufactures . . .	252,792,000
Breadstuffs	235,452,000
Unmanufactured cotton . .	228,647,000
Tobacco	170,028,000
Electrical machinery	102,136,000
Fruits and nuts	99,061,000
Copper and manufactures . . .	86,809,000
Chemicals	82,747,000
Wood and manufactures	55,886,000
Manufactured cotton	52,833,000
Coal	52,740,000
Paper and manufactures	37,355,000.
Non-metallic minerals** . . .	28,187,000
Rubber manufactures . . .	27,181,000
Books and maps	23,000,000
Leather and manufactures . . .	20,711,000
TOTAL DOMESTIC EXPORTS . . .	$3,057,169,000

* Other than electrical and industrial machinery

** Other than coal, marble, stone

Base Map by Permission of Denoyer-Geppert Company, Chicago

ents Aboard, 1930; Direct Investments, 1936.

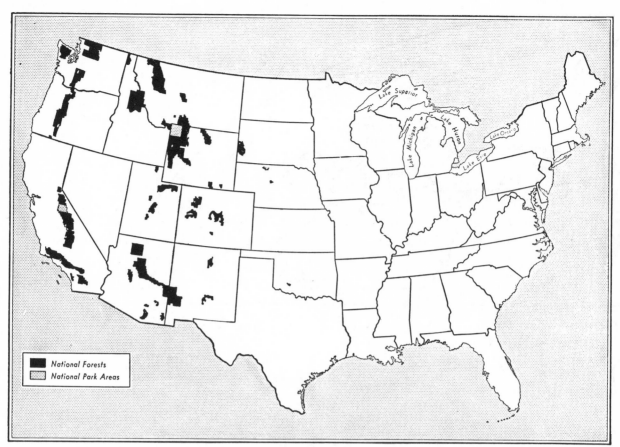

263

National Forests, 1900
Arizona, New Mexico and Oklahoma were still territories at this time

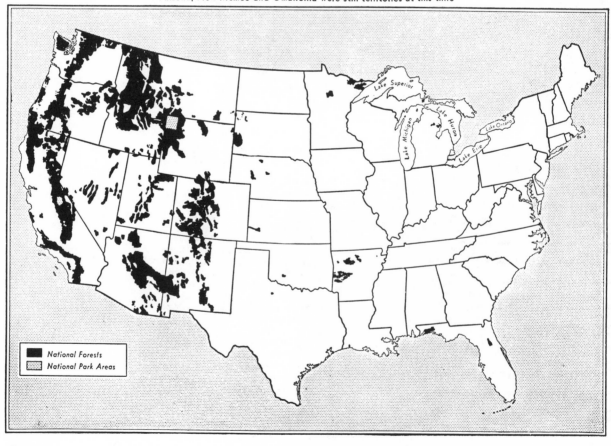

264

National Forests, 1910
Arizona and New Mexico were still territories at this time

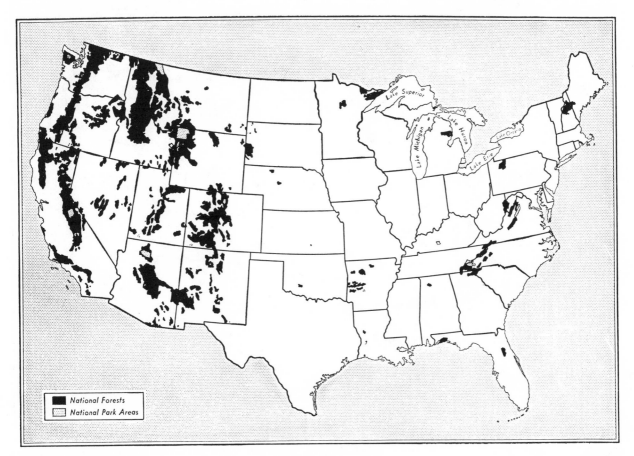

265   National Forests, 1930

National Forests
National Park Areas

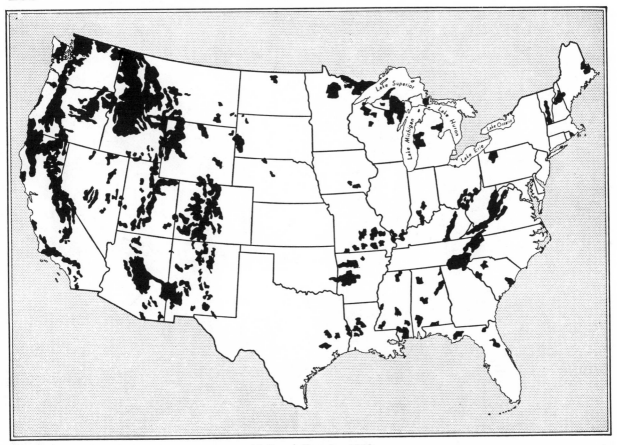

266   National Forests, 1950

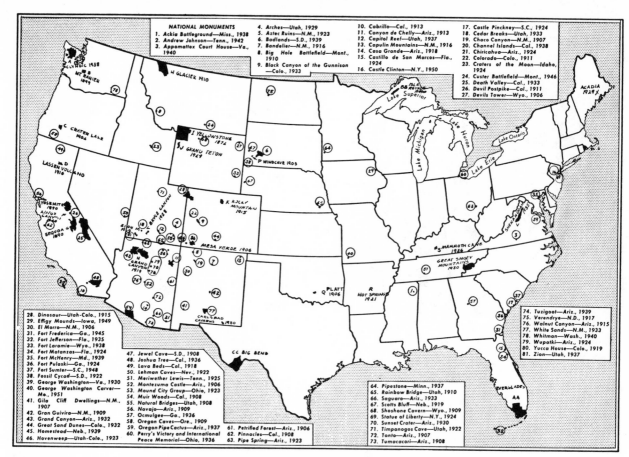

267

National Parks and National Monuments

Numbers = national monuments; Letters = national parks. Names and dates of establishment of the national parks are given on the map. National parks and monuments in Alaska and Hawaii are not included.

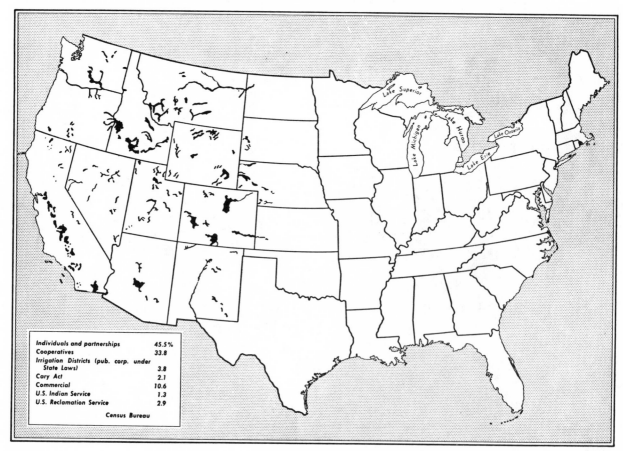

Individuals and partnerships	45.5%
Cooperatives	33.8
Irrigation Districts (pub. corp. under State Laws)	3.8
Cary Act	2.1
Commercial	10.6
U.S. Indian Service	1.3
U.S. Reclamation Service	2.9

Census Bureau

268

Irrigated Lands, 1910

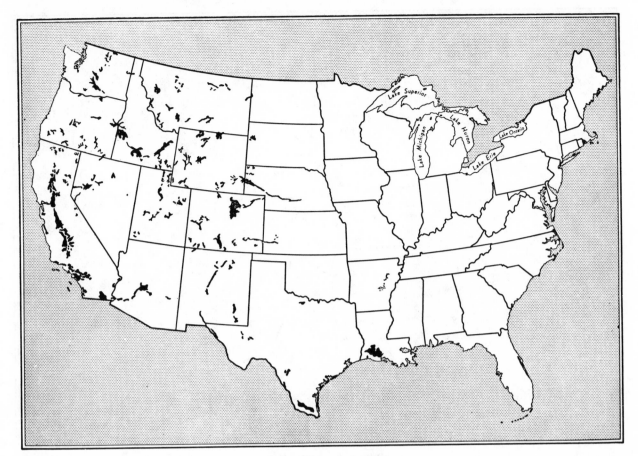

269

Irrigated Lands, 1930

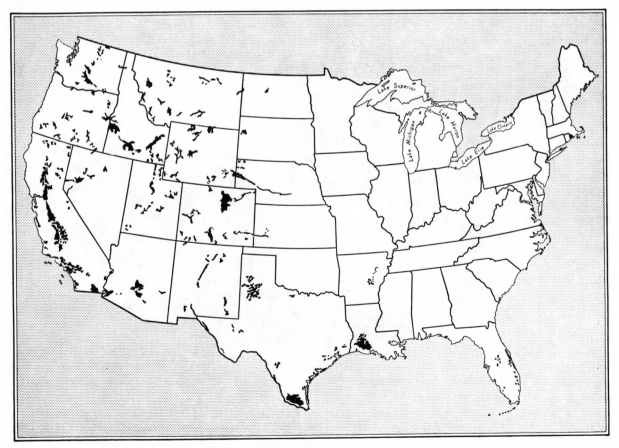

270

Irrigated Lands, 1950

[173]

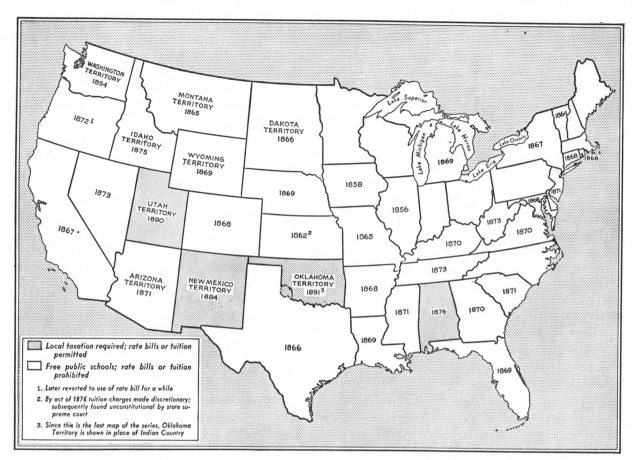

271   State Public School Legislation, 1875
Dates are those for establishment of free schools after 1854

Legend:

- Local taxation required; rate bills or tuition permitted
- Free public schools; rate bills or tuition prohibited

1. Later reverted to use of rate bill for a while
2. By act of 1876 tuition charges made discretionary; subsequently found unconstitutional by state supreme court
3. Since this is the last map of the series, Oklahoma Territory is shown in place of Indian Country

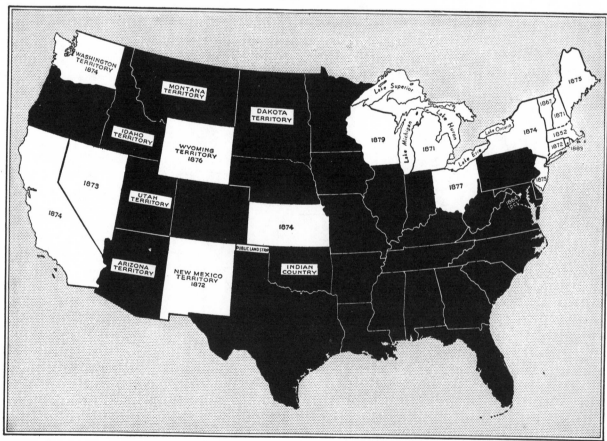

272   Compulsory School Attendance, 1880
Black states have no compulsory school attendance law. Dates represent the year school attendance became compulsory

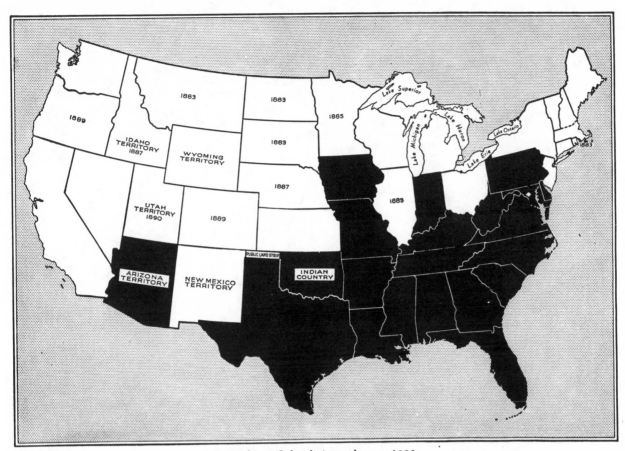

273 Compulsory School Attendance, 1890

Black states have no compulsory school attendance law. Dates represent the year school attendance became compulsory

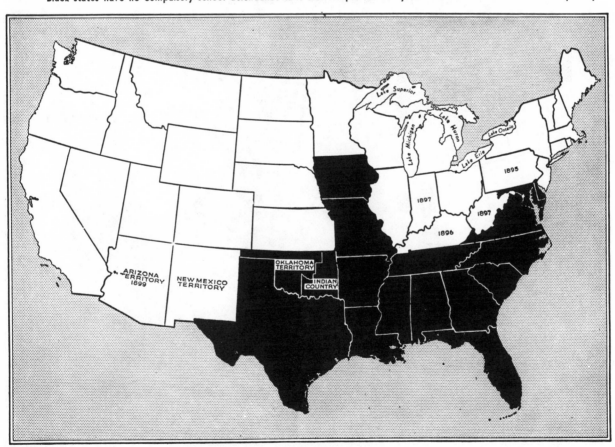

274 Compulsory School Attendance, 1900

Black states have no compulsory school attendance law. Dates represent the year school attendance became compulsory

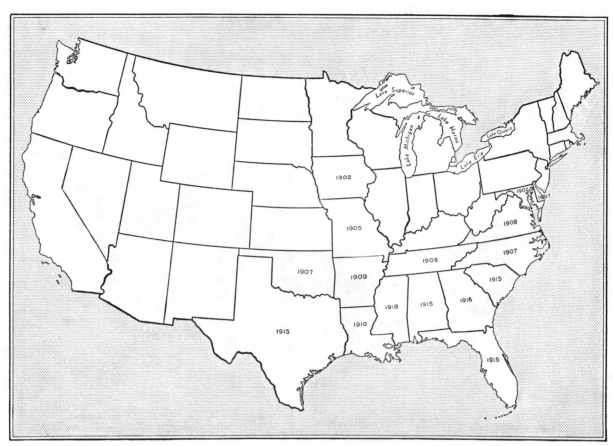

275

Compulsory School Attendance, 1920

Dates represent the year school attendance became compulsory

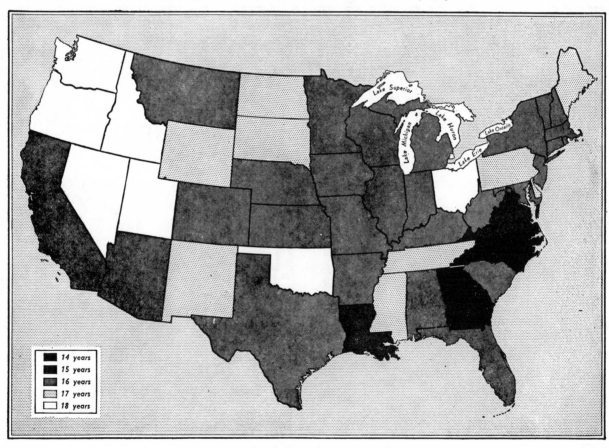

276

Compulsory School Attendance: Age Limits, 1940

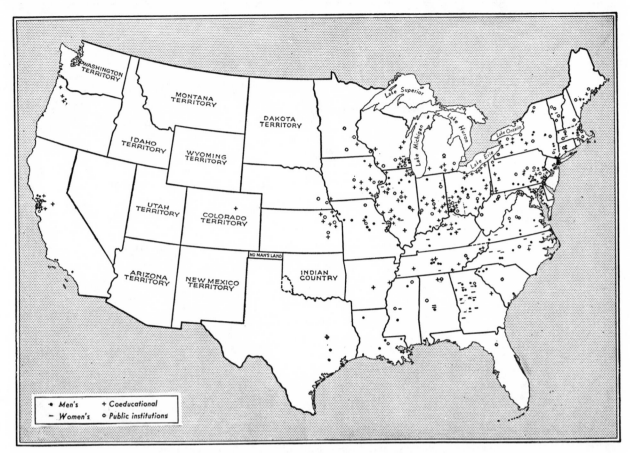

277 Universities, Colleges, and Other Institutions of Higher Learning, 1870
Location of symbols is only approximate, especially in urban centers

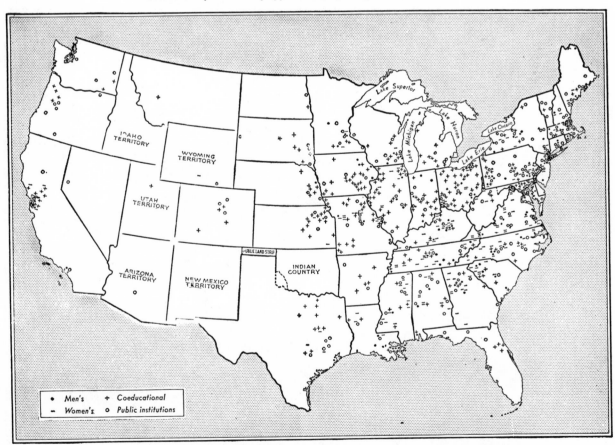

278 Universities, Colleges, and Other Institutions of Higher Learning, 1890
Location of symbols is only approximate, especially in urban centers

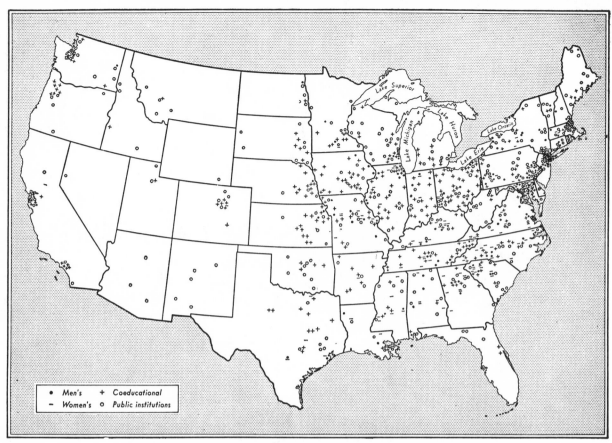

279 Universities, Colleges, and Other Institutions of Higher Learning, 1910
Arizona and New Mexico were still territories at this time
Location of symbols is only approximate, especially in urban centers

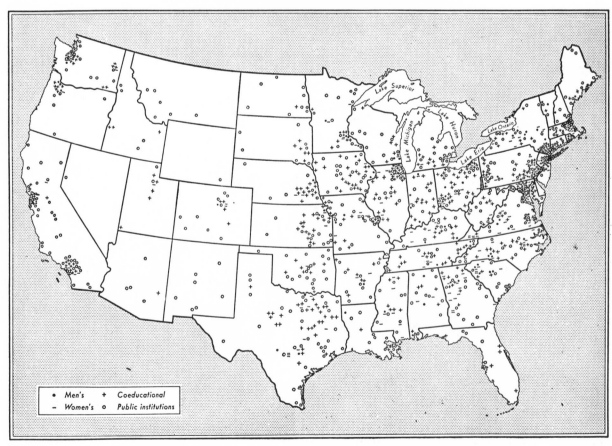

280 Universities, Colleges, and Other Institutions of Higher Learning, 1930
Location of symbols is only approximate, especially in urban centers

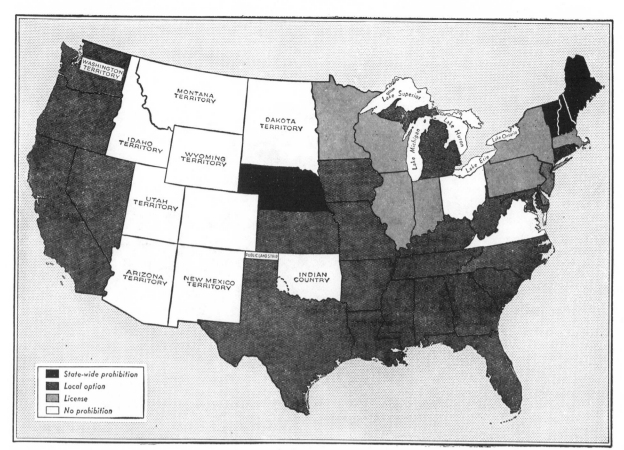

281

Prohibition, 1880

Prohibition on Indian Reservations not shown

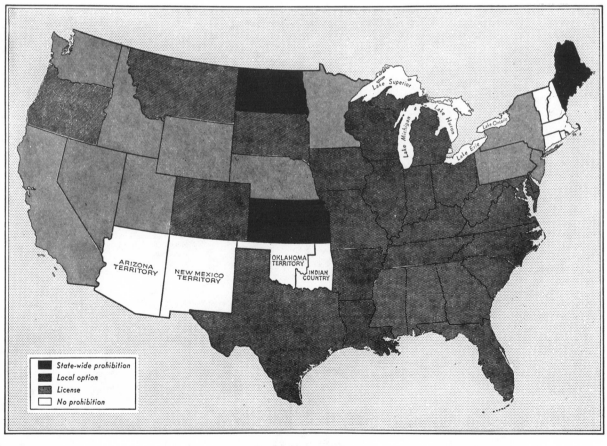

282

Prohibition, 1906

Prohibition on Indian Reservations not shown

[179]

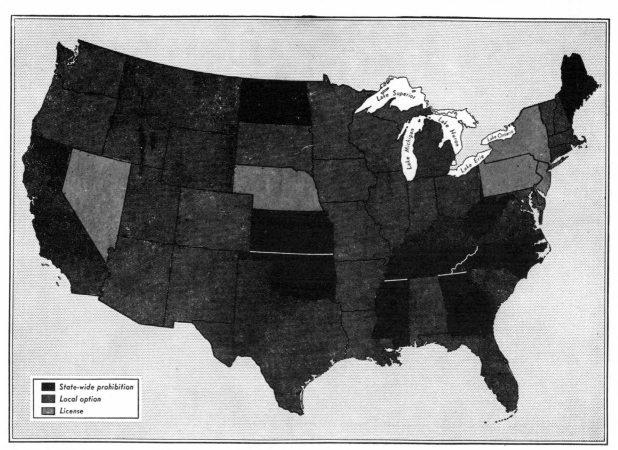

283 Prohibition, 1915

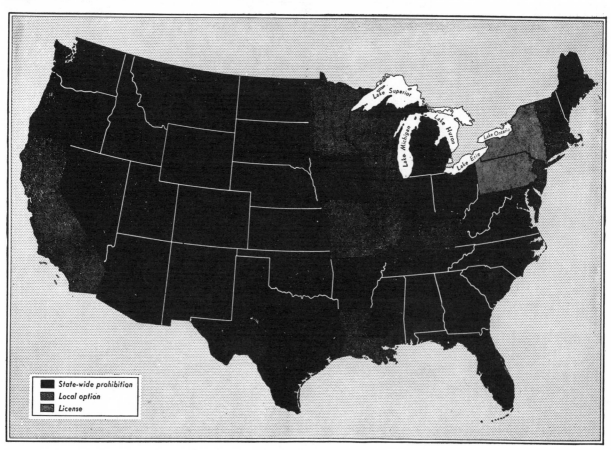

284 Prohibition, 1919

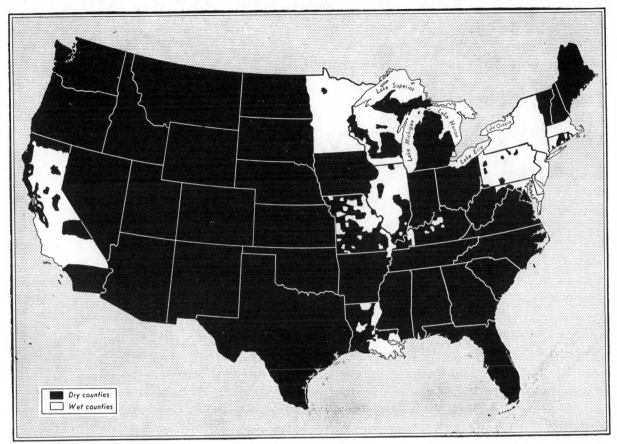

Dry Counties, 1919

285

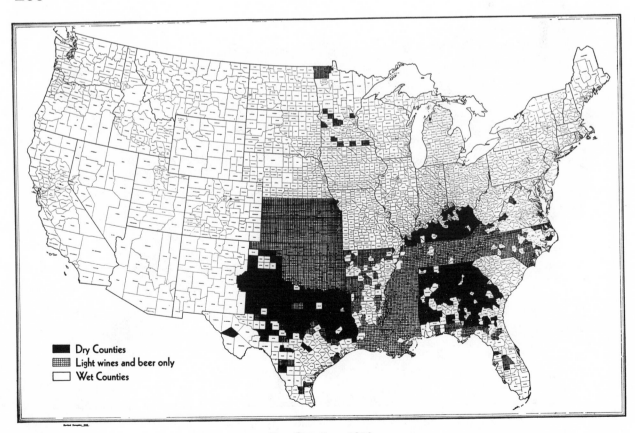

Dry Counties, 1950

286

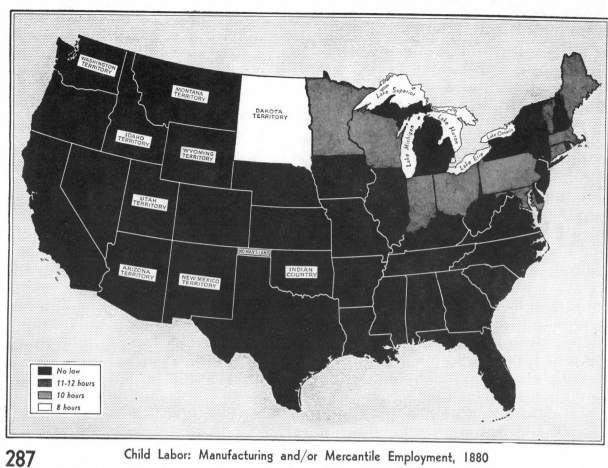

287   Child Labor: Manufacturing and/or Mercantile Employment, 1880

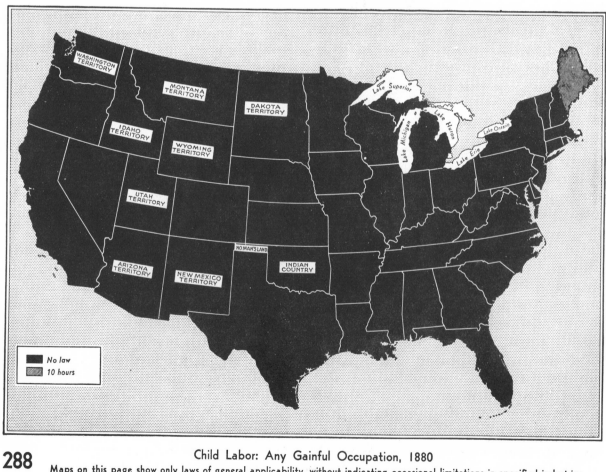

288   Child Labor: Any Gainful Occupation, 1880
Maps on this page show only laws of general applicability, without indicating occasional limitations in specified industries

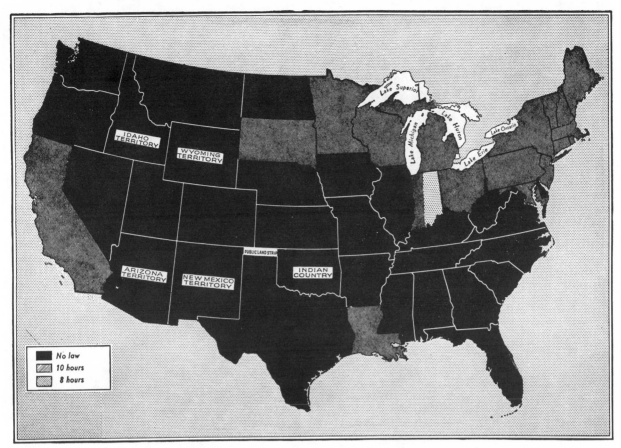

289 Child Labor: Manufacturing and/or Mercantile Employment, 1890

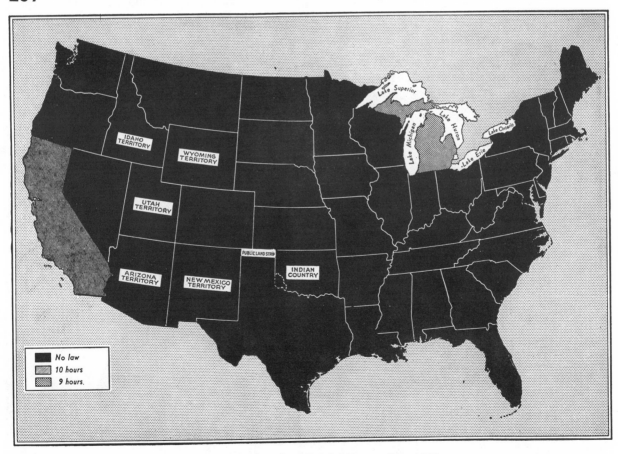

290 Child Labor: Any Gainful Occupation, 1890

Maps on this page show only laws of general applicability, without indicating occasional limitations in specified industries

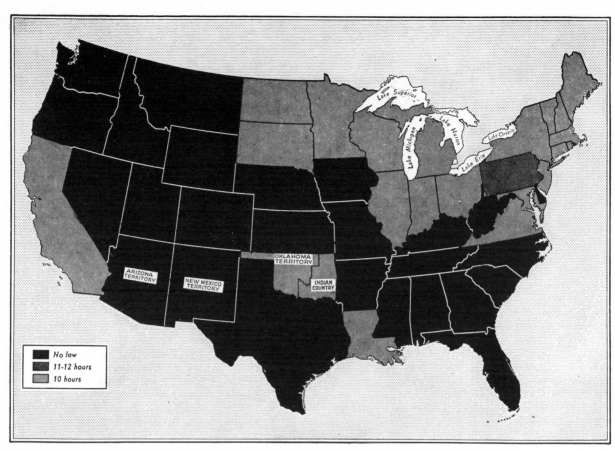

291   Child Labor: Manufacturing and/or Mercantile Employment, 1900

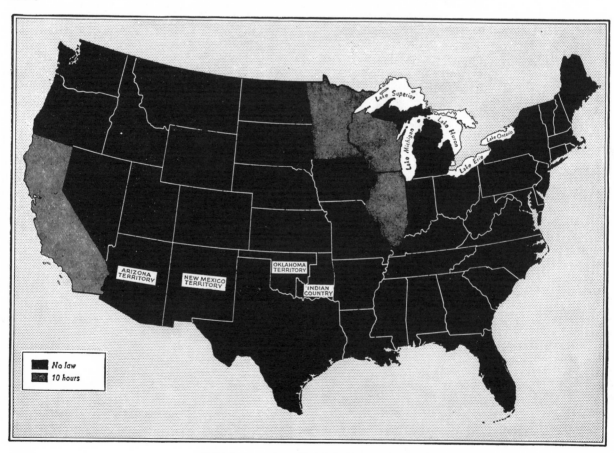

292   Child Labor: Any Gainful Occupation, 1900
Maps on this page show only laws of general applicability, without indicating occasional limitations in specified industries

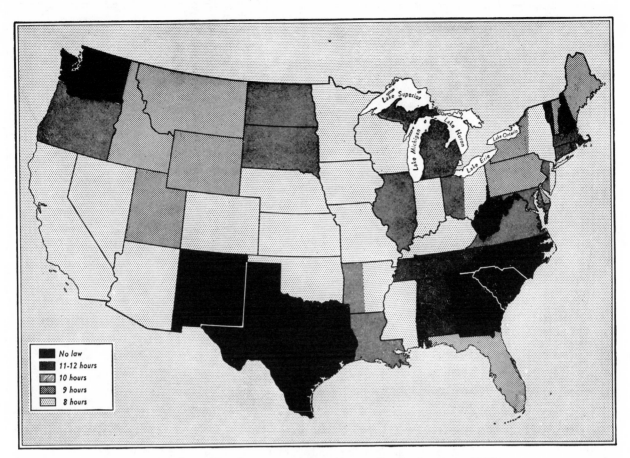

293   Child Labor: Manufacturing and/or Mercantile Employment, 1915

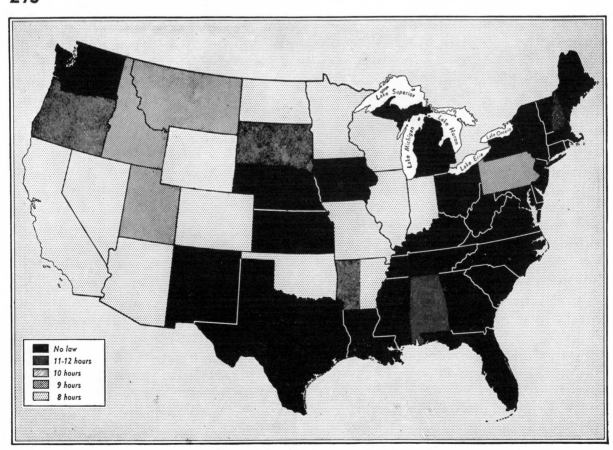

294   Child Labor: Any Gainful Occupation, 1915

Maps on this page show only laws of general applicability, without indicating occasional limitations in specified industries

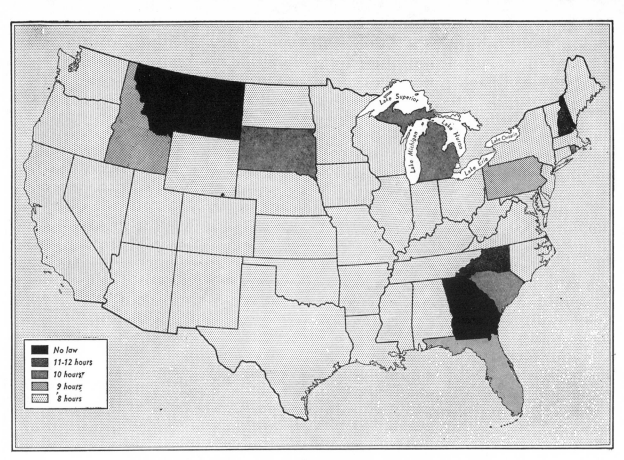

295   Child Labor: Manufacturing and/or Mercantile Employment, 1930

Legend:
- No law
- 11-12 hours
- 10 hours
- 9 hours
- 8 hours

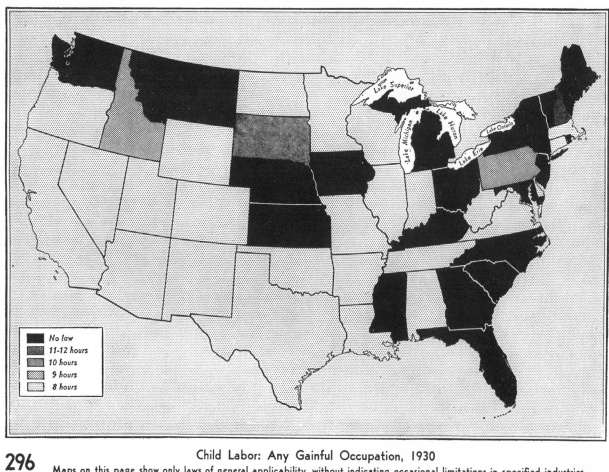

296   Child Labor: Any Gainful Occupation, 1930
Maps on this page show only laws of general applicability, without indicating occasional limitations in specified industries

Legend:
- No law
- 11-12 hours
- 10 hours
- 9 hours
- 8 hours

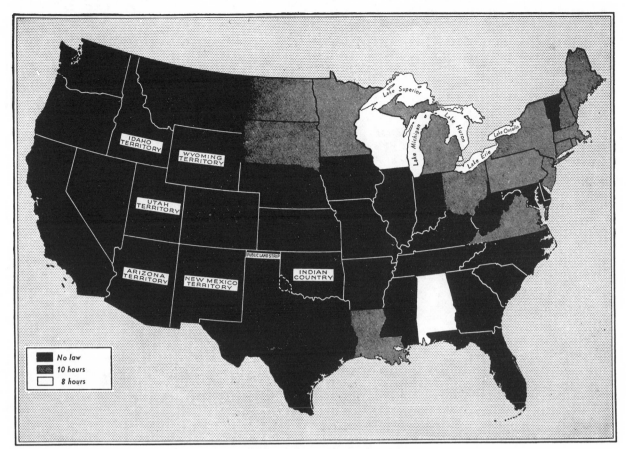

297   Women's Hours of Work, 1890

Legend (map 297):
- No law
- 10 hours
- 8 hours

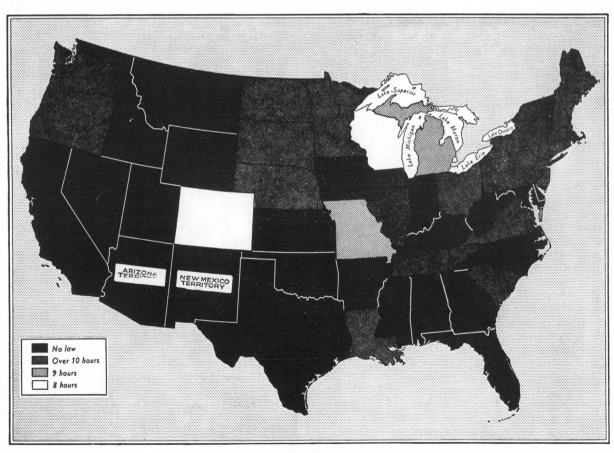

298   Women's Hours of Work, 1910

Legend (map 298):
- No law
- Over 10 hours
- 9 hours
- 8 hours

Maps on this page show only laws of general applicability, without indicating occasional limitations in specified industries

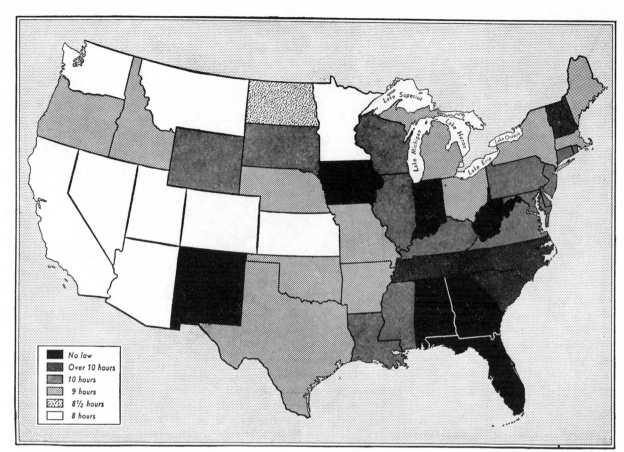

299   Women's Hours of Work, 1920

Legend (1920):
- No law
- Over 10 hours
- 10 hours
- 9 hours
- 8½ hours
- 8 hours

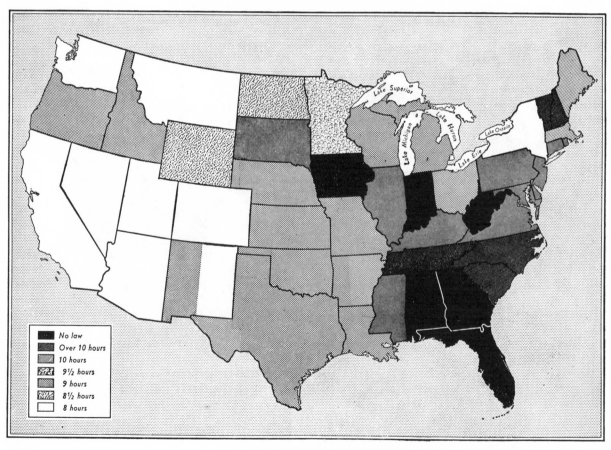

300   Women's Hours of Work, 1930

Legend (1930):
- No law
- Over 10 hours
- 10 hours
- 9½ hours
- 9 hours
- 8½ hours
- 8 hours

Maps on this page show only laws of general applicability, without indicating occasional limitations in specified industries

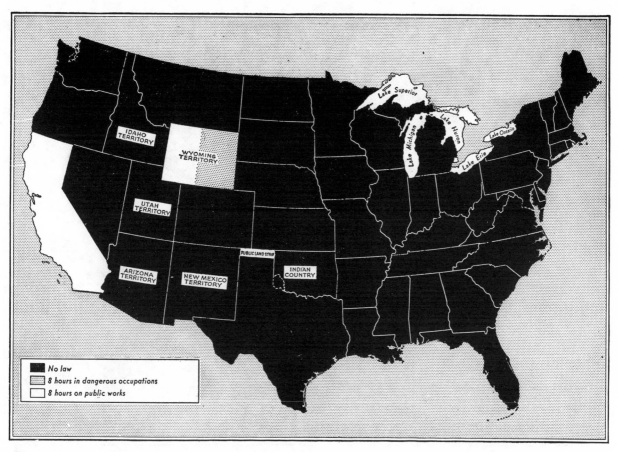

301　　Men's Hours of Work: Public Works and Dangerous Occupations, 1890

Legend (map 301):
- No law
- 8 hours in dangerous occupations
- 8 hours on public works

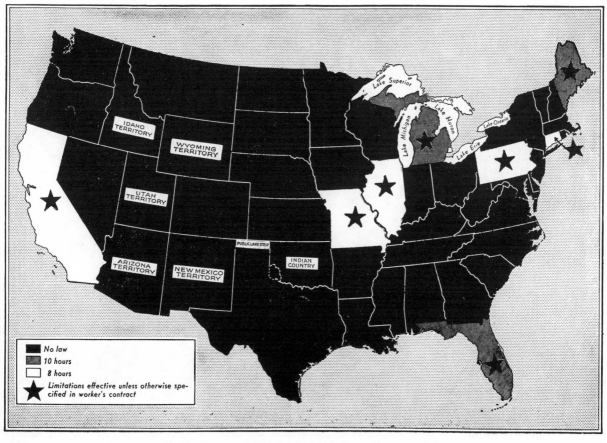

302　　Men's Hours of Work: General Occupations, 1890

No indication is made of occasional limitations in specified industries

Legend (map 302):
- No law
- 10 hours
- 8 hours
- ★ Limitations effective unless otherwise specified in worker's contract

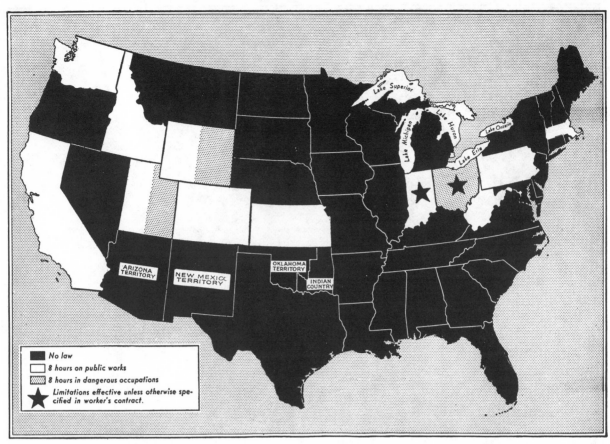

303   Men's Hours of Work: Public Works and Dangerous Occupations, 1900

Legend:
- No law
- 8 hours on public works
- 8 hours in dangerous occupations
- ★ Limitations effective unless otherwise specified in worker's contract.

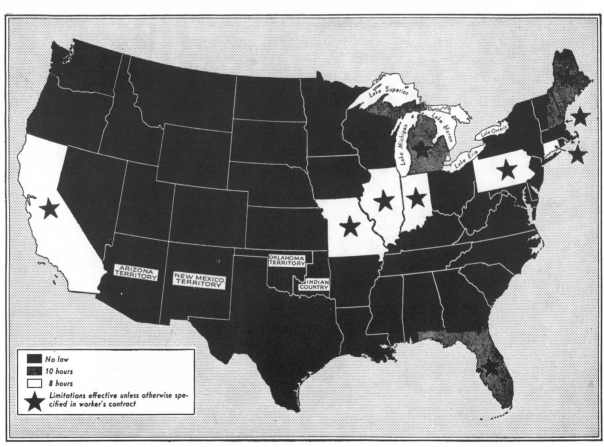

304   Men's Hours of Work: General Occupations, 1900
No indication is made of occasional limitations in specified industries

Legend:
- No law
- 10 hours
- 8 hours
- ★ Limitations effective unless otherwise specified in worker's contract

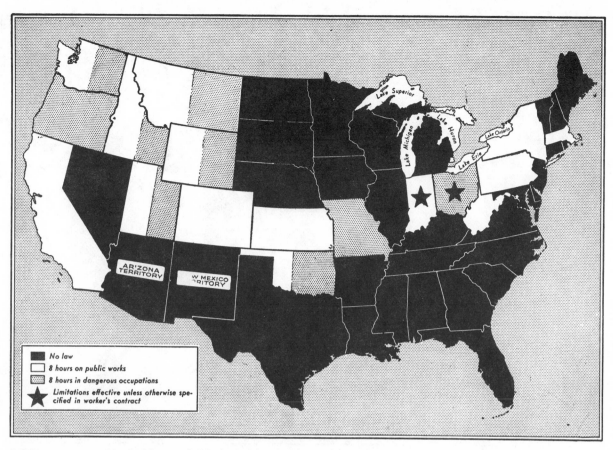

305   Men's Hours of Work: Public Works and Dangerous Occupations, 1910

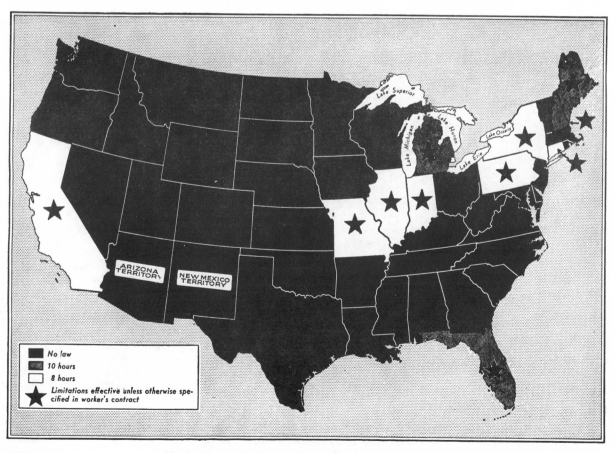

306   Men's Hours of Work: General Occupations, 1910

No indication is made of occasional limitations in specified industries

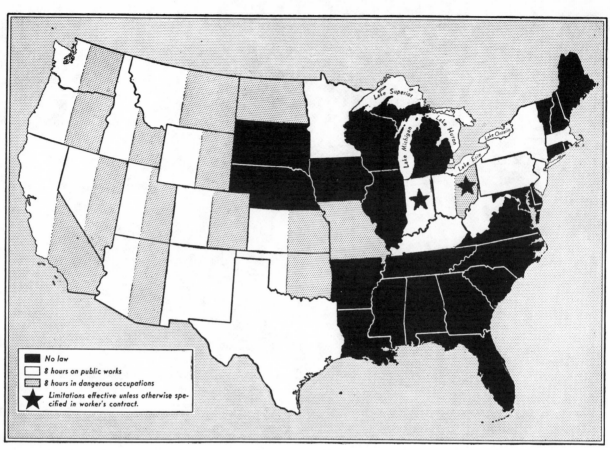

307   Men's Hours of Work: Public Works and Dangerous Occupations, 1920

Legend:
- ■ No law
- □ 8 hours on public works
- ▦ 8 hours in dangerous occupations
- ★ Limitations effective unless otherwise specified in worker's contract.

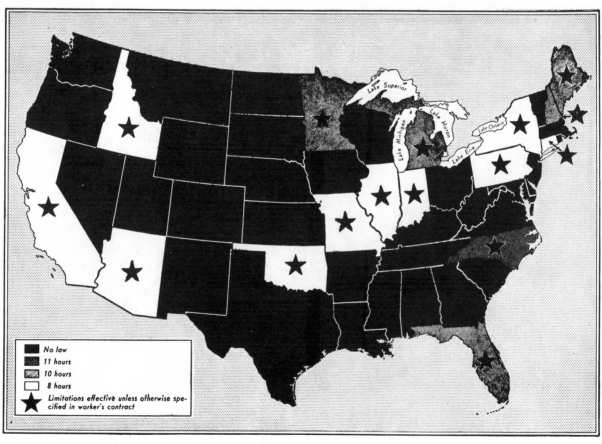

308   Men's Hours of Work: General Occupations, 1920

No indication is made of occasional limitations in specified industries

Legend:
- ■ No law
- ▨ 11 hours
- ▧ 10 hours
- □ 8 hours
- ★ Limitations effective unless otherwise specified in worker's contract

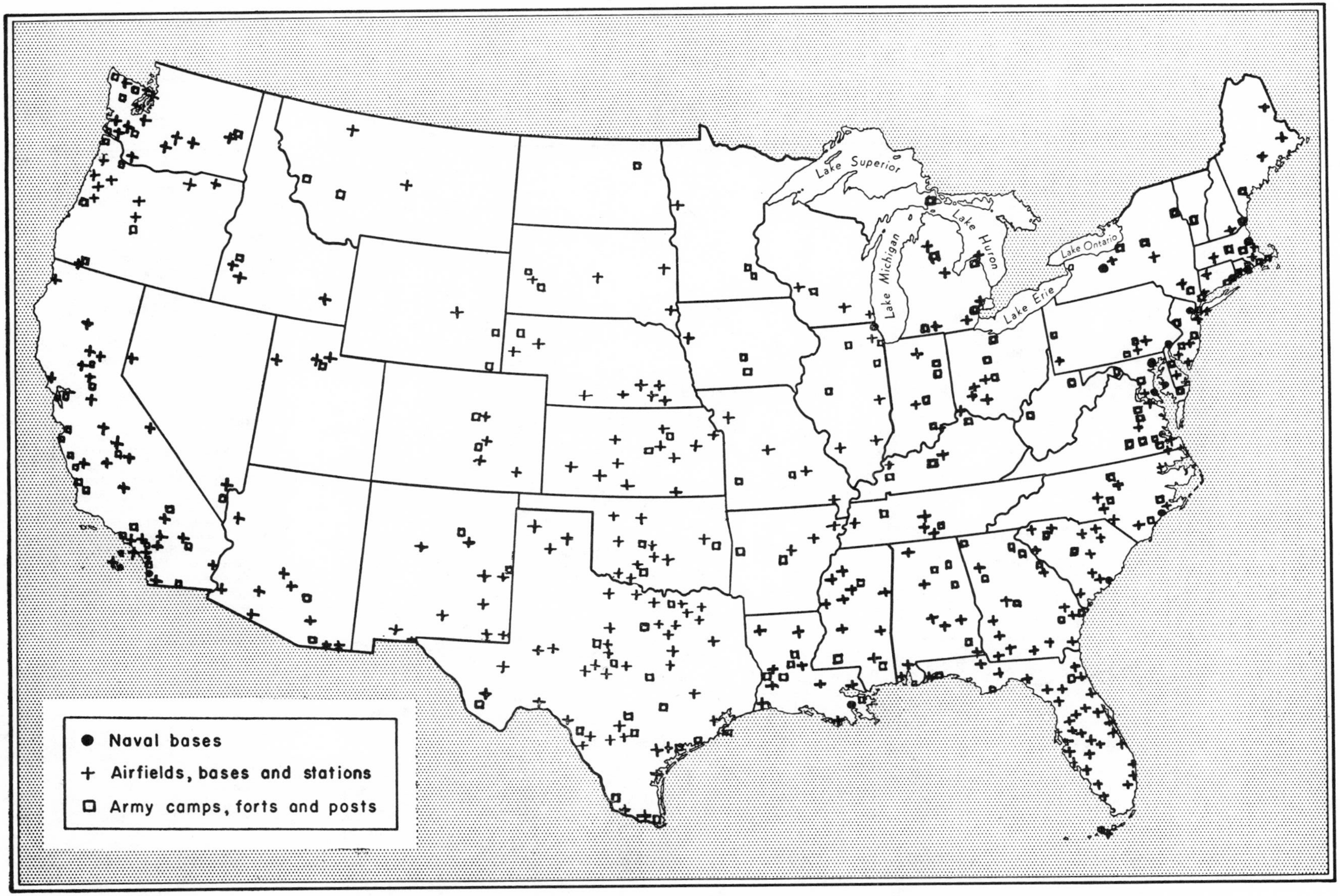

America in the Second World War: Army Camps, Naval Bases, and Airfields

Naval bases
Airfields, bases and stations
Army camps, forts and posts

309

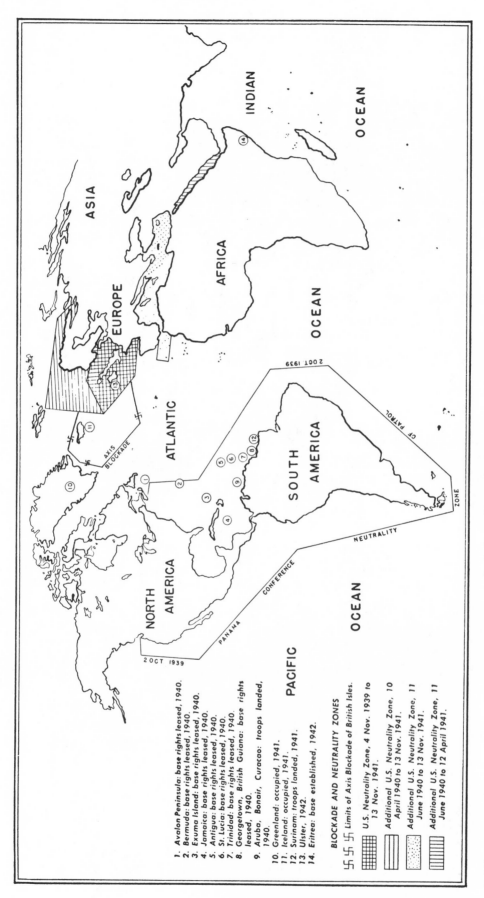

1. *Avalon Peninsula: base rights leased, 1940.*
2. *Bermuda: base rights leased, 1940.*
3. *Exuma Island: base rights leased, 1940.*
4. *Jamaica: base rights leased, 1940.*
5. *Antigua: base rights leased, 1940.*
6. *St. Lucia: base rights leased, 1940.*
7. *Trinidad: base rights leased, 1940.*
8. *Georgetown, British Guiana: base rights leased, 1940.*
9. *Aruba, Bonair, Curacao: troops landed, 1940.*
10. *Greenland: occupied, 1941.*
11. *Iceland: occupied, 1941.*
12. *Surinam: troops landed, 1941.*
13. *Ulster, 1942.*
14. *Eritrea: base established, 1942.*

BLOCKADE AND NEUTRALITY ZONES

卐 卐 卐 *Limits of Axis Blockade of British Isles.*

⊞ *U.S. Neutrality Zone, 4 Nov. 1939 to 13 Nov. 1941.*

▥ *Additional U.S. Neutrality Zone, 10 April 1940 to 13 Nov. 1941.*

▦ *Additional U.S. Neutrality Zone, 11 June 1940 to 13 Nov. 1941.*

▤ *Additional U.S. Neutrality Zone, 11 June 1940 to 12 April 1941.*

Prelude to War in the Atlantic, 1939-1941

310

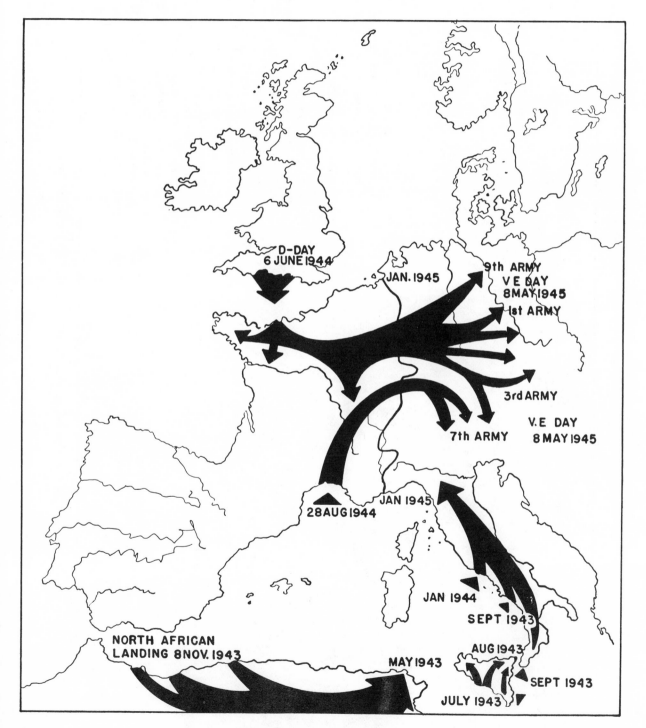

America in the Second World War: European and African Fronts

WAR IN THE PACIFIC
1941-1945

1. JAPANESE ATTACK PEARL HARBOR — 7 DEC. 1941
2. JAPANESE ATTACK PHILIPPINE IS. — 8 DEC. 1941
3. WAKE ISLAND FALLS — 23 DEC. 1941
4. BATTLE OF CORAL SEA — 7-8 MAY 1942
5. BATTLE OF MIDWAY — 3-6 JUNE 1942
6. SOLOMON ISLANDS CAMPAIGN — AUG. 1942-JUNE 1944
7. ALEUTIAN CAMPAIGN — AUG. 1942-AUG. 1943
8. BATTLE OF BISMARCK SEA — 2-4 MARCH 1943
9. GILBERT ISLAND OPERATIONS — NOV. 1943
10. MARSHALL IS. OPERATIONS — FEB. 1944
11. HOLLANDIA OPERATIONS — APRIL 1944
12. MARIANAS ISLANDS OPERATIONS — JUNE-AUG. 1944
13. WESTERN CAROLINES OPERATIONS — SEPT. 1944
14. LEYTE LANDINGS — OCT. 1944
15. BURMA CAMPAIGNS — DEC. 1944-AUG. 1945
16. LINGAYEN GULF LANDINGS — JAN. 1945
17. IWO JIMA OPERATIONS — FEB.-MAR. 1945
18. OKINAWA OPERATIONS — APRIL-JUNE 1945
19. BORNEO OPERATIONS — MAY-JULY 1945
20. PRE-INVASION OPERATIONS — JULY-AUG. 1945
21. JAPANESE SURRENDER — 2 SEPT. 1945

———— LINE OF FARTHEST JAPANESE ADVANCE 1942

America in the Second World War: The Fighting in the Pacific

312

[196]

APPENDICES

	Date of Admission	1770	1780	1790	1800	1810	1820	1830	1840	1850
New Hampshire		60,000	84,500	141,885	183,858	214,460	244,161	269,328	284,574	317,976
Massachusetts		265,000	307,000	378,787	422,845	472,040	523,287	610,408	737,699	994,514
Connecticut		175,000	203,000	237,946	251,002	261,942	275,248	297,675	309,978	370,792
Rhode Island		55,000	52,000	68,825	69,122	76,931	83,059	97,199	108,830	147,545
New York		160,000	200,000	340,120	589,051	959,049	1,372,812	1,918,608	2,428,921	3,097,394
New Jersey		110,000	137,000	184,139	211,149	245,562	277,575	320,823	373,306	489,555
Pennsylvania		250,000	335,000	434,373	602,365	810,091	1,049,485	1,348,233	1,724,033	2,311,786
Delaware		25,000	37,000	59,096	64,273	72,674	72,749	76,748	78,085	91,532
Maryland		200,000	250,000	319,728	341,548	380,546	407,350	447,040	470,019	583,034
Virginia		450,000	520,000	747,610	880,200	974,600	1,065,366	1,211,405	1,239,797	1,421,611
North Carolina		230,000	300,000	393,751	478,103	555,500	638,829	737,987	753,419	869,039
South Carolina		140,000	160,000	249,073	345,591	415,115	502,741	581,185	594,398	668,507
Georgia		26,000	55,000	82,548	162,686	252,433	340,989	516,823	691,392	906,185
Vermont	1791	—	—	—	154,465	217,895	235,981	280,652	291,948	314,120
Kentucky	1792	—	—	—	220,955	406,511	564,317	687,917	779,828	982,405
Tennessee	1796	—	—	—	105,602	261,727	422,823	681,904	829,210	1,002,717
District of Columbia	(1800)	—	—	—	14,093	24,023	33,039	39,834	43,712	51,687
Ohio	1803	—	—	—	—	230,760	581,434	937,903	1,519,467	1,980,329
Louisiana	1812	—	—	—	—	—	153,407	215,739	352,411	517,762
Indiana	1816	—	—	—	—	—	147,178	343,031	685,866	988,416
Mississippi	1817	—	—	—	—	—	75,448	136,621	375,651	606,526
Illinois	1818	—	—	—	—	—	55,211	157,445	476,183	851,470
Alabama	1819	—	—	—	—	—	127,901	309,527	590,756	771,623
Maine	1820	—	—	—	—	—	298,335	399,455	501,793	538,169
Missouri	1821	—	—	—	—	—	—	140,455	383,702	682,044
Arkansas	1836	—	—	—	—	—	—	—	97,574	209,897
Michigan	1837	—	—	—	—	—	—	—	212,267	397,654
Florida	1845	—	—	—	—	—	—	—	—	87,445
Texas	1845	—	—	—	—	—	—	—	—	212,592
Iowa	1846	—	—	—	—	—	—	—	—	192,214
Wisconsin	1848	—	—	—	—	—	—	—	—	305,391
California	1850	—	—	—	—	—	—	—	—	92,597
Minnesota	1858	—	—	—	—	—	—	—	—	—
Oregon	1859	—	—	—	—	—	—	—	—	
Kansas	1861	—	—	—	—	—	—	—	—	
West Virginia	1863	—	—	—	—	—	—	—	—	
Nevada	1864	—	—	—	—	—	—	—	—	
Nebraska	1867	—	—	—	—	—	—	—	—	
Colorado	1876	—	—	—	—	—	—	—	—	
North Dakota	1889	—	—	—	—	—	—	—	—	
South Dakota	1889	—	—	—	—	—	—	—	—	
Montana	1889	—	—	—	—	—	—	—	—	
Washington	1889	—	—	—	—	—	—	—	—	
Idaho	1890	—	—	—	—	—	—	—	—	
Wyoming	1890	—	—	—	—	—	—	—	—	
Utah	1896	—	—	—	—	—	—	—	—	
Oklahoma	1907	—	—	—	—	—	—	—	—	
New Mexico	1912	—	—	—	—	—	—	—	—	
Arizona	1912	—	—	—	—	—	—	—	—	
Totals		2,205,000	2,781,000	3,929,214	5,308,483	7,239,881	9,638,453	12,866,020	17,069,453	23,191,876

POPULATION, 1770-1950

1860	1870	1880	1890	1900	1910	1920	1930	1940	1950
326,073	318,300	346,991	376,530	411,588	430,572	443,083	465,293	491,524	533,242
1,231,066	1,457,351	1,783,085	2,238,947	2,085,346	3,336,416	3,852,356	4,249,614	4,316,721	4,690,514
460,467	537,454	622,700	746,258	908,420	1,114,756	1,380,631	1,606,903	1,709,242	2,007,280
174,620	217,353	276,531	345,506	428,556	542,610	604,397	687,497	713,346	791,896
3,880,735	4,382,759	5,082,871	6,003,174	7,268,894	9,113,614	10,385,227	12,588,066	13,479,142	14,830,192
672,035	906,096	1,131,116	1,444,933	1,883,669	2,537,167	3,155,900	4,041,334	4,160,165	4,835,329
2,906,215	3,521,951	4,282,891	5,258,113	6,302,115	7,665,111	8,720,017	9,631,350	9,900,180	10,498,012
112,216	125,015	146,608	168,493	184,735	202,322	223,003	238,386	266,505	318,085
687,049	780,894	934,943	1,042,390	1,188,044	1,295,346	1,449,661	1,631,526	1,821,244	2,343,001
1,596,318	1,225,163*	1,512,565	1,655,980	1,854,184	2,061,612	2,309,187	2,421,851	2,677,773	3,318,680
992,622	1,071,361	1,399,750	1,617,949	1,893,810	2,206,287	2,559,123	3,170,276	3,571,623	4,061,929
703,708	705,606	995,577	1,151,149	1,340,316	1,515,400	1,683,724	1,738,765	1,899,804	2,117,027
1,057,286	1,184,109	1,542,180	1,837,353	2,216,331	2,609,121	2,895,832	2,908,506	3,123,723	3,444,578
315,098	330,551	332,286	332,422	343,641	355,956	352,428	359,611	359,231	377,747
1,155,684	1,321,011	1,648,690	1,858,635	2,147,174	2,289,905	2,416,630	2,614,589	2,845,627	2,944,806
1,109,801	1,258,520	1,542,359	1,767,518	2,020,616	2,184,789	2,337,885	2,616,556	2,915,841	3,291,718
75,080	131,700	177,624	230,392	278,718	331,069	437,571	486,869	663,091	802,178
2,339,511	2,665,260	3,198,062	3,672,329	4,157,545	4,767,121	5,759,394	6,646,697	6,907,612	7,946,627
708,002	726,915	939,946	1,118,588	1,381,625	1,656,388	1,798,509	2,101,593	2,363,880	2,683,516
1,350,428	1,680,637	1,978,301	2,192,404	2,516,462	2,700,876	2,930,390	3,238,503	3,427,796	3,934,224
791,305	827,922	1,131,597	1,289,600	1,551,270	1,797,114	1,790,618	2,009,821	2,183,796	2,178,914
1,711,951	2,539,891	3,077,871	3,826,352	4,821,550	5,638,591	6,485,280	7,630,654	7,897,241	8,712,176
964,201	996,992	1,262,505	1,513,401	1,828,697	2,138,093	2,348,174	2,646,248	2,832,961	3,061,743
628,279	626,295	648,936	661,086	694,466	742,371	768,014	797,423	847,226	913,774
1,182,012	1,721,295	2,168,380	2,679,185	3,106,665	3,293,335	3,404,055	3,629,367	3,784,664	3,954,653
435,450	488,471	802,525	1,128,211	1,311,564	1,574,449	1,752,204	1,854,482	1,949,387	1,909,511
749,113	1,184,059	1,636,937	2,093,890	2,420,982	2,810,173	3,668,412	4,842,325	5,256,106	6,371,766
140,424	187,748	269,493	391,422	528,542	752,619	968,470	1,468,211	1,897,414	2,771,305
604,215	818,579	1,591,749	2,235,527	3,048,710	3,896,542	4,663,228	5,824,715	6,414,824	7,711,194
674,913	1,194,020	1,624,615	1,912,297	2,231,853	2,224,775	2,404,021	2,470,939	2,538,268	2,621,073
775,881	1,054,670	1,315,497	1,693,330	2,069,042	2,333,860	2,632,067	2,939,006	3,137,587	3,434,575
379,994	560,247	864,694	1,213,398	1,485,053	2,377,549	3,426,861	5,677,251	6,907,387	10,586,223
172,023	439,706	780,773	1,310,283	1,751,394	2,075,708	2,387,125	2,563,953	2,792,300	2,982,483
52,465	90,923	174,768	317,704	413,536	672,765	783,389	953,786	1,089,684	1,521,341
—	364,399	996,096	1,428,108	1,470,495	1,690,949	1,769,257	1,880,999	1,801,028	1,905,299
—	442,014	618,457	762,794	958,800	1,211,119	1,463,701	1,729,205	1,901,974	2,005,552
—	42,491	62,266	47,355	42,335	81,875	77,470	91,058	110,247	160,083
—	122,993	452,402	1,062,656	1,066,300	1,192,214	1,296,372	1,377,963	1,315,834	1,325,510
—	—	194,327	413,249	539,700	799,024	939,629	1,035,791	1,123,296	1,325,089
—	—	—	190,983	391,146	577,056	646,872	680,845	641,935	619,636
—	—	—	348,600	401,570	583,888	636,547	692,849	642,961	652,740
—	—	—	142,924	243,329	376,053	548,889	837,606	559,456	591,024
—	—	—	357,232	518,103	1,141,990	1,356,621	1,563,396	1,736,191	2,378,963
—	—	—	88,548	161,772	325,594	431,866	445,032	524,873	588,637
—	—	—	62,555	92,531	145,965	194,402	225,565	250,742	290,529
—	—	—	—	276,749	373,351	449,396	507,847	550,310	688,862
—	—	—	—	—	1,657,155	2,028,283	2,396,040	2,336,434	2,233,351
—	—	—	—	—	—	360,350	423,317	531,818	681,187
—	—	—	—	—	—	334,162	435,573	499,261	749,587
31,443,321	38,558,371	50,155,783	62,947,714	75,994,575	91,972,266	105,710,620	122,775,046	131,669,275	150,697,361

* West Virginia was separated from Virginia in 1863.

APPENDIX II
PRESIDENTIAL ELECTIONS

These tables are arranged so as to show the votes of one party in the same relative position throughout. Thus, after 1800, the first column shows, not necessarily the winning candidate, but the candidate of the Democratic party, while the second column shows the vote of the Whig and later of the Republican candidate. This gives the best possible chance to compare the shifts of voting strength between the parties from one election to the next. States are arranged in the order of their admission. Capitals mark the name of the successful candidate. Bold-face figures show the majority or plurality candidate in each state.

Only the electoral votes are given through 1824. Popular votes were taken in but a few of the states prior to that time, and where taken, the statistics are both hard to get and unreliable. Since prior to the passage of the Twelfth Amendment, members of the Electoral College put the names of two men on their ballots, the man receiving the highest number to become President, and the next highest, Vice-President, the names of both appear on the tally of the ballot through 1800. Up to that date, the name of the successful presidential candidate appears in capitals, that of the vice-presidential candidate in italicized capitals.

Correlation of these tables to the suffrage maps will be rewarding. The astounding increase of vote totals in many states between 1820 and 1828 is not to be accounted for by population increase alone. And there are many instances where small popular votes in states maintaining tax-paying qualifications yet having their electoral vote based on the total of the white population plus three-fifths of the slaves, had equal weight in the Electoral College with more democratic states casting much larger popular votes.

"LEGIS." indicates that the electors were chosen by the Legislature, not by popular vote. "UNAN." indicates that the successful candidate in that state had no formal opposition. "Maj." is used in the one case where the full vote totals appear to be unobtainable, but where the figure of the majority of the successful candidate over his opposition is available.

Owing to incomplete reporting by many states, the figures on minor party votes are inconclusive and incomplete. The official national totals of minor candidates are given below the totals of the major parties. The later figures are based on the official returns compiled by the Clerk of the House of Representatives. Returns in the early elections were taken from the *American* and the *Tribune Almanacs*. Electoral votes are published in the *Annals of Congress*, and for 1824 in the *Register of Debates*.

PRESIDENTIAL ELECTORAL VOTES TO 1824

	1788												1792					1796												
	WASHINGTON	ADAMS	Huntingdon	Jay	Hancock	Harrison	G. Clinton	Rutledge	Milton	Amesbury	Telfair	Lincoln	WASHINGTON	ADAMS	G. Clinton	Jefferson	Burr	ADAMS	JEFFERSON	Washington	T. Pinckney	Burr	S. Adams	Ellsworth	S. Johnston	Iredell	Jay	G. Clinton	C. C. Pinckney	J. Henry
New Hampshire	5	5											6	6				6						6						
Massachusetts	10	10											16	16				16			13			1			2			
Connecticut	7	5	2										9	9				9			4			4			1			
New Jersey	6	1		5									7	7				7			7									
Pennsylvania	10	8			2								15	14	1			1	14		2	13								
Delaware	3			3									3	3				3			3									
Maryland	6					6							8	8				7	4		4	3								2
Virginia	10	5		1	1		3						21		21			1	20	1		1	15					3	1	
South Carolina	7				1			6					8	7			1		8		8									
Georgia	5								2	1	1	1	4		4				4									4		
New York													12		12			12			10						2			
North Carolina													12		12			1	11	1		6			2	3				
Rhode Island													4	4				4			4									
Vermont													3	3				4			4									
Kentucky													4			4			4			4								
Tennessee																			3			3								
TOTALS	69	34	2	9	4	6	3	6	2	1	1	1	132	77	50	4	1	71	68	2	59	30	15	11	2	3	5	7	1	2

PRESIDENTIAL ELECTORAL VOTES TO 1824

	1800					1804		1808			1812		1816		1820		1824			
	JEFFERSON (D)	BURR (D)	Adams (F)	Pinckney (F)	Jay (F)	JEFFERSON (D)	Pinckney (F)	MADISON (D)	G. Clinton	Pinckney (F)	MADISON (D)	D. Clinton (F)	MONROE (D)	King (F)	MONROE (D)	J. Q. Adams	Jackson (D)	J. Q. ADAMS (NR)‡	Crawford (D)	Clay (NR)
New Hampshire			6	6		7				7		8	8		7	1		8		
Massachusetts			16	16		19				19		22		22	15			15		
Connecticut			9	9			9			9		9		9	9			8		
Rhode Island			4	3	1	4				4		4	4		4			4		
New York	12	12				19		13	6			29	29		29		1	26	5	4
New Jersey			7	7		8		8				8	8				8			
Pennsylvania	8	8	7	7		20		20			25		25		24		28			
Delaware			3	3			3			3		4		3				1	2	
Maryland	5	5	5	5		9	2	9		2	6	5	8		11		7	3	1	
Virginia	21	21				24		24			25		25		25				24	
North Carolina	8	8	4	4		14		11		3	15		15		15		15			
South Carolina	8	8				10		10			11		11		11		11			
Georgia	4	4				6		6			8		8		8				9	
Vermont			4	4		6		6			8		8		8			7		
Kentucky	4	4				8		7			12		12		12					14
Tennessee	3	3				5		5			8		8		7		11			
Ohio						3		3			7		8		8					16
Louisiana											3		3		3		3	2		
Indiana													3		3		5			
Mississippi															2		3			
Illinois															3		2	1		
Alabama															3		5			
Maine															9			9		
Missouri															3†					3
TOTALS	73*	73*	65	64	1	162	14	122	6	47	128	89	183	34	208	1	99	84	41	37

* Elected by the House of Representatives.
† Vote not allowed.
‡ Elected by the House of Representatives.

PRESIDENTIAL ELECTIONS, 1824–1940

	1824				1828		1832		1836	
	Jackson (D)	J. Q. ADAMS (NR)	Crawford (D)	Clay (NR)	JACKSON (D)	J. Q. Adams (NR)	JACKSON (D)	Clay (W)	VAN BUREN (D)	Others W, (etc.)
New Hampshire	643	4,170			20,692	24,076	25,486	19,010	18,722	6,228
Massachusetts		30,687	6,616		6,019	29,836	14,545	33,003	33,501	41,093†
Connecticut		7,587	1,978		4,448	13,829	11,269	17,755	19,234	18,466
Rhode Island		2,145	200		821	2,754	2,126	2,810	2,964	2,710
New York	LEGIS. SPLIT TICKET				140,763	135,413	168,497	154,896	166,815	138,543
New Jersey	10,985	9,110	1,196		21,950	23,758	23,856	23,393	26,347	26,802‡
Pennsylvania	36,100	5,440	4,206	1,609	101,652	50,848	90,983	66,716	91,475	87,111
Delaware	LEGIS. SPLIT TICKET				4,349	4,769	4,110	4,276	4,155	4,738‡
Maryland	14,523	14,632	3,646	695	24,578	25,759	19,156	19,160	22,167	25,852‡
Virginia	2,861	3,189	8,849	416	26,752	12,101	33,609	11,451	30,261	23,368
North Carolina	20,415	15,621			37,857	13,918	24,862	4,563	26,910	23,626
South Carolina	LEGIS.				LEGIS.		**		LEGIS.§	
Georgia			LEGIS.		18,709		20,750		22,126	24,930‖
Vermont		LEGIS.			8,205	24,784	7,870	11,152*	14,037	20,991‡
Kentucky	6,453			16,782	39,084	31,172	36,190	43,396	33,435	36,955‡
Tennessee	20,197	216	312		44,090	2,240	28,740	1,436	26,120	35,962‖
Ohio	18,457	12,280		19,255	67,597	63,396	81,246	76,349	96,948	105,405‡
Louisiana	LEGIS. SPLIT				4,605	4,007	4,049	2,528	3,653	3,383
Indiana	7,343	3,095		5,315	22,237	17,052	31,552	15,472	32,480	41,381‡
Mississippi	3,234	1,694	119		6,763	1,581	5,919		9,979	9,688
Illinois	1,901	1,542	219	1,047	6,763	1,581	14,147	5,429	18,007	14,983
Alabama	9,443	2,416	1,680	67	17,138	1,938	UNAN.		10,068¶	15,037
Maine	2,330	6,870			13,927	20,773	33,291	27,204	22,300	15,239
Missouri	987	311		1,401	8,232	3,422	5,192 maj.		10,995	8,337
Arkansas									2,400	1,238
Michigan									7,360	4,000
TOTALS	152,899	105,321	47,265	47,087	650,028	512,158	687,502	550,189	762,149	736,736

* Electoral vote cast for Wm. Wirt, Anti-Masonic.
** Legislature cast vote for Floyd.
† Electoral vote cast for Webster (W).
‡ Electoral vote cast for Harrison (W).
§ Electoral vote cast for Mangum.
‖ Electoral vote cast for H. White.
¶ Electoral vote cast for Van Buren (D).

Wirt 33,108.

	1840			1844			1848			1852		
	Van Buren (D)	HARRISON (W)	Birney (L)	POLK (D)	Clay (W)	Birney (L)	Cass (D)	TAYLOR (W)	Van Buren (FS)	PIERCE (D)	Scott (W)	Hale (FS)
New Hampshire	32,670	26,434	126	27,150	17,866	4,161	27,763	14,781	7,560	28,997	16,147	6,695
Massachusetts	51,948	72,874	1,621	52,985	66,872	10,830	35,284	61,072	38,133	46,880	56,063	29,993
Connecticut	35,296	31,601	174	29,841	32,842	1,943	7,046	30,314	5,005	33,249	30,359	3,160
Rhode Island	3,301	5,278	42	4,848	7,323	107	3,600	6,689	705	8,735	7,626	644
New York	212,519	225,812	2,798	237,588	232,473	15,812	114,592	218,551	120,519	262,083	234,882	25,329
New Jersey	31,034	33,362	69	37,495	38,318	131	36,880	40,009	849	44,305	38,556	350
Pennsylvania	143,676	144,019	343	167,535	161,203	3,126	172,661	186,113	11,263	198,568	179,122	8,524
Delaware	4,884	5,967		5,969	6,257		5,910	6,440	80	6,318	6,293	62
Maryland	28,752	33,528		33,676	35,984		34,528	37,702	125	40,022	35,077	54
Virginia	43,893	42,501		49,417	43,677		46,536	45,124	9	72,413	57,132	
North Carolina	34,218	46,676		39,287	43,232		38,869	43,519	85	39,744	39,058	59
South Carolina	LEGIS.			LEGIS.			LEGIS.			LEGIS.		
Georgia	31,933	40,264		44,155	42,106		44,736	47,603		34,705	16,660	
Vermont	18,009	32,445	319	18,041	26,700	3,957	10,948	23,122	13,857	13,044	22,173	8,621
Kentucky	32,616	58,489		51,980	61,262		49,720	67,141		53,806	57,068	265
Tennessee	48,289	60,391		59,915	60,039		58,419	64,705		57,018	58,898	
Ohio	124,782	148,157	903	149,061	155,113	8,050	154,783	138,356	35,494	169,220	152,526	31,682
Louisiana	7,617	11,297		13,417	12,818		15,380	18,273		18,647	17,255	
Indiana	51,695	65,308		70,181	67,867	2,106	74,745	69,907	8,100	95,299	80,901	6,934
Mississippi	16,995	19,518	149	25,188	19,193		26,555	25,821		26,876	17,548	
Illinois	47,476	45,537		55,515	45,612	3,579	56,629	53,215	15,804	80,597	64,934	9,966
Alabama	33,991	28,471		36,223	24,850		31,363	30,482		26,881	15,038	
Maine	46,201	46,612	194	45,719	34,378	4,836	40,195	35,273	12,157	41,609	32,534	8,030
Missouri	29,760	22,972		41,369	31,251		32,671	40,077		36,642	28,944	
Arkansas	6,049	4,363		9,546	5,504		9,300	7,588		12,173	7,401	
Michigan	21,098	22,907	321	27,703	24,223	3,632	30,687	23,940	10,389	41,842	33,860	7,237
Florida							3,238	4,539		4,318	2,875	
Texas							8,801	3,777		13,552	4,995	
Iowa							12,051	10,557	1,126	8,624	7,444	777
Wisconsin							15,001	13,747	10,417	33,658	22,240	8,814
California										39,665	34,971	100
TOTALS	1,128,702	1,274,783	7,609	1,335,834	1,297,033	62,270	1,222,455	1,362,031	291,678	1,590,490	1,378,589	157,296

	1856			1860				1864		1868	
	BUCHANAN (D)	Fremont (R)	Fillmore (A)	Douglas (D)	Breckenridge (SRD)	LINCOLN (R)	Bell (CU)	McClellan (D)	LINCOLN (U)	Seymour (D)	GRANT (R)
New Hampshire	32,567	38,158	414	25,811	2,112	37,519	441	32,871	36,400	31,224	38,191
Massachusetts	39,240	108,190	19,626	34,372	5,939	106,533	22,331*	48,745	126,742	59,408	136,477
Connecticut	34,995	42,715	2,615	15,522	14,641	43,792	3,291	42,285	44,691	47,600	50,641
Rhode Island	6,680	1,467	1,675	7,707*		12,244		8,718	14,349	6,548	12,993
New York	195,878	274,705	124,604	303,329*		353,804		361,986	368,735	429,883	419,883
New Jersey	46,943	28,531	24,115	62,801*		58,324		68,124	60,723	83,001	80,121
Pennsylvania	230,154	147,350	82,178	16,765	178,871*	268,030	12,776	276,316	296,391	313,382	342,281
Delaware	8,003	306	6,175	1,023	7,337	3,815	3,863	8,767	8,155	10,980	7,623
Maryland	39,115	281	47,462	5,966	42,482	2,294	41,760	32,739	40,153	62,357	30,438
Virginia	89,975	291	60,039	16,290	74,323	1,929	74,681				
North Carolina	48,246		36,886	2,701	48,539		44,990			84,090	96,226
South Carolina	LEGIS.				LEGIS.					45,237	62,301
Georgia	56,617		42,372	11,590	51,889		42,886			102,822	57,134
Vermont	10,577	39,561	511	6,849	218	33,808	1,969	13,321	42,419	12,045	44,167
Kentucky	72,917	369	65,822	25,651	53,143	1,364	66,058	64,301	27,786	115,889	39,566
Tennessee	73,638		66,178	11,350	64,709		69,274			26,311	56,757
Ohio	170,874	187,497	28,125	187,232	11,405	231,610	12,194	205,568	265,154	238,700	280,159
Louisiana	22,169		20,709	7,625	22,681		20,204			80,225	33,263
Indiana	118,672	94,816	23,386	115,509	12,295	139,033	5,306	130,233	150,422	166,980	176,552
Mississippi	35,665		24,490	3,283	40,797		25,040				
Illinois	104,279	96,280	37,451	160,215	2,404	172,161	4,913	158,730	189,496	199,143	250,293
Alabama	46,817		28,557	12,651	48,831		27,875			72,086	76,366
Maine	38,035	65,514	3,233	26,693	6,368	62,811	2,046	46,992	68,114	42,396	70,426
Missouri	58,164		48,524	58,801	31,317	17,028	58,372	31,678	72,750	59,788	85,651
Arkansas	21,908		10,816	5,227	28,732		20,094			19,078	22,152
Michigan	52,139	71,762	1,560	65,057	805	88,480	405	74,604	91,521	97,069	138,550
Florida	6,368		4,843	367	8,543		5,437			LEGIS.	
Texas	28,575		15,244		47,548		15,438*				
Iowa	36,241	44,127	9,944	55,111	1,048	70,409	1,763	49,596	89,075	74,040	120,399
Wisconsin	52,867	66,092	579	65,021	888	86,110	161	65,884	83,458	84,710	108,857
California	42,460	16,721	28,327	38,516	34,334	39,173	6,817	43,841	62,134	54,078	54,592
Minnesota				11,920	748	22,069	62	17,375	25,000	28,072	43,542
Oregon				3,951	5,006	5,270	183	8,457	9,888	11,125	10,961
Kansas								3,691	16,441	14,019	31,049
West Virginia								10,438	23,152	20,306	29,025
Nevada								6,594	9,826	5,218	6,480
Nebraska										5,439	9,729
TOTALS	1,850,960	1,334,553	885,960	1,365,976	847,953	1,857,610	590,631	1,811,754	2,223,035	2,703,249	3,012,833

* Fusion

	1872		1876			1880			1884	
	Greeley (D & LR)	GRANT (R)	Tilden (D)	HAYES (R)	Cooper (G)	Hancock (D)	GARFIELD (R)	Weaver (G)	CLEVELAND (D)	Blaine (R)
New Hampshire	31,425	37,168	38,510	41,540		40,797	44,856	528	39,198	43,254
Massachusetts	59,269	133,472	108,777	150,063		111,960	105,205	4,548	122,481	146,724
Connecticut	45,880	50,626	61,934	59,084	774	61,415	67,071	868	67,182	65,898
Rhode Island	5,329	13,665	10,712	15,787	60	10,779	18,195	236	12,391	19,030
New York	387,281	440,736	521,949	480,207	1,987	534,511	555,544	12,373	563,154	562,005
New Jersey	76,456	91,656	115,962	103,517		122,565	120,555	2,617	127,784	123,433
Pennsylvania	212,041	349,589	366,158	384,142	7,187	407,502	444,713	20,648	392,785	473,804
Delaware	10,208	11,115	13,381	10,572		15,181	14,138	121	16,976	13,053
Maryland	67,687	66,760	91,780	71,981		93,706	78,515	818	96,932	85,699
Virginia	91,654	93,468	139,670	95,558		128,568	84,020		145,497	139,356
North Carolina	70,004	94,769	125,427	108,417		124,208	115,874	1,126	142,592	125,068
South Carolina	22,703	72,290	90,906	91,870		112,312	58,071	566	69,890	21,733
Georgia	76,356	62,550	130,088	50,446		102,470	54,086	969	94,667	48,603
Vermont	10,927	41,481	20,350	44,428		19,316	45,567	1,215	17,331	39,514
Kentucky	99,995	88,766	159,690	97,156	1,994	149,068	106,306	11,499	152,961	118,122
Tennessee	94,218	84,930	133,166	89,596		130,381	98,760	5,405	133,324	124,093
Ohio	244,321	281,852	323,182	330,698	3,057	340,821	373,048	6,456	368,280	400,082
Louisiana	57,029	71,663	70,508	75,135		65,067	38,637	439	62,540	46,347
Indiana	163,632	186,147	213,526	208,011		225,552	232,164	12,986	244,900	238,463
Mississippi	42,288	82,175	112,173	52,605		75,750	34,854	5,797	76,510	43,509
Illinois	189,438	241,944	258,601	278,232	17,233	277,321	318,037	26,358	312,351	337,469
Alabama	79,444	90,272	102,002	68,230		91,185	56,221	4,642	93,951	59,591
Maine	29,087	61,422	49,823	66,300		65,171	74,039	4,408	52,140	72,209
Missouri	151,434	119,116	203,077	145,029	3,498	208,609	153,567	35,135	235,988	202,929
Arkansas	37,927	41,373	58,071	38,669		60,775	42,436	4,079	72,927	50,895
Michigan	77,020	136,199	141,095	166,534	9,060	131,301	185,190	34,895	149,835	192,669
Florida	15,427	17,763	22,923	23,849		27,964	23,654		31,766	28,031
Texas	66,500	47,406	104,755	44,800		156,428	57,893	27,405	225,309	93,141
Iowa	71,179	131,566	112,121	171,326	9,431	105,845	183,904	32,327	177,316	197,088
Wisconsin	86,477	104,992	123,927	130,068	1,509	114,634	144,897	7,980	146,453	161,135
California	40,718	54,020	75,845	78,614	44	80,426	80,348	3,392	89,288	102,416
Minnesota	35,211	55,708	48,587	72,955	2,389	53,315	93,902	3,267	70,065	111,685
Oregon	7,742	11,818	14,157	15,214		19,955	20,619	245	24,604	26,860
Kansas	32,390	67,048	37,902	78,354	7,770	59,801	121,549	19,851	90,132	154,406
West Virginia	29,533	32,323	55,584	41,392		57,391	46,243	9,079	67,331	63,913
Nevada	6,236	8,413	9,308	10,383		8,619	7,878		5,578	7,193
Nebraska	7,812	18,329	17,554	31,917	2,320	28,523	54,979	3,950	54,391	76,912
Colorado						24,647	27,450	1,435	27,723	36,290
TOTALS	2,834,079	3,597,070	4,284,885	4,033,950	81,740	4,442,035	4,449,053	307,306	4,911,017	4,848,334

O'Conner (NLR) 29,408 Smith (Pro) 9,552 Dow (Pro) 10,487 St. John (Pro) 151,809
Black (Pro) 5,608 Butler (G) 133,825

	1888		1892			1896	
	Cleveland (D)	HARRISON (R)	CLEVELAND (D)	Harrison (R)	Weaver (P)	Bryan (D & P)	McKINLEY (R)
New Hampshire	43,456	45,728	43,081	45,658	293	21,651	57,444
Massachusetts	151,905	183,892	176,858	202,927	3,348	121,385	278,976
Connecticut	74,922	74,586	82,395	77,032	809	56,740	110,285
Rhode Island	17,520	21,969	24,336	26,975	228	14,459	37,437
New York	635,965	650,338	654,900	609,459	16,436	551,513	819,838
New Jersey	151,508	144,300	171,066	156,101		133,695	221,371
Pennsylvania	446,633	526,091	452,264	516,011	8,714	433,228	728,300
Delaware	16,414	12,973	18,581	18,077		13,425	16,883
Maryland	106,168	99,986	113,866	92,736	796	104,746	136,978
Virginia	151,979	150,449	193,977	113,256	12,275	154,985	135,388
North Carolina	148,336	134,784	133,098	100,565	44,732	174,488	155,243
South Carolina	65,825	13,740	54,698	13,384	2,410	58,801	9,313
Georgia	100,472	40,453	129,386	48,305	42,937	94,733	60,107
Vermont	16,785	45,192	16,325	37,992	44	10,607	50,991
Kentucky	183,800	155,134	175,461	135,441	23,500	217,890	218,171
Tennessee	158,779	138,988	136,594	99,851	23,730	168,847	149,703
Ohio	396,455	416,054	404,115	405,187	14,852	477,497	525,991
Louisiana	85,032	30,701	87,662	27,903		77,175	22,037
Indiana	261,013	263,361	262,740	255,615	22,208	305,573	323,754
Mississippi	85,467	31,120	40,288	1,342	10,102	63,793	5,123
Illinois	348,371	370,475	426,281	399,288	22,207	464,523	607,130
Alabama	117,320	56,197	138,138	9,197	85,181	131,226	54,737
Maine	50,437	72,656	48,024	62,878	2,045	34,587	80,461
Missouri	261,943	236,252	268,188	226,918	41,213	313,576	239,333
Arkansas	86,717	60,245	87,834	46,974	11,831	110,103	37,512
Michigan	213,469	236,387	202,296	222,708	19,931	237,268	293,582
Florida	39,056	26,659	30,143		4,843	32,736	11,288
Texas	234,883	88,280	239,148	81,444	99,418	361,224	158,894
Iowa	179,877	211,598	196,367	219,795	20,595	289,293	223,741
Wisconsin	155,243	176,556	177,335	170,846	9,909	165,349	268,051
California	117,729	124,816	118,174	117,962	25,311	144,618	146,688
Minnesota	104,385	142,492	100,920	122,823	29,313	139,753	193,503
Oregon	26,522	33,291	14,243	35,002	26,965	46,739	48,779
Kansas	102,745	182,904		157,241	163,111	172,915	159,345
West Virginia	78,677	78,171	84,467	80,293	4,166	94,488	105,379
Nevada	5,149	7,088	714	2,711	7,264	8,376	1,938
Nebraska	80,542	108,425	24,943	87,227	83,134	115,999	103,064
Colorado	37,567	50,774		38,620	53,584	161,269	26,279
North Dakota				17,506	17,700	20,686	26,335
South Dakota			9,081	34,888	26,544	41,225	41,042
Montana			17,581	18,851	7,334	42,537	10,494
Washington			29,844	36,460	19,105	51,646	39,153
Idaho			2	8,799	10,520	23,135	6,314
Wyoming				8,454	7,722	10,375	10,072
Utah						64,607	13,491
Oklahoma							
New Mexico							
Arizona							
TOTALS	5,540,050	5,444,337	5,554,414	5,190,802	1,027,329	6,467,946	7,035,638

Fisk (Pro) 259,125 Bidwell (Pro) 271,058 Palmer (ND) 131,529
Streeter (UL) 146,897 Levering (Pro) 141,676
Cowdrey (UL) 2,418

	1900		1904		1908	
	Bryan (D)	McKINLEY (R)	Parker (D)	ROOSEVELT (R)	Bryan (D)	TAFT (R)
New Hampshire	35,489	54,798	33,905	54,180	33,655	53,149
Massachusetts	157,016	239,147	165,722	257,822	155,543	265,966
Connecticut	74,014	102,572	72,909	111,089	68,255	112,915
Rhode Island	19,812	33,784	24,839	41,605	24,706	43,942
New York	678,425	822,013	683,981	859,533	667,468	870,070
New Jersey	164,879	221,754	164,367	245,164	182,567	265,326
Pennsylvania	424,232	712,665	335,430	840,949	448,782	745,779
Delaware	18,386	22,535	19,359	23,712	22,071	25,114
Maryland	122,237	136,185	109,446	109,497	115,908	116,513
Virginia	146,080	115,865	86,548	47,880	82,946	52,573
North Carolina	157,752	133,081	124,121	82,625	136,995	114,937
South Carolina	47,283	3,579	52,563	2,554	62,200	3,965
Georgia	81,700	35,056	83,472	24,003	72,413	41,692
Vermont	12,849	42,596	9,777	40,459	11,496	39,552
Kentucky	234,899	226,801	217,170	205,277	244,092	235,711
Tennessee	145,356	123,180	131,653	105,369	135,608	118,324
Ohio	474,882	543,918	344,940	600,095	502,721	572,311
Louisiana	53,671	14,233	48,708	5,205	63,568	8,958
Indiana	309,584	336,063	274,345	368,289	338,262	348,993
Mississippi	51,706	5,753	53,374	3,187	60,287	4,363
Illinois	503,061	597,985	327,606	632,645	450,810	629,932
Alabama	96,368	55,634	79,857	22,472	74,374	25,308
Maine	36,823	65,435	27,648	64,438	35,403	66,987
Missouri	351,992	314,092	296,312	321,449	346,574	347,203
Arkansas	81,091	44,770	64,434	46,860	87,015	56,760
Michigan	211,685	316,269	135,392	364,957	175,771	335,580
Florida	28,007	7,314	27,046	8,314	31,104	10,654
Texas	267,432	130,641	167,200	51,242	217,302	65,666
Iowa	209,265	307,808	149,141	307,907	200,771	275,210
Wisconsin	159,279	265,756	124,107	280,164	166,632	247,747
California	124,985	164,755	89,404	205,226	127,492	214,398
Minnesota	112,901	190,461	55,187	216,651	109,401	195,843
Oregon	33,385	46,526	17,521	60,455	38,049	62,530
Kansas	162,601	185,955	86,174	212,955	161,209	197,216
West Virginia	98,807	119,829	100,881	132,628	114,418	137,869
Nevada	6,347	3,849	3,982	6,864	11,212	10,775
Nebraska	114,013	121,835	52,921	138,558	131,099	126,997
Colorado	122,733	93,039	100,105	134,687	126,644	123,700
North Dakota	20,531	35,808	14,273	52,595	32,885	57,680
South Dakota	39,544	54,530	21,969	72,083	40,266	67,536
Montana	37,145	25,373	21,773	34,932	29,326	32,333
Washington	44,833	57,456	28,098	101,540	58,691	106,062
Idaho	29,414	27,198	18,480	47,783	36,162	52,621
Wyoming	10,164	14,482	8,930	20,489	14,918	20,846
Utah	45,006	47,089	33,413	62,466	42,601	61,028
Oklahoma					122,363	110,474
New Mexico						
Arizona						
TOTALS	6,358,071	7,219,530	5,084,491	7,628,834	6,409,106	7,679,006

1900: Woolley (Pro) 209,166, Debs (Soc) 44,768. 1904: Swallow (Pro) 259,257, Debs (Soc) 402,400. 1908: Chafin (Pro) 252,683, Debs (Soc) 420,820

	1912			1916		1920	
	WILSON (D)	Taft (R)	Roosevelt (P)	WILSON (D)	Hughes (R)	Cox (D)	HARDING (R)
New Hampshire	34,724	32,927	17,794	43,781	43,725	62,662	95,196
Massachusetts	173,408	155,948	142,228	247,885	268,784	276,691	681,153
Connecticut	74,561	68,324	34,129	99,786	106,514	120,721	229,238
Rhode Island	30,412	27,703	16,878	40,394	44,858	55,062	107,463
New York	655,475	455,428	390,021	759,426	869,115	731,238	1,871,167
New Jersey	170,282	88,834	145,409	211,645	269,352	258,229	611,670
Pennsylvania	395,637	273,360	444,894	521,784	703,823	503,202	1,218,215
Delaware	22,631	15,997	8,886	24,753	26,001	39,911	52,858
Maryland	112,674	54,956	57,789	138,359	117,347	180,626	236,117
Virginia	90,332	23,288	21,777	102,824	49,356	141,670	87,456
North Carolina	144,507	29,139	69,130	168,383	120,890	305,447	232,848
South Carolina	48,357	536	1,293	61,846	1,550	64,170	2,244
Georgia	93,076	5,191	21,980	125,845	11,225	107,162	43,720
Vermont	15,334	23,332	22,132	22,739	40,295	20,919	68,212
Kentucky	219,584	115,512	102,766	269,990	241,854	456,497	452,480
Tennessee	130,335	59,444	53,725	153,282	116,223	206,558	219,829
Ohio	424,834	278,168	229,807	604,161	514,753	780,037	1,182,022
Louisiana	60,971	3,834	9,323	79,875	6,466	87,519	38,538
Indiana	281,890	151,267	162,007	334,063	341,005	511,364	696,370
Mississippi	57,227	1,595	3,645	80,422	4,253	69,277	11,576
Illinois	405,048	253,593	386,478	950,229	1,152,549	534,395	1,420,480
Alabama	82,438	9,732	22,680	99,409	22,809	103,254	74,690
Maine	51,113	26,545	48,495	64,127	69,506	58,961	136,355
Missouri	57,227	1,595	3,645	398,025	369,339	574,799	727,162
Arkansas	68,838	24,467	21,673	112,148	47,148	107,408	71,117
Michigan	150,751	152,244	214,584	285,151	339,097	233,450	762,865
Florida	36,417	4,279	4,535	55,984	14,611	90,515	44,853
Texas	219,489	26,745	28,530	286,514	64,999	288,767	114,260
Iowa	185,325	119,805	161,819	221,699	280,449	227,921	634,674
Wisconsin	164,228	130,695	62,460	193,042	221,323	113,422	498,576
California	283,436	3,914	283,610	466,200	462,394	229,191	624,992
Minnesota	106,426	64,334	125,856	179,152	179,544	142,994	519,421
Oregon	47,064	34,673	37,600	120,187	126,813	80,019	143,592
Kansas	143,663	74,845	120,210	314,588	277,658	185,464	369,268
West Virginia	113,046	56,667	78,977	140,403	143,124	220,789	282,007
Nevada	7,986	3,196	5,620	17,776	12,127	9,851	15,479
Nebraska	109,008	54,029	72,614	158,827	117,257	119,608	247,498
Colorado	114,232	58,386	72,306	178,816	102,308	104,936	173,248
North Dakota	29,555	23,090	25,726	55,206	53,471	37,422	160,072
South Dakota	48,942		58,811	59,191	64,217	35,938	110,692
Montana	27,941	18,512	22,456	101,063	66,750	57,372	109,430
Washington	86,840	70,445	113,698	183,388	167,244	84,298	223,137
Idaho	33,921	32,810	25,527	70,054	55,368	46,579	88,975
Wyoming	15,310	14,560	9,232	28,316	21,698	17,429	35,091
Utah	36,579	42,100	24,174	84,025	54,137	56,639	81,555
Oklahoma	119,156	90,786		148,113	97,233	215,808	243,404
New Mexico	22,139	17,900	8,347	33,693	31,163	46,668	57,634
Arizona	10,324	3,021	6,949	112,148	47,148	29,546	37,016
TOTALS	6,286,214	3,483,922	4,126,020	9,129,606	8,538,221	9,147,353	16,152,200

1912: Chafin (Pro) 208,923, Debs (Soc) 897,011, Reimer (Soc Lab) 29,079. 1916: Hanley (Pro) 220,506, Benson (Soc) 585,113, Reimer (Soc Lab) 13,403.
1920: Watkins (Pro) 189,408, Debs (Soc) 919,799, Christensen (FL) 265,411

	1924			1928		1932	
	Davis (D)	COOLIDGE (R)	La Follette (P) * (and Soc.)	Smith (D)	HOOVER (R) *(and Anti-Smith Democrat)	ROOSEVELT (D)	Hoover (R)
New Hampshire	57,201	98,575	8,993	80,715	115,404	100,680	103,629
Massachusetts	280,884	703,489	141,225	792,758	775,566	800,148	736,959
Connecticut	110,184	246,322	42,416	252,040	296,614	281,632	288,420
Rhode Island	76,666	125,286	7,628	118,973	117,522	146,604	115,266
New York	950,796	1,820,058	467,293*	2,089,863	2,193,344	2,534,959	1,937,963
New Jersey	298,043	676,277	109,028	616,517	926,050	806,630	775,684
Pennsylvania	409,192	1,401,481	307,567*	1,067,586	2,055,382	1,295,948	1,453,540
Delaware	33,445	52,441	4,979*	36,643	68,860	54,319	57,074
Maryland	148,072	162,414	47,157	223,626	301,479	314,314	184,184
Virginia	139,797	73,359	10,379	140,146	164,609	203,979	89,637
North Carolina	284,270	191,753	6,651	287,078	348,992	497,566	208,344
South Carolina	49,008	1,123	620	62,700	3,188	102,347	1,978
Georgia	123,200	30,300	12,691	129,602	99,360*	234,118	19,863
Vermont	16,124	80,498	5,964	44,440	90,404	56,266	78,984
Kentucky	374,855	398,966	38,465	381,070	558,064	580,574	394,716
Tennessee	158,404	130,882	10,656	167,343	195,388	259,817	126,806
Ohio	477,888	1,176,130	357,948	864,210	1,627,546	1,301,695	1,227,697
Louisiana	93,218	24,670	4,063	164,655	51,160	249,418	18,853
Indiana	492,245	703,042	71,700	562,691	848,290	862,054	677,184
Mississippi	100,475	8,546	3,494	124,539	27,153	140,168	5,180
Illinois	576,975	1,453,321	432,027	1,313,817	1,768,141	1,882,304	1,432,756
Alabama	112,966	45,005	8,084	127,797	120,725	207,910	34,675
Maine	41,964	138,440	11,382	81,179	179,923	128,907	166,631
Missouri	572,753	648,486	84,160	662,562	834,080	1,025,406	564,713
Arkansas	84,795	40,564	13,173	119,196	77,751	189,602	28,467
Michigan	152,238	874,631	122,014	396,762	965,396	871,700	739,894
Florida	62,083	30,633	8,625	101,764	144,168	206,307	69,170
Texas	484,605	130,023	42,881	341,032	367,036	760,348	97,959
Iowa	162,000	537,635	272,243	378,936	623,818	598,019	414,433
Wisconsin	68,115	311,614	453,678*	450,259	544,205	707,410	347,741
California	105,514	733,250	424,649*	614,365	1,147,929	1,324,157	847,902
Minnesota	55,913	420,759	339,192	396,451	560,977	600,806	363,959
Oregon	67,589	142,579	68,403	109,223	205,341	213,871	136,019
Kansas	156,319	407,671	98,461	193,003	513,672	424,204	349,498
West Virginia	257,232	288,635	36,723	263,784	375,551	405,124	330,731
Nevada	5,909	11,243	9,769	14,000	18,327	28,756	12,674
Nebraska	137,289	218,585	106,701	197,959	345,745	359,082	201,177
Colorado	75,238	195,171	69,945	133,131	253,872	250,877	189,617
North Dakota	13,858	94,931	89,922	106,648	131,441	178,350	71,772
South Dakota	27,214	101,299	75,355	102,660	157,603	183,515	99,212
Montana	33,805	74,138	65,876	78,578	113,300	127,286	78,078
Washington	42,842	220,224	150,727	156,772	335,844	353,260	208,645
Idaho	24,256	69,879	54,160	53,074	99,848	109,479	71,312
Wyoming	12,868	41,858	25,174	29,299	52,748	54,370	39,583
Utah	47,001	77,327	32,662	80,985	94,618	116,750	84,795
Oklahoma	255,798	226,242	41,141	219,174	394,046	516,468	188,165
New Mexico	48,542	54,745	9,543	48,211	69,645	95,089	54,217
Arizona	26,235	30,516	17,210	38,537	52,533	79,264	36,104
TOTALS	8,385,586	15,725,016	4,822,856	15,016,443	21,392,190	22,821,857	15,761,841

1924: Foster (W) 33,361, Faris (Pro) 57,551, Johns (Soc Lab) 38,958, Nations (A) 23,867, Wallace (CL) 2,778. 1928: Thomas (Soc) 267,420, Foster (C) 48,770, Varney (Pro) 20,106, Reynolds (Soc Lab) 21,603, Webb (FL) 6,390. 1932: Foster (C) 102,991, Upshaw (Pro) 81,869, Reynolds (Soc Lab) 33,275, Coxey (FL) 7,309, Harvey (Lib) 53,425

	1936			1940	
	ROOSEVELT (D & AL)	Landon (R)	Lemke (U)	ROOSEVELT (D & AL)	Willkie (R) * (and Ind. Dem.)
New Hampshire	108,460	104,642	4,819	125,292	110,127
Massachusetts	942,716	768,613	118,369	1,076,522	939,700
Connecticut	382,129	278,685		417,621	361,819
Rhode Island	165,238	125,031	19,569	181,746	138,432
New York	3,293,222	2,180,670		3,251,918	3,027,478
New Jersey	1,083,549	719,421	9,045	1,016,404	944,876
Pennsylvania	2,353,788	1,690,300	67,467	2,171,035	1,889,848
Delaware	69,702	54,014	442	74,599	61,440
Maryland	389,612	231,435		384,546	269,534
Virginia	161,083	76,366	233	160,198	82,895
North Carolina	616,141	223,283	2	609,015	213,633
South Carolina	113,791	1,646		95,470	1,727
Georgia	255,364	36,942		265,194	46,302*
Vermont	62,124	81,023		64,269	78,371
Kentucky	541,944	369,702	12,501	557,222	410,384
Tennessee	327,083	146,516	696	351,601	169,153
Ohio	1,747,122	1,127,709	132,212	1,733,139	1,568,773
Louisiana	292,894	36,791		319,751	52,446
Indiana	934,974	691,570	19,407	874,063	899,466
Mississippi	157,318	4,418		168,252	7,364
Illinois	2,282,999	1,570,393	86,439	2,142,934	2,047,240
Alabama	238,195	35,358	549	250,726	42,174
Maine	126,333	168,823	7,581	156,478	163,951
Missouri	1,111,043	697,891	14,630	958,746	871,009
Arkansas	146,765	32,039	4	158,622	42,121
Michigan	1,016,794	699,733	75,795	1,032,991	1,039,917
Florida	249,117	78,248		359,334	126,158
Texas	734,485	103,874	3,281	840,151	199,152
Iowa	621,756	487,977	29,687	578,800	632,370
Wisconsin	802,984	380,828	60,297	704,821	679,206
California	1,766,836	836,481		1,877,618	1,351,419
Minnesota	698,811	350,461		644,196	596,274
Oregon	266,733	122,706	21,831	258,415	219,555
Kansas	464,520	397,727	494	364,725	489,169
West Virginia	502,582	325,258		495,662	372,414
Nevada	31,925	11,923		31,945	21,229
Nebraska	347,454	248,731	12,847	263,677	352,201
Colorado	295,021	181,267	9,962	265,554	279,576
North Dakota	163,148	72,751	36,708	124,036	154,590
South Dakota	160,137	125,977		131,362	177,065
Montana	159,690	63,598	5,549	145,698	99,579
Washington	459,579	206,892	17,463	462,145	322,123
Idaho	125,683	66,256	7,684	127,842	106,553
Wyoming	62,624	38,739	1,653	59,287	52,633
Utah	150,246	64,550		154,277	93,151
Oklahoma	501,069	245,122		474,313	348,872
New Mexico	105,838	61,710	924	103,699	79,315
Arizona	86,722	33,433		95,267	54,030
TOTALS	27,476,673	16,679,583	882,479	27,243,466	22,304,755

1936: Browder (C) 80,150, Colvin (Pro) 37,847, Aiken (Soc Lab) 12,777, Thomas (Soc) 99,557. 1940: Browder (C) 46,251, Babson (Pro) 57,812, Aiken (Soc Lab) 14,861

	1944		1948			
	ROOSEVELT (D)	Dewey (R)	TRUMAN (D)	Dewey (R)	Thurmond (SR)	Wallace (P)
New Hampshire	119,663	109,916	107,995	121,299	7	1,970
Massachusetts	1,960,665	921,350	1,151,788	909,370	—	38,157
Connecticut	435,146	390,527	423,297	437,754	—	13,713
Rhode Island	175,356	123,487	188,736	135,787	—	2,619
New York	3,304,238*	2,987,647	2,780,204†	2,841,163	—	509,559
New Jersey	987,874	961,335	—	—	—	—
Pennsylvania	1,940,479	1,835,054	1,752,426	1,902,197	—	55,161
Delaware	68,166	56,747	67,813	69,588	—	1,050
Maryland	315,490	292,949	286,521	294,814	2,476	9,983
Virginia	242,276	145,243	200,786	172,070	43,393	2,047
North Carolina	527,399	263,155	459,070	258,572	69,652	3,915
South Carolina	90,601	4,547	34,423	5,386	102,607	154
Georgia	268,187	56,507	254,646	76,691	85,055	1,636
Vermont	53,820	71,527	45,557	75,926	—	1,279
Kentucky	472,589	392,448	466,756	341,210	10,411	1,567
Tennessee	308,707	200,311	270,402	202,914	73,815	1,288
Ohio	1,570,763	1,582,293	1,452,791	1,445,684	—	37,596
Louisiana	281,564	67,750	136,344	72,657	204,290	3,035
Indiana	781,403	875,891	807,833	821,079	—	9,649
Mississippi	158,515	3,742	19,384	5,043	167,538	225
Illinois	2,079,479	1,939,314	1,994,715	1,961,103	—	—
Alabama	198,918	44,540	—	40,930	171,443	1,522
Maine	140,631	155,434	111,916	150,234	—	1,884
Missouri	807,356	761,175	917,315	655,039	—	3,998
Arkansas	148,965	63,551	149,659	50,959	40,068	751
Michigan	1,106,899	1,084,423	1,003,448	1,038,595	—	46,515
Florida	339,377	143,215	281,988	194,280	89,755	11,620
Texas	821,605	191,425	750,700	282,240	106,909	3,764
Iowa	499,876	547,267	522,380	494,018	—	12,125
Wisconsin	650,413	674,532	647,310	590,959	—	25,282
California	1,988,564	1,512,965	1,913,134	1,895,269	1,228	190,381
Minnesota	589,864	527,416	692,966	483,617	—	27,866
Oregon	248,635	225,365	243,147	260,904	—	14,978
Kansas	287,458	442,096	351,902	423,039	—	4,603
West Virginia	392,777	322,819	429,188	316,251	—	3,311
Nevada	29,623	24,611	31,291	29,357	—	1,469
Nebraska	233,246	329,880	224,165	264,774	—	—
Colorado	234,331	268,731	267,288	239,714	—	6,115
North Dakota	100,144	118,535	95,812	115,139	374	8,391
South Dakota	96,711	135,365	117,653	129,651	—	2,801
Montana	112,556	93,163	119,071	96,770	—	7,313
Washington	486,774	361,689	—	—	—	—
Idaho	107,399	100,137	107,370	101,514	—	4,972
Wyoming	49,419	51,921	52,354	47,947	—	931
Utah	150,088	97,891	149,151	124,402	—	2,679
Oklahoma	401,549	319,424	452,782	268,817	—	—
New Mexico	81,389	70,688	105,464	80,303	—	1,037
Arizona	80,926	56,287	95,251	77,597	—	3,310
TOTALS	**24,776,864**	**22,006,285**	**24,105,812**	**21,970,065**	**1,169,021**	**1,157,172**

* Includes 496,405 American Labor and 329,235 Liberal votes cast in endorsement of Democratic candidate in New York State.
Thomas (Soc.) 80,473; Watson (Proh.) 74,758; Teichert (Soc. Lab.) 45,336.
† Includes 225,562 Liberal Party votes.
Thomas (Soc.) 139,521; Watson (Proh.) 103,343; Teichert (Soc. Lab.) 29,061; Dobbs (Soc. Workers) 13,613.

	1952	
	Stevenson (D)	EISENHOWER (R)
New Hampshire	106,663	166,289
Massachusetts	1,083,525	1,292,325
Connecticut	481,649	611,012
Rhode Island	203,293	210,935
New York	3,104,601*	3,952,815
New Jersey	1,015,902	1,374,613
Pennsylvania	2,146,269	2,415,789
Delaware	83,315	90,059
Maryland	395,337	499,424
Virginia	268,677	349,037
North Carolina	652,803	558,107
South Carolina	173,007	158,312
Georgia	452,323	198,979
Vermont	43,355	109,717
Kentucky	495,729	495,029
Tennessee	443,710	446,147
Ohio	1,600,302	2,100,456
Louisiana	345,027	306,925
Indiana	801,530	1,136,259
Mississippi	172,553	112,966
Illinois	2,013,920	2,457,327
Alabama	275,075	149,231
Maine	118,806	322,353
Missouri	929,830	959,429
Arkansas	226,300	177,155
Michigan	1,230,657	1,551,529
Florida	444,950	544,036
Texas	970,128	1,102,878
Iowa	451,513	808,906
Wisconsin	622,175	979,744
California	2,197,548	2,897,310
Minnesota	608,458	763,211
Oregon	270,579	420,815
Kansas	273,296	616,302
West Virginia	453,578	419,970
Nevada	31,688	50,502
Nebraska	188,057	421,603
Colorado	245,504	379,782
North Dakota	76,694	191,712
South Dakota	90,426	203,857
Montana	106,213	157,394
Washington	492,845	599,107
Idaho	95,081	180,707
Wyoming	47,934	81,047
Utah	135,564	194,190
Oklahoma	430,939	518,045
New Mexico	105,661	132,170
Arizona	108,527	152,042
TOTALS	**27,311,316**	**33,927,549**

* Includes 416,711 Liberal votes cast in endorsement of Democratic candidate in New York State.

IMMIGRATION BY COUNTRY OF ORIGIN, 1831-1950

	1831-40	1841-50	1851-60	1861-70	1871-80	1881-90	1891-1900	1901-10	1911-20	1921-30	1941-50
Austra-Hungary				7,800	72,969	353,722	592,707	2,145,266	896,342	63,548	3,469*
Belgium	22	5,094	4,738	6,734	7,221	20,174	18,167	41,635	33,746	15,846	12,189
Bulgaria							160	39,280	22,533	2,945	375
Czechoslovakia									3,426	102,194	8,347
Denmark	1,063	539	3,749	17,094	31,771	88,132	50,231	65,285	41,983	32,430	5,393
France	45,575	77,262	76,358	35,984	72,201	50,463	30,770	73,739	61,897	49,610	38,809
Germany	152,454	434,626	951,667	787,468	717,182	452,970	505,152	341,498	143,945	412,202	226,578§
Greece						2,053	15,979	167,519	184,201	51,084	8,973
Italy	2,253	1,870	9,231	11,728	55,762	307,310	651,893	2,045,877	1,109,524	455,315	57,661
Netherlands	1,412	8,251	10,789	9,102	16,541	53,701	26,758	48,262	43,718	26,946	14,860
Norway ⎱	1,201	13,903	20,931	109,298	95,323	176,586	95,014	190,505	66,393	68,531	10,100
Sweden ⎰					115,922	391,776	226,266	249,534	95,074	97,249	10,665
Poland†	—	—	1,164	2,027	12,970	51,806	96,720	—	4,813	227,734	7,571
Roumania						5,938	12,750	53,008	13,311	67,646	1,076
Russia‡	646	656	1,621	4,536	52,254	265,089	602,011	1,597,306	921,957	78,433	548
Spain ⎱	2,954	2,759	10,353	8,493	5,266	4,418	8,731	27,935	68,611	28,958	2,898
Portugal ⎰					4,627	11,917	27,323	69,149	89,732	29,994	7,423
Switzerland	4,821	4,644	25,011	23,286	28,293	81,988	31,179	34,922	23,091	29,676	10,547
Turkey in Europe						1,185	3,786	119,256	77,210	14,659	580
United Kingdom											
England	7,611	32,092	247,125	222,277	437,706	644,680	216,726	388,017	249,944	157,420	112,252
Ireland	207,381	780,719	914,119	435,778	456,871	655,482	388,416	339,065	146,181	220,591	25,377
Scotland	2,667	3,712	38,331	38,768	87,564	149,869	44,188	120,469	78,357	159,781	16,131
Wales	185	1,261	6,319	4,313	6,631	12,640	10,557	17,464	13,107	13,012	3,209
Not Specified	65,347	229,979	132,199	349,538	16,142	168	67		18,238	22,983	11,813
Other Europe	96	155	116	210	658	1,346	122	665			
Total Europe	495,688	1,597,522	2,453,821	2,074,434	2,274,874	4,783,413	3,655,673	8,175,296	4,407,336	2,427,787	621,704
Canada and New-foundland ¶			59,304	153,878	383,640	393,304	3,311	179,226	742,185	924,515	171,718
Mexico ¶			3,078	2,191	5,162	1,913	971	49,642	219,004	459,287	60,589
Central America			449	95	157	404	549	8,192	17,159	15,769	21,665
South America			1,224	1,397	1,128	2,304	1,075	17,280	41,899	42,215	21,831
West Indies			10,660	9,046	13,957	29,042	33,066	107,548	123,424	74,899	49,725
Total America			74,715	166,607	404,044	426,967	38,972	361,888	1,143,671	1,516,685	354,804**
China	8	35	41,397	64,301	123,200	61,711	14,799	20,005	21,270	29,907	16,709
Japan							25,942	129,797	83,837	33,462	1,555
Turkey in Asia							26,799	77,393	79,389	19,165	218
Other Asia	40	47	61	308	603	6,669	3,696	15,772	8,055	14,866	13,298
Total Asia	48	82	41,458	64,609	123,803	68,380	71,236	243,567	192,559	97,400	31,780
Africa			210	312	358	857	350	7,368	8,443	6,286	7,367
Australia, Tasmania, New Zealand				36	9,886	7,017	2,740	11,975	12,348	8,299	13,805
Pacific Islands					1,028	5,557	1,225	1,049	1,079	427	5,437
All other countries			29,169	17,969	700	780	14,063	33,523#	1,147	228	142
Total Immigration	495,736	1,597,604	2,599,373	2,323,967	2,814,783	5,292,980	3,784,259	8,834,666	5,766,583	4,057,112	1,035,039

* Hungary only.
† From 1899-1919 Poland is included with Austria-Hungary, Germany and Russia.
‡ Including Finland 1831-1920.
§ Includes Austria 1938-45: Austria 1946-50: 24,860.
¶ No reports from 1886-1893.
\# Includes 32,807 persons returning to their homes in U.S. After 1906 such aliens have been considered non-immigrants.
** Includes other Americas.

APPENDIX IV

RAILROAD MILEAGE, 1840-1950

1840	2,818	1880	93,267	1920	252,845
1850	9,021	1890	167,191	1930	249,052
1860	30,626	1900	198,964	1940	233,670
1870	52,922	1910	249,992	1950	223,779

APPENDIX V

INITIATIVE, REFERENDUM, AND RECALL

	INITIATIVE	REFERENDUM	RECALL State-wide	RECALL Local	RECALL Judicial
Alabama	1907	1907			
Arkansas	1910	1911			
Arizona	1911	1911	1912		
California	1911–12	1911–12	1911		
Colorado	1910	1910	1912		
Idaho	1911–12	1911–12	1912 §		
Indiana		1901 †			
Kansas			1914		
Louisiana			1914 §		
Maryland		1915			
Massachusetts	1918	1918			
Michigan	1908 ¶	1908 ¶			
	1913	1913	1913 §		
Mississippi	1908	1908			
Missouri	1908	1908			
Montana	1906 ‡	1906 ‡			
Nebraska	1911–12	1911–12			
Nevada	1911–12	1904	1912		
New Mexico		1911			
North Dakota	1914	1914	1920		
Ohio	1912	1912	1913	1911	
Oregon	1902	1902	1908		1908
South Carolina					1910
South Dakota	1898	1898			
Utah	1900*	1900†		1907	
Washington	1911–12	1911–12	1912 §	1907	
Wisconsin			1926	1911	

* Ineffective: legislation has failed to render available the provision in the constitution.
† Impractical and ineffective.
‡ Modified.
¶ Conditional.
§ Except Judges.

INDEX

Index

Since the primary purpose of the index is to help the user locate the place or places in which he is interested, the territorial abbreviations appearing after most place names are designed to help that search, even if strict accuracy of terminology is thereby sacrificed. This is particularly true in Colonial Spanish America, where non-Spanish terms such as "Spanish Central America" and "Spanish South America" are used in place of the more euphonious but less well known "Nueva España," "Nueva Leon," "Nueva Estremadura," or "Castillo del Oro." Similarly in Canada "Ont." (Ontario) refers to the territory embraced within the borders of Ontario today, but is used also instead of upper and lower Canada throughout the period of British control of that area.

Since the secondary purpose of the index is to increase the instruction the *Atlas* is intended to offer, old-time geographical terminology is used in colonial America except in the Spanish areas. Thus one may find "Vincennes" listed as "Fr. Ill." in one place, referring to the French term for that region, the "Illinois Country"; in another as "P.Q." for the period when the town was governed by the British who, by the act of 1774, assigned that territory to the Province of Quebec; still later, of course, as "Ind." for Indiana. This device, though it produces some startling juxtapositions in the index, should prove helpful to the teacher who works with his or her class through the index.

Meaning of abbreviations used in the index are obvious.

All numbers refer to maps, not pages

Baranof Is., Alaska, 3
Barcelona, Sp., 213
Barents Sea, 305
Baton Rouge, La., 1, 9; in the Revolution, 49; in the Civil War, 158, 159
Baton Rouge arsenal, La., 157
Bastidas, route of, 21
Baxter Springs, Kan., and the Shawnee Trail, 226
Bay City, Mich., 1
Bay of Fundy, Can., 3
Bayonne, Fr., and U.S. in World War I, 213
Beaufort, S.C., 29
Beaufort Sea, 3
Beausejour, Can., in the Seven Years' War, 34
Bedford, Va., in the Revolution, 51
Belcher Is., Can., 3
Belen, Sp. Mex., 35
Belfast, Me., 1; in the War of 1812, 95
Bellefonte, Pa., and nearby canal, 117
Bell, route of, 59
Bennett Is., Siberia, claimed by U.S., 261n
Bennington, Vt., 1; in the Revolution, 47
Benton, Mont., see Ft. Benton
Bentonville, N.C., in the Civil War, 161
Bent's Fort, Colo., 58, 59; in the Mexican War, 97
Bergen, N. Neth. (N.J.), 24
Bering Sea, 2, 3
Bermejo R., S.A., 4
Berkeley, charter grant to, 25
Berlin, Ohio, in the Civil War, 159
Bermuda, 2; U.S. airline connections to, 258; U.S. base at, 310
Beverswyck, N. Neth. (N.Y.), 24
Bienville, route of, 30
Big Bend National Park Project, Tex., 267
Big Hole Battlefield National Monument, Mont., 267
Big Horn Mts., 2
Bilbao, Sp., 213
Bill of Rights, see Constitution (First ten amendments)
Billings, Mont., 1
Binghamton, N.Y., 1
Birmingham, Ala., 1, 7
Bisbee, Ariz., 1, 6
Bismarck, N. Dak., 1
Bismarck Sea, battle of, 312
Bitterroot Range, Mont., etc., 2
Bituminous coal deposits, U.S., 8
Black Canyon of the Gunnison National Monument, Colo., 267
Blackfeet Indians, Mont., 19
Black Hills, S. Dak., 2, 6
Black River Canal, N.Y., 118
Black Rock Desert, 2
Black Rock, N.Y., in the War of 1812, 94
Black Sea, 305
Blackstock, S.C., in the Revolution, 50
Blackstone Canal, Mass.-R.I., 117

Black Warrior incident, 127n
Blanca Bay, Arg., 4
Blockade Zones, World War II, 312
Bloody Marsh, Ga., in the War of the Austrian Succession, 32
Blue Mts., 2
Blue Ridge Mts., N.C.-Va., 2
Blunt, route of, in the Civil War, 158
Bogotá, Col., 4
Boise, Ida., 1; *see also* Ft. Boise
Bolivia, 4
Bonaire, D.W.I., 4; intervention in, 262, 310
Bonin Is., claimed by U.S., 127n
Boonesboro, Ky., 58
Boone's Wilderness Trail, Ky., 58
Boothia Penin., 3
Bosque, route of, 35
Bordeaux, Fr., disembarkation port, World War I, 213
Borneo, in World War II, 312
Boston, Mass., 1, 22, 27; in the War of the League of Augsburg, 28; in the War of the Spanish Succession, 30; in the Revolution, 46, 48; in the War of 1812, 95; branch of First Bank of the U.S. at, 111; Second Bank, 112; and Underground Railway, 146; embarkation port, World War I, 212; Federal Reserve Bank, 250
Boston Mts., 2
Botwood, Nfld., 3
Boulder, Colo., 1
Bounty lands, for Revolutionary soldiers, 53; for veterans of the War of 1812, 95
Bourgemont, route of, 32
Boxer Rebellion, China, sites of U.S. intervention in, 261n
Boyd, route of, in the Revolution, 49
Braddock, route of, in the Seven Years' War, 34
Braddock's Road, Pa.-Md., 58
Bradstreet, route of, in Seven Years' War, 34
Bragg, routes of, in the Civil War, 158
Branco R., Brazil, 4
Brandenburg, Ky., in the Civil War, 159
Brandywine, Pa., in the Revolution, 47
Brant, route of, in the Revolution, 48
Brazil, 4
Brazito, N. Mex., in the Mexican War, 97
Brazos R., Tex., 2, 97
Brest, Fr., disembarkation port, World War I, 213
Breuckelen (Brooklyn), N. Neth. (N.Y.), 22, 24
Brewster, Mass., in the War of 1812, 95
Briar Creek, Ga., in the Revolution, 49
Bridgeport, Conn., 1
Bristol Bay, Alaska, 3
Bristol, Eng., disembarkation port, World War I, 213
British colonies and charter grants, 1660, 22; 1700, 25; 1750, 26; colonies, 1763–1775, 36
British Columbia, prov. of, 3
British Guiana, 4; U.S. base at Georgetown, 310

British Isles, U.S. troops in, World War II, 311
Brock, route of, in the War of 1812, 93
Brooklyn (Breuckelen), N. Neth. (N.Y.), 22, 24
Brown, Jacob, route of, in the War of 1812, 95
Brownsville, Tex., 1
Brunswick, Ga., 1; in the War of the Austrian Succession, 32; and Brunswick Canal, 118
Brunswick, Me., 26
Brunswick Canal, Ga., 118
Bruselas, Sp. C.A., 21
Bryce Canyon National Park, Utah, 267
Buchanan, Va., terminus of James River and Kanawha Canal, 118
Buell, route of, in the Civil War, 158
Buena Vista, Cal., Naval Oil Reserve, 9
Buena Vista, Mex., in the Mexican War, 97
Buenos Aires, Arg., 4
Buffalo, N.Y., 1, 58; in the War of 1812, 95; branch of Second Bank of the U.S. at, 112; and nearby canals, 117; and Underground Railway, 146
Bull Run, Va., in the Civil War, 157
Burgoyne, routes of, in the Revolution, 46, 47
Burma, in World War II, 312
Burnside, routes of, in the Civil War, 159
Butler, route of, in the Revolution, 48
Butterfield Overland Mail, 116
Butte, Mont., 1, 6

Cabot, routes of, 20
Cabot Str., 3
Cabral, route of, 20
Cabrillo, route of, 21
Cabrillo National Monument, Cal., 267
Caddo Indians, Tex.-La., 19
Cagayan Sulú and Sibitú, purchased from Spain, 261n
Cahokia, Fr. Ill., 30; P.Q., in the Revolution, 48
Cairo, Ill., and Underground Railway, 146; in the Civil War, 158
Caldwell, Kan., and Chisholm Trail, 226
Calgary, Alb., 3
California, Alta., 35
California Cut-off, 58
California, Lower, 98
California, Oregon, and Mexico Steamship Co., routes of, 261
California Trail, 58
Callao, Peru, 4
Calumet, Mich., 6
Calvert (Lord Baltimore), charter grant to, 22
Camarga, Mex., in the Mexican War, 97
Cambridge City, Ohio, and White Water Canal, 118
Cambridge, Mass., in the Revolution, 46
Camden, Ark., in the Civil War, 160
Camden, N.J., 1
Camden, S.C., 1; in the Revolution, 50
Camp Beauregard, La., 212
Camp Bowie, Tex., 212

Camp Cody, N. Mex., 212
Camp Cooper, Tex., 58
Camp Custer, Mich., 212
Camp Devens, Mass., 212
Camp Dix, N.J., 212
Camp Dodge, Iowa, 212
Camp Doniphan, Okla., 212
Camp Fremont, Cal., 212
Camp Funston, Kan., 212
Camp Gordon, Ga., 212
Camp Grant, Ill., 212
Camp Greene, N.C., 212
Camp Hancock, Ga., 212
Camp Jackson, S.C., 212
Camp Kearny, Cal., 212
Camp Lee, Va., 212
Camp Logan, Tex., 212
Camp MacArthur, Tex., 212
Camp McClellan, Ala., 212
Camp Meade, Md., 212
Camp Pike, Ark., 212
Camp Sevier, S.C., 212
Camp Shelby, Miss., 212
Camp Sheridan, Ala., 212
Camp Sherman, Ohio, 212
Camp Taylor, Ky., 212
Camp Travis, Tex., 212
Camp Upton, N.Y., 212
Camp Wadsworth, S.C., 212
Camp Wheeler, Ga., 212
Campbell, routes of, in the Revolution, 48, 49
Campeche Bay, 2
Campos, Brazil, 4
Canada, 3, 305; physical features of, 2, 3; invasion of, 1775-6, 126; 1812-13, 126; first reciprocity treaty with, 127n; revolts of Papineau and Mackenzie, 127n; Alaska border dispute, 209; Fenian raids against, 261n; Riel rebellion, 261n; free navigation of St. Lawrence to U.S. 261n
Canadian R., U.S., 2
Canals, to 1837, 117; 1837-60, 118; after 1860, 254; see also by specific name
Canal Zone, leased by U.S., 261n
Canton, China, 126
Canton, Miss., in the Civil War, 160
Canyon De Chelly National Monument, Ariz., 267
Cape Anne, Mass., 2
Cape Blanco, Arg., 4
Cape Blanco, Ore., 2
Cape Breton Island, N. Sco., 3
Cape Charles, Va., 2
Cape Chidley, Lab., 3
Cape Cod, Mass., 2
Cape Corrientes, Col., 4
Cape do São Roque, Brazil, 4
Cape Farewell, Greenland, 2, 3
Cape Fear, N.C., 2

All numbers refer to maps, not pages

Cape Fear R., N.C., 2
Cape Flattery, Wash., 2
Cape Frio, Brazil, 4
Cape Hatteras, N.C., 2
Cape Henry, Va., 2
Cape Horn, S.A., 4
Cape Huacas, Peru, 4
Cape Mendocino, Cal., 2
Cape Race, Nfld., 2, 3
Cape Sable, Fla., 2
Cape Sable, N. Sco., 3
Cape San Blas, Fla., 2
Cape Tennyson, Can., 3
Capital export, see Investments abroad
Capitol Reef National Monument, Utah, 267
Capulin Mountain National Monument, N. Mex., 267
Caracas, Ven., 4
Caranchua Indians, Tex., 19
Caribbean Sea, 2, 305; Spanish explorations and settlements in, 21
Carlsbad Caverns National Park, N. Mex., 267
Carmen, Mex., in the Mexican War, 97
Carolina proprietors, charter grants to, 25
Carolinas, 22
Caroline Is., in World War II, 312
Caroline incident, 127n
Carson City, Nev., 1
Cartagena, Col., 4
Carteret, charter grant to, 25
Cartier, routes of, 20
Cartwright, Lab., 3
Casa Grande Ruins National Monument, Ariz., 267
Casas Grandes, Sp. Mex., 35
Casco, Me., in the War of the League of Augsburg, 28; in the War of the Spanish Succession, 30
Castillo de San Marcos National Monument, Fla., 267
Castillo del Oro (C.A.), 21
Castillo, route of, 35
Castle Clinton National Monument, N.Y., 267
Castle Pinckney National Monument, S.C., 267
Catawba Indians, Ga.-S.C., 19
Cattle areas, 1700, 39; 1775, 40; 1860, 105; 1890, 227; 1920, 228; 1940, 230; 1950, 229
Cattle trails, 226
Cauca R., Col., 4
Cayenne, Fr. Guiana, 4
Cayuga Indians, N.Y., 19
Cayuga-Seneca Canal, N.Y., 118
Cedar Bluff, Ala., in the Civil War, 159
Cedar Breaks National Monument, Utah, 267
Cedar Rapids, Iowa, 1
Cenis Indians, Tex., 19
Central Cordillera, S.A., 4
Cessions of Western lands, see Land Cessions
Cervera, route of, in the Spanish-American War, 207
Chaco Canyon National Monument, N. Mex., 267
Chaco, S.A., 4

Chaleur Bay, Can., 3
Champagne-Marne sector, World War I, 213
Champlain, routes of, 28
Champlain-Hudson Canal, N.Y., 117
Chancellor and Willoughby, route of, 20
Chancellorsville, Va., in the Civil War, 159
Channel Islands National Monument, Cal., 267
Charcas, Sp. Mex., 21
Charity schools, see Schools, Free
Charlesfort, Carolina, 28
Charleston, S.C., 1, 25, 27, 30; in the Revolution, 46, 49, 50, 51; branch of First Bank of the U.S. at, 111; Second Bank, 112; and domestic routes of slave trade, 146; in the Civil War, 161
Charleston, W. Va., 1
Charleston arsenal, S.C., 157
Charleston-Santee Canal, S.C., 117
Charlestown, S.C., see Charleston
Charlotiana, 53
Charlotte, N.C., 33; in the Revolution, 50
Charlottesville, Va., 31; in the Revolution, 51
Charlottetown, P.E.I., 3
Charter grants, 1660, 22; 1700, 25; 1750, 26; to Berkeley and Carteret, 25; Conn. Co., 25; Council for New England, 22; De Mont's Government, 22; Gen. Oglethorpe, 26; Lord Baltimore, 22; Lord Hopton, 22; Mason and Gorges, 22; Mass. Bay Co., 22; Sir Robert Heath, 22; Sir (Lord) William Alexander, 22, 22n; the Carolina Proprietors, 25; Virginia (London) Co., 22; Virginia (Plymouth) Co., 22; William Penn, 25
Chateau Thierry, Fr., and U.S. in World War I, 213
Chateauguay, N.Y., in the War of 1812, 94
Chattahoochee R., 2, 60, 62
Chattanooga, Tenn., 1; in the Civil War, 158, 159, 160
Chaudiere R., P.Q., 3
Chaumont, Fr., and U.S. in Word War I, 213
Chehalis Indians, Wash., 19
Chemung Canal, N.Y., 117
Chenango Canal, N.Y., 117
Cheraw, S.C., in the Revolution, 50
Cherbourg, Fr., and U.S. in World War I, 213
Cherry Valley, N.Y., in the Revolution, 48
Cherokee Indians, Tenn.-N.C., 19
Chesapeake and Ohio Canal, 118
Chesapeake Bay, 2
Chester, Ill., and Underground Railway, 146
Chester, Pa., 1
Chesterfield Inlet, Keewatin, 3
Cheyenne, Wyo., 1, 226; and mail routes, 116
Cheyenne Indians, Wyo., 19
Chicago, Ill., 1; and Underground Railway, 146
Chickamauga, Ga., in the Civil War, 159
Chickasaw Bayou, Miss., in the Civil War, 158
Chickasaw Indians, Ala.-Miss.-Tenn., 19
Chickasaw Landing, Ala., in the Civil War, 161
Chicora, Sp. Fla., 35

Chicoutimi, P.Q., 3
Chihuahua, Mex., 1, 59; in the Mexican War, 97
Child labor, in any gainful occupation, 1880, 288; 1890, 290; 1900, 292; 1915, 294; 1930, 296; in mercantile and manufacturing establishments, 1880, 287; 1890, 289; 1900, 291; 1915, 293; 1930, 295.
Chile, 4; crisis with, 1891, 261*n*
Chillicothe, Ohio, branch of Second Bank at, 112
China, U.S. interventions in, 127, 261; in Boxer Rebellion, 261*n*
Chincha Is., Peru, 127*n*
Chinook Indians, Wash., 19
Chippewa Indians, Minn.-Wisc., 19
Chippewa, Ont., in the War of 1812, 95
Chiricahua National Monument, Ariz., 267
Chisholm Trail, 226
Choctaw Indians, Miss., 19
Chouteau's Landing, Mo., 58
Christianhaab, Greenland, 3
Chrysler's Farm, Ont., in the War of 1812, 94
Chugach Mts., Alaska, 3
Church, route of, in the War of the Spanish Succession, 30
Churchill R., Can., 2, 3
Cienfuegos, Cuba, U.S. airline connections to, 258
Cincinnati, Ohio, 1, 58; in the War of 1812, 94; branch of Second Bank at, 112; and Underground Railway, 146; in the Civil War, 159
Circuit Court boundaries, *see* Courts
Civil War, campaigns of 1861, 157; 1862, 158; 1863, 159; 1864, 160; 1865, 161; line of Northern occupation, 1861, 157; 1862, 158; 1863, 159; 1864, 160; Southern opposition to secession, 148
Clark, and Lewis, route of, 59
Clark, George Rogers, routes of, in the Revolution, 48, 49; land grant to, 53
Clark's Ferry, Pa., and nearby canals, 117
Clatsop Indians, Ore., 19
Cleveland, Ohio, 1, 7, 58; and Underground Railway, 146; Federal Reserve Bank, 258
Clinton, Sir Henry, routes of, in the Revolution, 46, 47, 49, 50, 51
Clinton, James, route of, in the Revolution, 48
Coahuilteco Indians, Tex., 19
Coal deposits, U.S., 8
Coalport Canal, Pa., 117
Coast Mts., Can., 3
Coast Range, U.S., 2
Cockburn, route of, in War of 1812, 95
Coeur d'Alène, Idaho, 6
Cold Harbor, Va., in the Civil War, 160
Colleges and Universities, 1775, 43; 1800, 134; 1830, 136; 1850, 137; 1870, 277; 1890, 278; 1910, 279; 1930, 280
Collingwood, Ont., and the Underground Railway, 146
Collins Line, route of, 127
Colendonck, N. Neth. (N.Y.), 24

Colima, Sp. Mex., 21
Colombia, 4, 305; (New Granada), Panama transit treaty with, 1846, 127*n*; coaling station contract, 127*n*
Colombian Steamship Co., subsidized routes of, 262
Colonies, British, 1660, 22; 1700, 25; 1750, 26; 1763–75, 36
Colorado National Monument, Colo., 267
Colorado Negro R., Arg., 4
Colorado Plateau, 2
Colorado R., Ariz., etc., 2
Colorado R., Tex., 2
Colorado Springs, Colo., 1
Colorado Territory, 90, 165
Columbia, Ga., in the Civil War, 161
Columbia, Pa., and nearby canals, 117, 118
Columbia R., Wash., 72
Columbia, S.C., 129
Columbus, routes of, 20, 21
Columbus, Ohio, 1, 58
Colville Indians, Wash., 19
Colville R., Alaska, 2
Comanche Indians, 19
Compañía Exploradora, route of Col. Morgan's, 35
Company's Canal, La., 118
Compulsory school attendance, *see under* Schools
Comstock Lode, Nev., 6
Concepcion, Chile, 4
Concord, N.H., 1
Confederate arsenals, 1861, 157
Confederate States of America, 155
Congress, *see* Senate, or House
Congress Lands, 53
Connecticut, cession of western lands, 56
Connecticut Co., charter grant, 25
Connecticut R., 2
Connecticut, Western Reserve of, 53
Constitution, distribution of vote on ratification of, 57; ratification of first ten amendments, 82; 11th amend., 83; 13th amend., 162; 14th amend., 163; 15th amend., 164; 16th amend., 198; 17th amend., 199; 18th amend., 200; 19th amend., 201; 20th amend., 202; 21st amend., 203
Continental divide, 72, 209
Cook Inlet, Alaska, 3
Coos Indians, Ore., 19
Copper, U.S. deposits, 6
Copper R., Alaska, 3
Coral Sea, battle of, 312
Cordoba, Arg., 4
Cordova, route of, 21
Corinth, Miss., in the Civil War, 158
Corn, 1840, 101; 1860, 102; 1890, 217; 1920, 218; 1950, 219
Corn Is., Nic., leased, 262*n*
Cornwallis, routes of, in the Revolution, 46, 50, 51
Coro, Ven., 4

All numbers refer to maps, not pages

[216]

All numbers refer to maps, not pages

Dollar Steamship Co., subsidized routes of, 262
Dolores, Sp. Mex., 35
Dolores, Sp. Tex., 35
Dominguez and Escalante, route of, 35
Dominica, 21
Dominican Republic, intervention in, 262n
Dominion of New England, 25n
Doniphan, route of, in the Mexican War, 97
Dover, Del., 1; and Underground Railway, 146
Dover, N.H., 22
Downie, route in the War of 1812, 95
Drainage basins, U.S., 5
Drake, Sir Francis, routes of, 20
Drought frequency, U.S., 16
Dubawnt R., Can., 3
Dubuque, Iowa, 1
Duluth, Minn., 1, 7
Duluth, route of, 28
Dunbar, route of, 59
Dunmore, attack on Newport by, 46
Durango, Sp. Mex., 21
Durham, N.C., 1
Durham Station, N.C., in the Civil War, 161
Dutch Guiana (Surinam), 4
Du Tisné, route of, 32

Early settlements, Dutch, 23, 24; English, 23, 24, 25, 27, 29, 31, 33; French, 28, 30, 32, 34; Spanish, 21, 35; Swedish, 23
East Cape, Alaska, 3
East Florida, British, 36
East New Jersey, 25
Easter Is., 305
Eastern Cordillera, S.A., 4
Eastern Division Canal, Pa., 117
Eastern Steamship Lines, subsidized routes of, 262
Easton, Pa., and nearby canals, 117
Ebenezer, Ga., 26
Ecuador, 4, 305
Edenton (Queen Anne's Creek), N.C., 29
Effigy Mounds National Monument, Ia., 267
Egg Island, Gulf of St. Lawrence, 30
Egypt, 305
El Caney, Cuba, battle of, 207
Elcano, route of, 20
Elections, Presidential, 1788–1952, Appendix II
Electric power transmission lines, 1923, 243; 1935, 244; 1950, 245
Elgin, Ill., 1
Elizabethtown, N.J., 25
Elkhart, Ind., 1
Ellesmere Is., Can., 3
Elmira, N.Y., 1
El Morro National Monument, N. Mex., 267
El Paso, Tex., 1, 9; Sp. Tex., 35; in the Mexican War, 97; and mail routes, circa 1858, 116
Embargo, House vote on, 91

Embarkation ports, World War I, 212
Embarrass R., Minn., 73
Endicott Mts., Alaska, 2, 3
England, see Great Britain
English expansion, to 1697, 27; to 1713, 29; to 1744, 31; to 1763, 33
English R., Ont., 3
Enumerated goods, 41
Equator, in S.A., 4
Erie, Pa., 1, 58; see also Presqu'Isle
Erie Canal, N.Y., 58, 117
Erie (Pa.) Canal, Pa., 118
Erie Indians, Ohio-Pa., 19
Erie Triangle, ceded by New York to U.S., 56
Eritrea, U.S. base at, 310
Erosion areas, U.S., 13
Escalante, route of, 35
Esopus, N. Neth. (N.Y.), 24
Espanola (Haiti), 21
Espejo, route of, 21
Espinoza, route of, 21
Espiritu Santo, Sp. Mex., 21
Essequibo R., S.A., 4
Europe, U.S. airline connections to, 258; see also names of specific countries
Evansville, Ind., 1; and Underground Railway, 146
Everglades National Park Project, Fla., 267
Everett, Wash., 1
Exeter, N.H., 22, 27
Expansion, U.S., 1775–1830, 126; 1830–1860, 127; 1904–1942, 258; English, to 1697, 27; to 1713, 29; to 1744, 31; to 1763, 33; French, to 1697, 28; to 1713, 30; to 1744, 32; to 1763, 34
Explorations, in Caribbean and Mexico, 19, 21; English, 20; French, 20; Portuguese, 20; routes of, 1492–1587, 20; Spanish, 20; French in Gt. Lakes and Miss. Valley, 28; in New Mexico, etc., 35; U. S. in West, 59
Exports and imports, colonial, 41; 1800, 126; 1850, 127; 1900, 261; 1938, 262
Export Steamship Corp., subsidized routes of, 262
Exuma Is., B.W.I., U.S. base at, 310

Fagundes, route of, 20
Fairfield Canal, N.C., 254
Fairfield, Conn., in the Revolution, 49
Falkland Is., S.A., 4, 305
Fall River, Mass., 1
Falls of the Ohio, 2
Fallen Timbers, Ohio, battle site, 53
Falmouth, Eng., disembarkation point, World War I, 213
Falmouth, Va., in the Civil War, 159
Farming, regionalized types of, 12; see also Cattle, Corn, Crop Areas, Drought Frequency, Farm Tenancy, Improved Acreage, Rice, Soil Regions, Tobacco, Wheat
Farmington Canal, Conn., 117

All numbers refer to maps, not pages

Ft. Leavenworth, Kan., 58; in the Mexican War, 97
Ft. Le Boeuf, Que., 34
Ft. Levis, Que., in the Seven Years' War, 34
Ft. Ligonier, Pa., 34
Ft. Lookout, S. Dak., 58
Ft. Loudoun, Pa., 33, 34
Ft. Loyal, Me., 27; in the War of the League of Augsburg, 28
Ft. Mackinac, Mich., in War of 1812, 93
Ft. Mackinac, Que., 30
Ft. Macon, N.C., in the Civil War, 158
Ft. Malden, P.Q., in the Revolution, 48; Ont., in War of 1812, 93, 94
Ft. Mandan, N. Dak., 58
Ft. Manhac, La., in the Revolution, 49
Ft. Massac, La., 34
Ft. Massachusetts, Mass., in the War of the Austrian Succession, 32
Ft. Matanzas National Monument, Fla., 267
Ft. Maurepas, La., 30
Ft. Maurepas, W. Can., 32
Ft. McHenry, Md., in the War of 1812, 95
Ft. McHenry National Park, Md., 267
Ft. Meigs, Ohio, in the War of 1812, 94
Ft. Miami, Fr. Ill., 30; N. W. Terr., 52
Ft. Michipicton, Que., 32
Ft. Mimms massacre, 94
Ft. Montgomery, N.Y., in the Revolution, 47
Ft. Moore, Ga., 31
Ft. Nassau, N. Neth., 23, 24
Ft. Necessity, Pa., 34
Ft. New Elfsborg, N. Swe., 23
Ft. New Gothenburg, N. Swe., 23
Ft. New Korsholm, N. Swe., 23
Ft. Niagara, N.Y., Que., 28, 34; in the Revolution, 48, 52; in the War of 1812, 94
Ft. Nicholson, N.Y., 29
Ft. Nisqually, Wash., 58
Ft. Orange, N. Neth., 24
Ft. Orleans, Fr. Ill., 32
Ft. Osage, Mo., 58
Ft. Oswego, N.Y., 31, 32
Ft. Ouiatanon, Fr. Ill., 32
Ft. Panmure (Natchez), La., in the Revolution, 49
Ft. Pentagoet, Me., 27
Ft. Pickens, Fla., in the Civil War, 157
Ft. Pierre, S. Dak., 58, 59
Ft. Pillow, Tenn., in the Civil War, 160
Ft. Pitt, Pa., 33, 53; in the Revolution, 48
Ft. Presqu'Isle, Que., 34
Ft. Prince George, S.C., 33
Ft. Prudhomme, La., 28
Ft. Pulaski, Ga., in the Civil War, 158, 159
Ft. Pulaski National Monument, Ga., 267
Ft. Raddison, Que., 28
Ft. Randall, Neb., 58
Ft. Redstone, Pa., in the Revolution, 48

Ft. Reliance, Mackenzie Dist., 3
Ft. Richelieu, Que., 28
Ft. Riley, Kan., 58
Ft. Ripley, Minn., 58
Ft. Rosalie, La., 32
Ft. Rouge, W. Can., 32
Ft. Rouillé, Que., 32, 34
Ft. Royal, Me., in the War of the League of Augsburg, 28
Ft. St. Antoine, Fr. Ill., 28
Ft. St. Charles, W. Can., 32
Ft. St. Croix, Fr. Ill., 28
Ft. Ste. Genevieve, La., 32
Ft. St. Jean, Que., 28
Ft. St. John, Que., 34
Ft. St. Joseph, Fr. Ill., 28
Ft. St. Joseph, Que., 28; in the Revolution, 51
Ft. St. Louis, Fr. Ill., 28
Ft. St. Louis, La., 28, 30
Ft. St. Nicholas, Fr. Ill., 28
Ft. St. Pierre, W. Can., 32
Ft. St. Phillip, La., in the War of 1812, 95
Ft. St. Vrain, Colo., 58
Ft. Saratoga, N.Y., 29
Ft. Scott, Ga., in First Seminole War, 95
Ft. Shirley, Pa., 33
Ft. Smith, Ark., 58, 59; and mail routes, *circa* 1858, 116
Ft. Snelling, Minn., 58, 59
Ft. Stanwix, N.Y., 33; in the Revolution, 47
Ft. Stephenson, Ohio, in the War of 1812, 94
Ft. Sumter, S.C., in the Civil War, 157; National Monument, 267
Ft. Sunbury, Ga., in the Revolution, 49
Ft. Tadoussac, Que., 28
Ft. Tecumseh, S. Dak., 58
Ft. Ticonderoga, N.Y., 1, 33; in the Seven Years' War, 32; in the Revolution, 46, 47
Ft. Tombecbé, La., 32
Ft. Toulouse, La., 32
Ft. Trinity, N. Neth., 23
Ft. Uintah, Utah, 58
Ft. Union, N. Mex., 58; in the Civil War, 157, 160
Ft. Vancouver, Wash., 58, 59
Ft. Venango, Que., 34
Ft. Vincennes, Fr. Ill., 32
Ft. Wagner, S.C., in the Civil War, 159
Ft. Walla Walla, Wash., 58, 59
Ft. Washita, Ind. Co., 58
Ft. Wayne, Ind., 1, 58; P.Q., in the Revolution, 48
Ft. Western, Me., 33
Ft. William, Ont., 3
Ft. William, Ore., 58
Ft. William Henry, N.Y., 33; in the Seven Years' War, 34
Ft. Williams, N.Y., 33
Ft. Worth, Tex., 1; and the Shawnee Trail, 226
Ft. Yuma, Ariz., 58

All numbers refer to maps, not pages

Fortress Monroe, Va., in the Civil War, 157
Fossil Cyacid National Monument, S. Dak., 267
Fowler, route of, 59
Foxe Channel, Can., 3
France, U.S. boundary proposals by, after the Revolution, 52; U.S. forces in, 213, 262, 311
Franchise qualifications, 1775, 42; 1780, 74; 1790, 75; 1800, 76; 1820, 77; 1830, 78; 1840, 79; 1850, 80; 1860, 81; 1870, 186; 1880, 187; 1900, 188; 1910, 189; 1950, 190; literacy requirement, 196; alien enfranchisement, 197; *see also* Women's Suffrage
Frankfort, Ky., 1, 58; and domestic routes of slave trade 146; in the Civil War, 158
Franklin, Dist. of, Can., 3
Franklin, state of, 53
Franklin, Tenn., in the Civil War, 160
Fraser R., Can., 2, 3
Fredericksburg, Va., in the Civil War, 158, 159
Frederickshaab, Greenland, 3
Frederickton, Md., in the War of 1812, 95
Fredericton, N.B., 3
Freeman, route of, 59
Free Schools, *see* Schools, Free
Fremont, routes of explorations, 59; route of in the Mexican War, 97
French and Indian War (Seven Years' War), 34
French and Indian Wars, 28, 30, 32, 34
French expansion, to 1697, 28; to 1713, 30; to 1744, 32; to 1763, 34
French Guiana, 4
French invasion of Mexico, 261n
French Louisiana, W. Fla. border of, 60
Fresno, Cal., 1
Frobisher, route of, 20
Frobisher Bay, Can., 3
Fronteras, Sp. Mex., 35
Frontier of settlement, 1660, 22; 1700, 25; 1750, 26; 1775, 37; after 1790 *see* Population, density of
Fundy, Bay of, 3
Fur trade routes, Indian, *circa* 1750, 33

Gadsden Purchase, 127n
Galapagos Is., 4
Galleons, Spanish, routes of, 20
Galveston, Tex., 1, 9; in the Mexican War, 97; and domestic routes of slave trade, 146
Galveston and Brazos Canal, Tex., 118
Galvez, routes of, in the Revolution, 49, 50, 51
Garces, route of, 35
Gardoqui's proposed lines of W. Florida, 61
Garfield, route of, in Civil War, 158
Gary, Ind., 1, 7
Gas, Natural, *see* Natural Gas
Gaspé Penin., P.Q., 3
Gates, routes of, in the Revolution, 47, 50
General Grant National Park, Cal., 267
Genesee Turnpike, N.Y., 58

Genesee Valley Canal, N.Y., 118
Genoa, Italy, 213
Georgetown, Br. Guiana, 4; U.S. base at, 310
Georgetown, S.C., in the Civil War, 161
George Washington Birthplace National Monument, Va., 267
George Washington Carver National Monument, Mo., 267
Georgia, military lands, 53; cession of western lands, 55
Georgia, Sts. of, 3
Georgia Co. lands, 53
Georgia Mississippi Co. lands, 53
Georgian Bay, Lake Huron, 3
German-born population, *see under* Population
Germantown, Pa., in the Revolution, 47
Germany, World War I, European battlefront, 213; Rhineland occupation, 258n; World War II, 311
Gettysburg, Pa., in the Civil War, 159
Ghent, Belg., 213
Gila Cliff Dwellings National Monument, N. Mex., 267
Gila R., 97
Gilbert Is., in World War II, 312
Glacier National Park, Mont., 267
Glasgow, Scot., disembarkation port, World War I, 213
Gloucester, Mass., 22, 27; in the War of 1812, 95
Godhavn, Greenland, 3
Godthaab, Greenland, 3
Gold, U. S. deposits, 6
Goldfield, Nev., 6
Goldsboro, N.C., in the Civil War, 161
Good Hope, Mackenzie Dist., 3
Gordillo, route of, 21
Gorges, charter grant to, 22
Grain areas, 1700, 39; 1775, 40; *see also* Wheat
Grace Steamship Co., subsidized routes of, 262
Granada, Sp. C.A. (Nic.), 21
Gran Chaco, S.A., 4
Grand Canyon National Monument, Ariz., 267
Grand Canyon National Park, Ariz., 267
Grande R., Brazil, 4
Grande R., Bol., 4
Grand Forks, N. Dak., 1
Grand Rapids, Mich., 1
Grand Teton National Park, Wyo., 267
Gran Quivira National Monument, N. Mex., 267
Grant, routes of, in the Civil War, 158, 159, 160, 161
Graves, route of, in the Revolution, 51
Grays Harbor, Wash., 2
Great Bear Lake, Can., 3
Great Britain, *see also* British Colonies; English expansion; Revolution; Trade; in Nicaragua, 261n; in Venezuela, 261n; U.S. forces in, 262, 311
Great Corn Is., Nic., leased, 262
Great Harbor, Conn., 27
Great Lakes, 2
Great National Road, 58
Great Salt Lake, Utah, 2

All numbers refer to maps, not pages

Great Salt Lake Desert, Utah, 2
Great Sand Dunes National Monument, Colo., 267
Great Slave Lake, Can., 2, 3
Great Smoky Mountains National Park, N.C.-Tenn., 267
Great Warrior Path, 33
Green R., Ky., 53
Greenbriar R., W. Va., 53
Greene, routes of, in the Revolution, 50, 51
Greenland, 3, 305; occupied by U.S., 310
Green Mts., Vt., 2
Greensboro, N.C., 1
Greenwich, Conn., 22
Grenada, 4
Greytown, Nic., bombarded, 127n; and Polk Corollary, 217n; British seize customs at, 261n
Grierson, route of, in the Civil War, 159
Grijalva, route of, 21
Guadalajara, route of, 35
Guadalupe (El Paso), Sp. Tex., 35
Guadalupe (Guadeloupe), Sp. Mex., 21
Guadeloupe (Guadelupe), 21
Guadeloupe Hidalgo, Mex., in the Mexican War, 97
Guale, Sp. Fla., 21, 35
Guam, annexed, 261n; invaded by Japan, 312
Guano Is., 261n
Guantanamo, Cuba, U.S. naval base, 262n
Guapore R., S.A., 4
Guatemala, Sp. C.A., 21; intervention in, 262n
Guevara, route of, 20
Guayaquil, Ec., 4
Guayaquil, Gulf of, 4
Guayamas, Sp. Mex., 35; Mex., in the Mexican War, 97
Guevavi, Sp. Mex., 35
Guilford, N.C., in the Revolution, 51
Gulf Mail Steamship Co., subsidized routes of, 262
Gulf of Alaska, 3
Gulf of California, Mex., 2
Gulf of Darien, Col., 2, 4
Gulf of Fonseca, C.A., 127n; naval lease in, 262
Gulf of Guayaquil, Ec., 4
Gulf of Honduras, C.A., 2
Gulf of Mexico, 2
Gulf of Panama, 4
Gulf of San Jorge, Arg., 4
Gulf of San Matias, Arg., 4
Gulf of Trieste, Ven., 4
Gulf of Venezuela, 4
Gulf oil field, 9
Gulfport, Miss., 1
Gunnison National Monument, Black Canyon of the, Colo., 267

Hackensack, N. Neth. (N.J.), 24
Hackensack R., N. Neth. (N.J.), 24
Hadley, Mass., 27
Hague, Neth., 213

Haiti, 2, 21; Mole of St. Nicholas offered to U.S. by, 261n; protectorate question, 261n; intervention in, 262n
Halifax, N. Sco., 3; embarkation port, World War I, 212
Hamilton, route of, in the Revolution, 48
Hamilton, Ont., 1, 3; in the War of 1812, 94
Hamilton R., Lab., 3
Hampden, raids in the War of 1812, 95
Hampshire and Hampden Canal, Mass., 117
Hampton, route in the War of 1812, 94
Harbor Grace, Nfld., 3
Harper's Ferry, W. Va., 1; in the Civil War, 158
Harrisburg, Pa., 1
Hartford, Conn., 1, 24, 27; in the Revolution, 46; branch of Second Bank of the U.S. at, 112; and Underground Railway, 146
Hartford, Treaty of, shown, 56
Hatteras Inlet, N.C., in the Civil War, 158
Havana, Cuba, 21; in the Spanish-American War, 207; U.S. airline connections to, 258
Haverhill, Mass., in the War of the Spanish Succession, 30
Havre de Grace, Md., in the War of 1812, 95; and Susquehanna and Tidewater Canal, 118
Hawaii, 305; early protectorate and base, 127n; U.S. airline connections to, 258; relations with, 1867–1898, 261n
Hawkesbury, N. Sco., 3
Hay River, Can., 3
Heath, Sir Robert, charter grant to, 22
Heemstede (Hempstead), N. Neth. (N.Y.), 24
Helena, Ark., in the Civil War, 160
Helena, Mont., 1, 6
Heligoland, Ger., 213
Hempstead (Heemstede), N. Neth. (N.Y.), 22, 24
Henrietta Is., Siberia, claimed by U.S., 261n
Hennepin, routes of, 28
Herkimer, route of, in the Revolution, 47
Hermosillo, Mex., 1
Herron, route of, in the Civil War, 158
Highways, see Roads and Highways
Hillsboro, N.C., in the Revolution, 51
Hindman, route of, in the Civil War, 158
Hoboken, N. Neth. (N.J.), 24
Hocking Canal, Ohio, 118
Hojeda, routes of, 20, 21
Hollandia, in World War II, 312
Holly Springs, Miss., in the Civil War, 158
Holyoke, Mass., 1
Homestead National Monument, Neb., 267
Honduras, canal treaties, 127n; interventions in, 262n
Honolulu, T.H., U.S. airline connections to, 258
Hood, route of, in the Civil War, 160
Hooker, routes of, in the Civil War, 159
Hopedale, Lab., 3
Hopi Indians, Ariz., 19

Hopton, Lord, charter grant to, 22
Horseshoe Bend, Ala., in the War of 1812, 95
Hot Springs, Ark., 1
Hot Springs National Park, Ark., 267
Hours of work, men, in general occupations, 1890, 302; 1900, 304; 1910, 306; 1920, 308; in public works and dangerous occupations, 1890, 301; 1900, 303; 1910, 305; 1920, 307
Hours of work, women, limitations on, 1850, 139; 1890, 297; 1910, 298; 1920, 299; 1930, 300
House vote, on passage of the Embargo, 91; on war resolution, 1812, 92; on the Mexican War, 96; on resolution declaring war with Spain, taken prior to submission of Senate amendments, Apr. 13, 1898, 206; on entry into World War I, 210
Houston, Tex., 1, 9
Hovenweep National Monument, Utah-Colo., 267
Howe brothers, routes of, in the Revolution, 46, 47, 48, 49
Howland Is., claimed by U.S., 261n
Hudson Bay, Can., 2, 3
Hudson, R., N.Y., 2
Hudson Str., Can., 2, 3
Hull, route of, in the War of 1812, 93
Hungary, 305
Huntington, N.Y., 22; in the Revolution, 49
Huntington, Pa., and nearby canals, 117
Huntsville, Ala., in the War of 1812, 95

Iceland, 2; occupied by U.S., 310
Ichuse, Sp. Fla., 21, 35
Idaho City, Ida., 6
Idaho Territory, 165
Iguassu Falls, Brazil, 4
Illinois Indians, Ill., 19
Illinois-Indiana oil field, 9
Illinois-Michigan Canal, 118
Illinois R., Ill., 2
Illinois-Rock Island Canal, Ill., 254
Illinois Territory, 92
Immigration by country of origin, 1831–1950, Appendix III
Imports and exports, colonial, 41; 1800, 126; 1850, 127; 1900, 261; 1938, 262
Improved Acreage, 1850, 107; 1870, 231; 1880, 232; 1900, 233; 1910, 234; land in harvested crops, 1920, 235; acreage in harvested crops, 1950, 236
Income tax, ratification of 16th amend. to the Constitution, 198
Independence, Mo., 59; and mail routes, circa 1850, 116
Indian cession, line of, 1790, 63; 1810, 65; 1830, 67; 1850, 69
Indian fur trade routes, circa 1750, 33
Indian Ocean, 305
Indian tribes, U.S., 19
Indiana Territory, 85, 92
Indianapolis, Ind., 1, 58

Indigo areas, 40
Industrial areas, see Manufacturing areas
Initiative, Referendum and Recall, see Appendix V
Inter-coastal Waterways, 254
Interpositions of force, see Expansion, U.S.
Interventions, see Expansion, U.S.
Investments abroad, 1900, 261; 1938, 262
Iowa Indians, Iowa, 19
Iowa Territory, 68
Iquitos, Peru, 4
Ireland, Northern, U.S. troops in, 311
Irish-born population, see under Population
Iron, U.S. deposits, 7
Iron works, 1775, 38
Irondequoit Bay, N.Y., 28
Ironton, Ohio, and Underground Railway, 146
Iroquois Indians, N.Y.-Pa., 19
Irrigated lands, 1910, 268; 1930, 269; 1950, 270
Island No. 10, Miss. R., in the Civil War, 158
Isle de Lobos, Mex., in the Mexican War, 97
Isle of Orleans, La., 60, 62
Isle of Pines, Cuba, 2; claimed by U.S., 261n
Isle Royal, Mich., 73
Isle Royal National Park Project, Mich., 267
Isthmus of Tehuantepec, Mex., 2
Italy, U.S. forces in, 262n, 310
Iwo Jima, in World War II, 312

Jackson, Miss., 1; and domestic routes of slave trade, 146; in the Civil War, 159, 160
Jackson, Tenn., in the Civil War, 160
Jackson's Florida campaign, 1818, 95
Jacksonville, Fla., 1; in the Civil War, 158, 159, 160
Jamaica, B.W.I., 2; U.S. base at, 310
Jamaica (Rustdorf), N. Neth. (N.Y.), 24
James Bay, Can., 2, 3
James R., Va., 2
James River and Kanawha Canal, Va., 118
James River Canal, Va., 117
Jamestown, Va., 22, 27
Japan, in World War II, 312
Japan, Sea of, 305
Japan, Sts. of Shimonoseki bombarded, 261n
Jeanette Is., Siberia, claimed by U.S., 261n
Jefferson City, Mo., 1
Jenkins Ferry, Ark., in the Civil War, 160
Jenkinson, route of, 20
Jequitinhonha R., Brazil, 4
Jersey City, N.J., 1
Jewel Cave National Monument, S. Dak., 267
John Day R., Ore., 72
Johnson, route of, in the Seven Years' War, 34
Johnston Is., claimed by U.S., 261n
Joliet, route of, 28
Joliet, Ill., 1
Jonesboro, Tenn., in the Civil War, 161
Joplin, Mo., 1, 6

All numbers refer to maps, not pages

Joshua Tree National Monument, Cal., 267
Joutel, route of, 28
Juana (Cuba), 21
Juan de Fuca, Sts. of, 2, 3; island in, seized by U.S., 127n
Julianehaab, Greenland, 3
Juman, Sp. Tex., 35
Junction Canal, Pa., 118
Junction City, Kan., and the Western Shawnee Trail, 226
Juneau, Alaska, 3, 209
Juniata Division Canal, Pa., 117
Jurua R., Brazil, 4

Kanagawa, Treaty of, 127n
Kansas City, Mo., 1; and the Overland Mail, 116; and cattle country, 226; Federal Reserve Bank, 250
Kansas R., 2
Kansas Territory, 70
Kaskaskia, Fr. Ill., 30; P.Q., in the Revolution, 48, 49
Kearny, route of, in the Mexican War, 97
Keewatin, Dist. of, 3
Kem, USSR, U.S. forces at, 262n
Kennebec R., Me., 2
Kent Island, Md., 27
Kentucky, lands relinquished to, 55
Kentucky R., 53
Kettle Creek, Ga., in the Revolution, 49
Kettleman Hills oil fields, Cal., 9
Key West, Fla., in the Spanish-American War, 207
Khabarovsk, USSR, U.S. forces at, 262n
Kickapoo Indians, Wisc.-Ill., 19
Kievits Hoeck, N. Neth. (Conn.), 24
King George's War (War of the Austrian Succession), 32
King William's War (War of the League of Augsburg), 28
Kingman Reef, claimed by U.S., 261n
Kings Mountain, S.C., in the Revolution, 50
Kingston, N.Y., and Delaware and Hudson Canal, 117
Kingston, Ont., 3; and Underground Railway, 146
Kino, Fr., route of, 35
Kiowa Indians, Colo., etc., 19
Kittaning Path, 33
Klamath Indians, Ore., 19
Klikitat Indians, Wash., 19
Klondike region, 3, 209
Knoxville, Tenn., 1, 58; and domestic routes of slave trade, 146; in the Civil War, 158, 159, 161
Knyphausen, route of, in the Revolution, 50
Kodiak Is., Alaska, 2, 3
Korea, Ping-Yang forts bombarded, 261n
Kuskokwim R., Alaska, 2, 3

La Bahia, Sp. Tex., 35
La Bahia del Espiritu Santo, Sp. Tex., 35
Labor, see Hours of Work, Child Labor
Labrador, 3

La Cosa, routes of, 21
La Croix Lake, Ont., 73
LaFayette, route of, in the Revolution, 51
La Florida, 35
La Grange, Tenn., in the Civil War, 159
La Harpe, route of, 32
La Havre, Fr., disembarkation port in World War I, 213
Laird R., Can., 2, 3
Lake Athabaska, Can., 2, 3
Lake Borgne, La., in the War of 1812, 95
Lake Dos Patos, Brazil, 4
Lake Erie, U.S.-Can., 2
Lake Huron, U.S.-Can., 2
Lake Manitoba, Man., 2, 3
Lake Maracaibo, Ven., 2, 4
Lake Melville, Lab., 3
Lake Michigan, U.S., 2
Lake Nipigon, Ont., 2, 3
Lake Nipissing, Ont., 3, 52
Lake of the Woods, 2, 3
Lake Okeechobee, Fla., 2
Lake Ontario, Can.-U.S., 2
Lake Saranaga, Ont., 73
Lake Superior, Can.-U.S., 2
Lake Superior-Rainy Lake border dispute, 1826-42, 73
Lake Titicaca, S.A., 4
Lake Winnedago, Ont., 73
Lake Winnipeg, Man., 2, 3
Lake Winnipegosis, Man., 2, 3
Lake Wollaston, Can., 2
La Junta, Sp. Mex., 35
Lampazos, Sp. Mex., 35
Land cessions, New York, 54; Georgia, 55; Virginia, 55; Connecticut, 56; Massachusetts, 56; New Hampshire, 56; North Carolina, 56; South Carolina, 56
Land grants to railroads, 253, 254
Land in Cultivation, see Improved Acreage
Land retirement areas, U.S., 14
Lands End, Eng., 213
Lansing, Mich., 1
La Pallice, Fr., and U.S. in World War I, 213
La Paz, Bol., 4
La Paz, Sp. Mex., settlements at, 21; in the Mexican War, 97
La Plata, Arg., 4
La Pointe, Que., 28
La Purissima Concepcion, Sp. Cal., 35
Laramie, Wyo., 1
Laredo, Sp. Tex., 35
La Salle, Ill., 254
La Salle, routes of, 28
La Soledad, Sp. Cal., 35
Las Palmas, claimed by U.S., 261n
Lassen Pass, Cal., 58
Lassen Volcanic National Park, Cal., 267
Laurentian Mts., Can., 2

All numbers refer to maps, not pages

Lava Beds National Monument, Cal., 267
La Verendrye bros., routes of, 32
Lawrence, Kan., 1; and Underground Railway, 146
Lawrence, Mass., 1
Lead, S. Dak., 6
Lead, U.S. deposits, 6
Leadville, Colo., 6
Leavenworth, Kan., 1; and the Overland Mail, 116
Lebanon, Ky., in the Civil War, 159
Lee, routes of, in the Civil War, 158, 159
Lehman Caves National Monument, Nev., 267
Léon, Sp. C.A., 21
Léon, Sp. Mex., 21
Les Sables d'Olenne, Fr., and U.S. in World War I, 213
Lesser Antilles, 4
Le Sueur, route of, 30
Lethbridge, Alb., 3
Levis, P.Q., 3
Lewis and Clark, route of, 59
Lexington, Ky., branch of Second Bank at, 112; in the Civil War, 158
Leyte, P.I., landings at, in World War II, 312
Liberia, financial protectorate, 262n
Lignite deposits, U.S., 8
Lima-Indiana oil field, 9
Lima, Peru, 4
Lincoln, route of, in the Revolution, 49
Lincoln, Neb., 1
Lingayen Gulf, P.I., in World War II, 312
Liquor license, see Prohibition
Literacy qualification for the suffrage, 196
Little Colorado R., 2
Little Corn Is., Nic., leased, 262n
Little Rock, Ark., 1; in the Civil War, 160
Little Rock arsenal, Ark., 157
Little Slave Lake, Alb., 2, 3
Liverpool, Eng., disembarkation port, World War I, 213
Lovos Is., Peru, 127n
Local option, see Prohibition
London, Eng., disembarkation port, World War I, 213
London, Ont., 3
Long, routes of, 59
Long Beach, Cal., 1
Long Island, N.Y., 2
Lopez expedition, Cuba, 127n
Loreto, Sp. Mex., 35
Lorraine, prov. of, 213
Los Adaes, Sp. Tex., 35
Los Ais, Sp. Tex., 35
Los Angeles, Cal., 1, 9; Sp. Cal., 35; Cal., 58, 59; in the Mexican War, 97; and mail routes, circa 1854, 116
Los Cayos (Bahamas), 21
Louisbourg, Can., 3; in War of the Austrian Succession, 32
Louisiana, Fr., border with W. Fla., 60; Sp., 35; border with W. Fla., 61; Territory of, 88

Louisville, Ky., 1; branch of Second Bank at, 112; and Underground Railway, 146
Louisville-Portland Canal, Ky.-Ohio, 117
Lowell, Mass., 1
Lower California, Sp., 98
Lower California Penin., Mex., 2
Lower Shawnee Town, 33
Lundy's Lane, Ont., in the War of 1812, 95
Luxemburg, duchy of, 213
Lynchburg, Va., 1; in the Civil War, 161
Lyon, Fr., and U.S. in World War I, 213
Lyon, route of, in the Civil War, 157

McClellan, routes of, in the Civil War, 158
McCulloch, route of, in the Civil War, 157
McDowell, route of, in the Civil War, 157
Mackenzie, Dist. of, 3
Mackenzie, revolt of, Can., 127n
Mackenzie R., Can., 2, 3
McLernand, route of, in the Civil War, 159
Macon, Ga., in the Civil War, 160, 161
McPherson, Mackenzie Dist., 3
Madagascar, 305
Madeira Is., 41
Madeira R., Brazil, 4
Madison, Wisc., 1
Magdalena R., Col., 4
Magellan, route of, 20
Magnetic Pole, North, 3
Maine, British occupation of, in War of 1812, 95
Maine, border proposals, 1782–3, 52; border dispute, 1821–42, 71; award by King of the Netherlands, 1831, 71
Malinger R., Ont., 73
Mallets, routes of, 32
Mamor R., Bol., 4
Mammoth Cave National Park, Ky., 267
Manaos, Brazil, 4
Manchester, Eng., disembarkation port, World War I, 213
Manchester, N.H., 1
"Manifest Destiny," 127
Manila, P.I., U.S. airline connections to, 255
Manila Bay, P.I., battle of, 207n
Manitoba, prov. of, 3
Manitoulin Is., Ont., 3
Manufacturing areas, 1775, 38; 1810, 108; 1840, 109; 1860, 110; 1900, 246; 1940, 247; 1947, 248
Manzanillo, Mex., in the Mexican War, 97
Maranhao, Brazil, 4
Marañon R., S.A., 4
March, route of, in the War of the Spanish Succession, 30
Marianas Is., in World War II, 312
Marietta, N.W. Terr., 53; Ohio, 1
Marion, routes of, in the Revolution, 50, 51
Maroni R., S.A., 4

All numbers refer to maps, not pages

All numbers refer to maps, not pages

Montpelier, Vt., 1
Montreal, P.Q., 1, 3, 9; Que., in the War of the League of Augsburg, 28; in the War of the Spanish Succession, 30; in the Seven Years' War, 34; P.Q., in the Revolution, 46, 47; in the War of 1812, 95; telegraph line to, 122; and Underground Railway, 146; embarkation port, World War I, 212
Moore, campaign against St. Augustine, 1702, 30
Moosejaw, Sask., 3
Moosonee, Ont., 3
Morgan, Compañía Exploradora, route of, 35
Morgan, route of, 59
Morgan, route of, in the Civil War, 159
Mormon migration, route of, 58
Morocco, 305
Morris Canal, N.J., 117
Morristown, N.J., in the Revolution, 47, 50
Moscoso, route of, 21
Moultrie, route of, in the Revolution, 49
Mound City Group National Monument, Ohio, 267
Mt. Aconcagua, S.A., 4
Mt. Chimborazo, Ec., 4
Mt. Cotopaxi, Ec., 4
Mt. Hubbard, Alaska, 3
Mt. Illampu, Bol., 4
Mt. Illimani, Bol., 4
Mt. Rainier National Park, Wash., 267
Mt. St. Elias, Alaska, 3, 209
Mt. Vernon arsenal, Miss., 157
Mt. Whipple, Alaska, 209
Muir Woods National Monument, Cal., 267
Munson Steamship Line, subsidized routes of, 262
Murfreesboro, Tenn., in the Civil War, 159
Murmansk, USSR, U.S. forces at, 262n
Murray, route of, in the Seven Years' War, 34
Muscle Shoals, Ala., 1
Muskingum Canal, Ohio, 118

Nantes, Fr., and U.S. in World War I, 213
Narantsouck Mission, Me., 32
Narragansett Indians, R.I.-Mass., 19
Nashua, N.H., 1
Nashville, Tenn., 1, 58; and domestic routes of slave trade, 146; in the Civil War, 158, 159, 160
Nassau, Bahamas, U.S. airline connections to, 258
Natal, Brazil, 4
Natchez, Miss., 58; and domestic routes of slave trade, 146
Natchitoches, La., 32, 59
National Army camps, World War I, 212
National Cattle Trail, proposed, 226
National Forests, 1900, 263; 1910, 264; 1930, 265; 1950, 266
National Guard Camps, World War I, 212
National Monuments, 267
National Parks, 267
National Road, Old (or Great), 58

Natural Bridges National Monument, Utah, 267
Natural Gas, U.S. fields, 9
Natural Resources, U.S., gold, silver, zinc, lead, copper, 6; iron, 7; coal, 8; oil and natural gas, 9
Nauvoo, Ill., 58
Navajo Indians, Ariz.-N. Mex., 19
Navajo National Monument, Ariz., 267
Navassa Is., claimed by U.S., 127n, 261n
Navy, North Sea mine field, World War I, 213; bases, 305
Nebraska Territory, 70
Negro, see Abolition, Slavery, Population—Negro
Negro R., Brazil, 4
Nelson R., Can., 2, 3
Nemacolins Path, 33
Neosho, Mo., and mail routes, circa 1858, 116
Neutrality Zones, World War II, 310
Nevada Territory, 90
New Amsterdam, N. Neth. (N.Y.), 24
New Amstel, N. Neth. (Del.), 23
Newark, N.J., 1, 25
New Bedford, Mass., 1; in the War of 1812, 95; and the Underground Railway, 146
New Bern, N.C., 1, 29; and the Underground Railway, 146; in the Civil War, 158, 159
New Bern-Beaufort Canal, N.C., 254
New Brunswick, N.J., and Delaware and Raritan Canal, 118
New Brunswick, prov. of, 3
Newburyport, Mass., 1; in the Revolution, 46
New Castle, N. Neth., 23; Del., 25
New England, Dominion of, 25n; United Cols. of, 22n
Newfoundland, 2, 3; U.S. base at Avalon Penin., 310
Newfoundland Banks, 41
New Granada, Panama transit rights, 127n
New Hampshire, cession of Vermont claims, 56; for "New Hampshire Grants," see Vermont
New Haven, Conn., 1; in the Revolution, 49; and the Underground Railway, 146
New Haven colony, 22
New Inverness, Ga., 26
New Jersey, East, 25; West, 25
New London, Conn., 1, 22; in the Revolution, 51; in the War of 1812, 94, 95; base at, 305
New Mexico, Sp., 35, 98
New Mexico Territory, 70, 90, 122, 165
New Netherland, 22; northern part, 24, southern part, 23
New Orleans, La., 1, 9, 32, 58, 60; in the Revolution, 49, 50; in the War of 1812, 95; branch of First Bank of the U.S. at, 111; Second Bank, 112; and domestic routes of slave trade, 146; in the Civil War, 158, 159
New Orleans and Orleans Bank Canal, La., 117
New Paltz, N. Neth. (N.Y.), 24
Newport, R.I., 22, 27; in the Revolution, 46, 48, 49, 51
Newport, Va., in the Revolution, 46
Newport News, Va., 1; embarkation port, World War I, 212

Newspapers, 1725, 44; 1775, 45; 1800, 135; 1860, 138
New Sweden, 23
Newton, Kan., and the Chisholm Trail, 226
Newtown (Wilmington), N.C., 31
New Utrecht, N. Neth., 24
New York, charter borders, 22; cession of western lands, 54; military lands, 53
New York, N.Y., 1; in the Revolution, 48, 49, 50, 51; branch of First Bank of the U.S. at, 111; Second Bank, 112; and Underground Railway, 146; Federal Reserve Bank, 246; embarkation port, World War I, 212
New York and Cuba Mail Steamship Co., subsidized routes of, 262
New York and Pennsylvania Canal, 118
New York and Puerto Rico Steamship Co., subsidized routes of, 262
Nez Perce Indians, Ida.-Mont., 19
Nicaragua, interventions in, financial protectorate, 258n, 305n; British in, 261n; Vanderbilt Transfer, mentioned, 58; Corn Is. lease, 262n; Gulf of Fonseca base, 262n
Nicaraguan Canal, Hise treaties, 127n, 261n
Nicholls, route of, in the War of 1812, 95
Nicholson, route of, in the War of the Spanish Succession, 30
Nickel deposits, Sudbury, Ont., 6
Nicolet, route of, 28; 1838-9, 59
Nicuesa, route of, 21
Nieu Amsterdam, N. Neth., 24
Nieu Utrecht, N. Neth., 24
Ninety-six, S.C., in the Revolution, 50, 51
Niteroi, Brazil, 4
No Man's Land, Okla., 165
Nombre de Dios (Pan.), 4; Sp. C.A., 21
Nome, Alaska, 3
Norfolk, Va., 1; in War of 1812, 94, 95; branch of First Bank of the U.S. at, 111; Second Bank, 112; and domestic routes of slave trade, 146; and Underground Railway, 146; in the Civil War, 158; and Albemarle-Chesapeake Canal, 250
Norridgewock, Me., 31
North Africa, U.S. landings, World War II, 311
North Carolina, military lands, 53; cession of western lands, 56
North Magnetic Pole, 3
North Platte R., Neb., etc., 2
North Saskatchewan R., Can., 2, 3
North Sea minefield, World War I, 213
Northampton, Mass., and Hampshire and Hampden Canal, 117
Northern Division Canal, Pa., 117
Northwest posts, 52, 126
Northwest Territories, Can., 3
Norton Sd., Alaska, 2
Norwalk, Conn., in the Revolution, 49
Norwegian-born population, *see under* Population
Nova Scotia, prov. of, 2, 3

Noyon, Fr., in World War I, 213
Nueces R., Tex., 2, 97
Nueva Andalusia, Sp. C.A., 21
Nueva España, 21
Nueva Estremadura, Sp. Mex., 21
Nueva Galicia, Sp. Mex., 21
Nueva Leon, Sp. Mex., 21
Nunivak Is., Alaska, 3

Oakland, Cal., 1, 9; and mail routes, *circa* 1850, 116
Ocampo, route of, 21
Ocean Steam Navigation Co., routes of, 127
Oceanic and Oriental Navigation Co., subsidized routes of, 262
Ocmulgee National Monument, Ga., 267
Ogallala, Neb., and Western Trail, 226
Ogden, Utah, 1
Ogdensburg, N.Y., 1
Ohio and Pennsylvania Canal, 118
Ohio Canal, Ohio, 58, 117
Ohio Co. lands, 53
Ohio R., 2, 58
Ohio Territory, 85
Oil fields, U.S., 9
Ojeda (Hojeda), route of, 20, 21
Okinawa, in World War II, 312
Okkak, Lab., 3
Oklahoma City, Okla., 1
Oklahoma Territory, 168
Old National Road, 58
Olean, N.Y., and Genesee Valley Canal, 118
Olympia, Wash., 1
Olympic National Park, Wash., 267
Omaha, Neb., 1, 58; and the Overland Mail, 116
Omaha Indians, Neb., 19
Oman, 305
Oñate, routes of, 21, 35
Oneida Indians, N.Y., 19
Onondaga Indians, N.Y., 19
Ontario, prov. of, 3
Oregon border dispute, 1826-72, 72
Oregon Caves National Monument, Ore., 267
Oregon Country, 66; border problem, 127n; northern limits, 209
Oregon Territory, 69, 122
Oregon Trail, 58
Organ Pipe Cactus National Monument, Ariz., 267
Orinoco R., S.A., 4
Oriskany, N.Y., in the Revolution, 47
Orkney Is., G.B., 213
Orleans, Territory of, 88
Osage Indians, Kan.-Mo., 19
Osawatomie, Kan., and Underground Railway, 146
Ostend Manifesto, 127n
Oswego, N.Y., 1, 52; in the Seven Years' War, 34; in the Revolution, 47; and Oswego Canal, 117; and Underground Railway, 146

Oswego Canal, N.Y., 117
Ottawa, Ont., 1, 3
Ottawa Indians, Mich., 19
Ottawa R., Can., 2, 3
Otissingen (Flushing), N. Neth. (N.Y.), 24
Ouachita Mts., 2
Overland Mail, 116
Oxford, Miss., in the Civil War, 158
Ozark Mts., Ark., 2

Paanpack (Troy), N. Neth. (N.Y.), 24
Pacific Argentine Brazil Line, subsidized routes of, 262
Pacific Mail Steamship Co., routes of, 127
Pacific Ocean, 2
Packenham, route in the War of 1812, 95
Paducah, Ky., in the Civil War, 158, 160
Pago Pago, Samoa, base at, 261n
Painted Desert, Ariz., 2
Paiute Indians, Nev.-Utah, 19
Palm Beach, Fla., 1
Palmyra Is., claimed by U.S., 261n
Panama, early American transit facilities at, 127n; interventions in, 262n
Panama Canal, 2; transit rights in treaty of 1846, 127n
Panama City, Pan., 4, 305; Sp. C.A., 21
Panama Conference neutrality zone, World War II, 310
Panama, Gulf of, 4
Panama Mail Steamship Co., subsidized routes of, 262
Panama Railroad, 127n; mentioned, 58
Panuco R., Mex., 97
Panzacola (Pensacola), Sp. Fla., 35
Paonia Reclamation Project, Colo., 264
Papineau, revolt of, Can., 127n
Para, Brazil, 4
Para R., Brazil, 4
Paracima Mts., S.A., 4
Paraguay, 4; punitive expedition against, 127n
Paraguay R., S.A., 4
Paramaribo, Surinam, 4
Paraná R., S.A., 4
Paranahyba R., Brazil, 4
Parecis Mts., S.A., 4
Paria Bay, Ven., 4
Parima Mts., S.A., 3
Paris, Fr., and U.S. in World War I, 213
Paris, Peace of, 52
Parnahyba R., Brazil, 4
Parral, Sp. Mex., 35
Parras, Mex., in the Mexican War, 97
Parras, Sante Marie de, Sp. Mex., 21
Passaic R., N. Neth. (N.J.), 24
Patagonia, Arg., 4
Paterson, N.J., 1
Patterson, route of, in the Mexican War, 97
Pattie, route of, 59
Patzcuaro, Sp. Mex., 21
Paulus Hoeck (Hook), N. Neth. (N.J.), 24

Pauper Schools, *see* Schools, Free
Pawnee Indians, Kan.-Neb., 19
Pawtucket and Lowell Canal, R.I.-Mass., 117
Pea Ridge, Ark., in the Civil War, 158
Peace of Paris, 52
Peace R., Can., 2, 3
Pearl Harbor, T.H., acquired, 261n; attacked, 312
Pearl R., Miss., 2, 60, 62
Pecos, Sp. N. Mex., 35
Pecos R., N. Mex.-Tex., 2
Peekskill, N.Y., in the Revolution, 47, 51
Peking, China, and Boxer Rebellion, 261n
Pemaquid, Me., 27; in the War of the League of Augsburg, 28
Peninsula Campaign, Civil War, 158
Penn, William, charter grant to, 25
Penn's Neck Canal, 254
Pennsylvania, charter borders, 25; donation and depreciation lands, 53; lands relinquished to by Conn., 56
Penobscot, Me., 27
Penobscot Indians, Me., 19
Penobscot R., Me., 2
Pensacola, Fla., 1, 30; Sp. Fla., 35, 60; in the Revolution, 51; in the War of 1812, 95; in the Seminole War, 95; in the Civil War, 158, 159
Peoria, Ill., 1
Pepperell, route of, in the War of the Austrian Succession, 32
Pequot Indians, Mass.-Conn., 19
Perdido R., Fla., 2, 60, 62
Pernambuco, Brazil, 4
Perry, route of, on Lake Erie, War of 1812, 94
Perry's Victory and International Peace Memorial National Monument, Ohio, 267
Perryville, Ky., in the Civil War, 158
Pershing's pursuit of Villa, 262n
Peru, 4
Peterboro, Ont., 3
Petersburg, Va., 1; in the Revolution, 51; and domestic routes of slave trade, 146; in the Civil War, 161
Petrified Forest National Monument, Ariz., 267
Petroleum, U.S. fields, 9
Philadelphia, Pa., 1, 7, 25, 27; in the Revolution, 47, 48; and Delaware Division Canal, 117; and Underground Railway, 146; embarkation port, World War I, 212; Federal Reserve Bank, 250
Philippine Is., annexed, 261n; insurrection, 262n; in World War II, 312
Phips, route of, in the War of the League of Augsburg, 28
Phoenix, Ariz., 1
Pickawillany, 33
Pickawillany Trail, 33
Pickens, route of, in the Revolution, 49
Piedmont region, U.S., 2
Pierre, S. Dak., 1; *see also* Ft. Pierre
Pigeon R., Ont., 73

Pike, routes of, 59
Pike's Peak, Colo., 59
Pilcomayo R., S.A., 4
Pima Indians, Ariz., 19
Pineda, routes of, 20, 21
Ping-Yang forts, Korea, bombarded, 261*n*
Pinnacles National Monument, Cal., 267
Pinzon, routes of, 20, 21
Pipelines, U.S., 9
Pipe Spring National Monument, Ariz., 267
Pipestone National Monument, Minn., 267
Piscatauqua, Me., 27
Pitiqui, Sp. Mex., 35
Pittsburgh, Pa., 1, 7, 9, 58; branch of Second Bank at, 112; *see also* Ft. Pitt
Pizzaro, beginning of route of, 21
Placerville, Ida., 6
Platt National Park, Okla., 267
Plata R., S.A., 4
Platte R., U.S., 2
Plattsburg, N.Y., in the War of 1812, 94, 95
Pleasant Hill, La., in the Civil War, 160
Plymouth Colony, 22
Plymouth, Eng., disembarkation port, World War I, 213
Plymouth, Mass. Bay, 27; in the War of 1812, 95
Pocomtuck Indians, Mass., 19
Point au Fer, N.Y., 52
Point Barrow, Alaska, 2, 3
Point Conception, Cal., 2
Point de Aguja, Peru, 4
Ponca Indians, Neb.-Dak., 19
Pony Express, 116
Population, density of, 1790, 63; 1800, 64; 1810, 65; 1820, 66; 1830, 67; 1840, 68; 1850, 69; 1860, 70; 1870, 165; 1880, 166; 1890, 167; 1900, 168; 1910, 169; 1930, 170; 1950, 171; Dutch origin, 1775, 37; English origin, 1775, 37; foreign-born, proportion to total population, 1860, 174; 1880, 175; 1900, 176; German origin, 1775, 37; German-born, proportion to total population, 1880, 183; 1900, 184; 1930, 185; Irish-born, proportion to total population, 1880, 180; 1900, 181; 1930, 182; Negro (Free Negro), 1860, 145; proportion to population, 1900, 172; 1930, 173; Scots-Highland origin, 1775, 37; Scots-Irish origin, 1775, 37; Swedish and Norwegian-born, proportion to total population, 1880, 177; 1900, 178; 1930, 179; totals by states, Appendix I
Porcupine R., Alaska, 3
Port Arthur, Ont., 3
Port Gibson, Miss., in the Civil War, 159
Port Hudson, La., in the Civil War, 159
Port Nelson, Man., 3
Port Royal, N. Sco., in the War of the Spanish Succession, 30
Port Royal, S.C., 25; in the War of the Spanish Succession, 30; in the Civil War, 157, 158, 159

Porter, route of, in the Civil War, 160
Portland, Me., 1, 9; branch of Second Bank at, 112; and the Underground Railway, 146; embarkation port in World War I, 212
Portland, Ore., 1; and mail routes, *circa* 1861, 116; *see also* Ft. William
Porto Alegre, Brazil, 4
Porto Bello, Pan., 4
Portola, route of, 35
Portsmouth, Eng., 213
Portsmouth, N.H., 1; branch of Second Bank at, 112
Portsmouth, Ohio, and the Underground Railway, 146
Post Roads, 1804, 114; 1834, 115; Overland Mail and Pony Express, 116
Potomac, circumnavigation of globe by, 127*n*
Potomac R., Md.-Va., 2
Potosí, Bol. 4
Pottawatomie Indians, Mich., 19
Poughkeepsie, N.Y., 1
Pourée, route of, in the Revolution, 51
Power transmission lines, 1923, 243; 1935, 244; 1950, 245
Powhattan Indians, Va., 19
Prairie du Chien, Wisc., 58, 59
Prairie Grove, Ark., in the Civil War, 158
Precipitation, U.S., 15
Presidential Elections, 1788–1952, Appendix II
Presqu'Isle (Erie), Que., 34; Pa., in War of 1812, 94
Prestonburg, Ky., in the Civil War, 158
Prevost, route of, in the Revolution, 49; in the War of 1812, 94, 95
Price, routes of, in the Civil War, 158, 160
Primeria Alta, Sp. Cal., 35
Prince Edward Island, prov. of, 3
Prince George, B.C., 3
Prince of Wales Is., Alaska, 209
Prince Rupert, B.C., 3
Princeton, N.J., in the Revolution, 47
Prince William Sd., Alaska, 3
Proclamation Line of 1763, 36
Proctor, route of, in the War of 1812, 94
Prohibition, 1846, 132; 1856, 133; 1880, 281; 1906, 282; 1915, 283; 1919, 284; dry counties, 1919, 285; 1950, 286; ratification of the 18th amend., 200; repeal (21st amend.), 203
Providence, Md., 22
Providence, R.I., 1, 22; branch of Second Bank at, 112
Providence Plantations colony, 22
Public Domain, *see* Land cessions
Public Land Strip (Okla.), 166
Public Schools, *see* Schools
Puebla, Mex., in the Mexican War, 97
Pueblo, Colo., 1
Pueblo Indians, N. Mex., 19
Puerto, Santiago (Jamaica), 21
Puerto Rico, 2, 21; in the Spanish-American War, 207*n*; annexed, 261*n*

Puget Sd., Wash., 72
Purus R., Brazil, 4
Put-in-Bay, Ohio, 94
Putumayo R., S.A., 4

Qualla Battoo, Sumatra, 127*n*
Qu'Appelle R., Can., 3
Quebec, P.Q., 1, 3; Que., in the War of the League of
    Augsburg, 28; in the Seven Years' War, 34; P.Q., in
    the Revolution, 46; embarkation port, World War I,
    212
Quebec, prov. of, 3, 53
Quebec Act of 1774, 36
Queen Anne's Creek (Edenton), N.C., 29
Queen Anne's War (War of the Spanish Succession),
    30
Queen Charlotte Is., B.C., 3
Queenstown Heights, Ont., in War of 1812, 93
Queretaro, Sp. Mex., 21
Quexaltenango, Sp. Mex., 21
Quitman expedition, 127*n*
Quito, Ec., 4
Quito Sueño Is., claimed by U.S., title established, 261*n*
Quivira, 35

Railroads, 1840, 119; 1850, 120; 1860, 121; 1870, 251;
    1880, 252; land grants to, 253, 254; mileage by dec-
    ades, Appendix IV
Rainbow Bridge National Monument, 267
Rainfall, U.S., 15; drought frequency, 16
Rainy Lake, 3, 73
Rainy R., Can.-U.S., 73
Raisin R., Mich., 94
Raleigh, N.C., 1
Ramsey's Mill, N.C., in the Revolution, 51
Rapid City, S. Dak., 6
Rates of travel, 1800, 123; 1830, 124; 1860, 125; 1930,
    260
Rawdon, route of, in the Revolution, 51
Rayvenal boundary proposals after the Revolution, 52
Recall (Initiative and), *see* Appendix V
Reading, Pa., 1; and nearby canals, 117
Recife, Brazil, 4
Reclamation, irrigated areas, 1910, 268; 1930, 269;
    1950, 270
Red R., U.S., 2, 97
Red R., Can., 3
Referendum (Initiative and), *see* Appendix V
Regina, Sask., 3
Reims, Fr., in World War I, 213
Reindeer Lake, Sask., 3
Reno, Nev., 1
Rensselaerswyck, N. Neth. (N.Y.), 24
Republican R., U.S., 2
Revolt of Mackenzie, Upper Canada, 127*n;* of Papi-
    neau, Lower Canada, 127*n;* of Riel, Can., 257*n*

Revolutionary War Campaigns 46, 47, 48, 49, 50, 51;
    Peace of Paris, 52
Reykjavik, Iceland, 3
Rhineland, occupation of, after World War I, 262*n*
Rhode Island and Providence Plantations, 25
Rice areas, 1775, 40
Richelieu R., P.Q., 3
Richmond, Va., 1, 31, 58; in the Revolution, 50; branch
    of Second Bank of the U.S. at, 112; and domestic
    routes of slave trade, 146; in the Civil War, 158, 160,
    161; Federal Reserve Bank at, 250
Richmond Canal, Va., 117
Rich Mountain, W. Va., in the Civil War, 157
Ridgefield, Conn., in the Revolution, 47
Ridley expedition, 127*n*
Riel rebellion, Can., 261*n*
Rigaud, route of, in the War of the Austrian Succession,
    32
Rio de Janeiro, Brazil, 4
Rio Grande, U.S.-Mex., 97
Rio Grande do Sul, Brazil, 4
Ripley, Ohio, and Underground Railway, 146
Roads and highways, land grants to wagon roads, 253;
    U.S. highways, 1925, 256; 1935, 257; *see also* Post
    Roads; *see also* by specific name
Roanoke, Va., 1
Roanoke Is., Carolina, 2, 22, 27; in the Civil War, 158
Roanoke R., N.C., 2
Robertson Trail, 58
Rochambeau, routes of, in the Revolution, 51
Rochester, N.Y., 1, 58; and nearby canals, 117
Rochefort, Fr., and U.S. in World War I, 213
Rock Island, Ill., 250
Rocky Mts., 2; Can., 3
Rocky Mountain National Park, Colo., 267
Romaine R., P.Q., 3
Roncador Cay, claimed by U.S., 261*n*
Roncador Mts., Brazil, 4
Roosevelt Steamship Co., subsidized routes of, 262
Rosario, Arg., 4
Rosario, Sp. Tex., 35
Rosecrans, routes of, in the Civil War, 157, 159
Ross, route of, in the War of 1812, 95
Rotterdam, Neth., 213
Rouen, Fr., and U.S. in World War I, 213
Rouse's Point, N.Y., 1
Rui, route of, 35
Rush-Bagot agreement, 126*n*
Russia, Ukase of 1821, 126*n;* Archangel expedition,
    262*n;* U.S. forces in, after World War I, 262*n*
Rustdorf (Jamaica), N. Neth. (N.Y.), 24
Rutland, Vt., 1

Saar basin, Ger., 213
Saavedra, route of, 20
Sabine Cross Roads, La., in the Civil War, 160
Sabine R., Tex.-La., 2, 97

Sac and Fox Indians, Wisc., 19
Sacketts Harbor, N.Y., in the War of 1812, 94
Saco, Me., 22, 27
Sacramento, Cal., 1; in the Mexican War, 97; and mail routes, *circa* 1858, 116
Sacramento Mts., Mex., 2
Sagadahoc, Me., 27
Saguaro National Monument, Ariz., 267
Saguenay R., P.Q., 3
St. Augustine, Fla., 1; Sp. Fla., 21, 35; attacked 1702, 30; in the War of the Austrian Succession, 32; in the Civil War, 158, 159
St. Bartholomew Is., W.I., purchase contemplated, 261*n*
St. Catherines, Ont., and the Underground Railway, 146
St. Denis, route of, 32
St. Denis, La., 30
St. Eustatius Is., W.I., 2
St. Francis de Sales, Que., 28
St. Francis Xavier, Fr. Ill., 28
St. Ignace, Que., 28
St. John R., Me., 2
St. Johns, Nfld., 3; embarkation port, World War I, 212
St. Johns, P.Q., in the Revolution, 46
St. Joseph, Mo., and the Overland Mail, 116
St. Lawrence Is., Alaska, 2, 3
St. Lawrence R., 2, 3; free navigation of secured, 261*n*
St. Leger, route of, in the Revolution, 47
St. Louis, Mo., 1, 9, 58, 59; in the Revolution, 5; branch of Second Bank of the U.S. at, 112; and mail routes, *circa* 1858, 116; Federal Reserve Bank, 250
St. Louis R., Minn., 73
St. Lucia, B.W.I., 2; U.S. base at, 310
St. Marks, Fla., in the First Seminole War, 95
St. Mary's, Md., 22, 27
St. Maurice R., P.Q., 3
St. Mihiel sector, Fr., World War I, 213
St. Nazaire, Fr., disembarkation port, World War I, 213
St. Paul, Minn., 1
St. Petersburg, Fla., 1
St. Pierre Is., 3
St. Xavier del Bac, Sp. Mex., 35
Salado R., Arg., 4
Salem, Mass , 27
Salem, N.J., 25
Salem, Ore., 1
Salinan Indians, Cal., 19
Salisbury, N.C., 58; and domestic routes of slave trade, 146; in the Civil War, 161
Salmon Falls, N.H., in the War of the League of Augsburg, 28
Saltillo, Sp. Mex., 21; in the Mexican War, 97
Salt Lake City, Utah, 1, 6, 58, 59; and mail routes, *circa* 1851, 116
Saludo R., Arg., 4
Samana Bay, S. Dom., 2; negotiations re, 261*n*
Samoa, 305; negotiations re, 261*n*

Sampson, route of, in the Spanish-American War, 207
San Antonio de Bejar, Sp. Tex., 35
San Antonio, Sp. Fla., 21, 35
San Antonio, Tex., 1; and mail routes, 1854, 116; and cattle trails, 226
San Augustin, Sp. Tex., 35
San Blas, Mex., in the Mexican War, 97
San Buenaventura, Sp. Cal., 35
San Carlos Borromeo, Sp. Cal., 35
San Diego, Cal., 1, 59; in the Mexican War, 97; and mail routes, *circa* 1857, 116
San Diego de Alcala, Sp. Cal., 35
San Dionysio, Sp. Cal., 35
San Esteban, Sp. Mex., 21
San Felipé, Sp. Mex., 21
San Felipe Orista, Sp. Fla., 35
San Fernando Re de España, Sp. Cal., 35
San Francisco, Cal., 1, 6; (de Assisi), 35, 59; and mail routes, *circa* 1858, 116; Federal Reserve Bank, 250
San Francisco de la Espada, Sp. Tex., 35
San Francisco de los Nechas, Sp. Tex., 35
San Francisco de los Tejas, Sp. Tex., 35
San Francisco de Solano, Sp. Cal., 35
San Francisco do Borja, Sp. Mex., 35
San Geronimo, Sp. Mex., 21
San Jacinto, Tex., battle site, 97
San José, Mex., in the Mexican War, 97
San José, Sp. Cal., 35
San Juan, Sp. Mex., 21
San Juan Bautista, P.R., 21
San Juan Bautista, Sp. Cal., 35
San Juan Capistrano, Sp. Cal., 35
San Juan de los Caballeros, Sp. N. Mex., 35
San Juan Hill, Cuba, battle of, 207
San Luis, Sp. Fla., 35
San Luis, Sp. Mex., 21
San Luis, Sp. Tex., 35
San Luis Bautista, Sp. Tex., 35
San Luis Obispo, Sp. Cal., 35
San Luis Obispo Bay, Cal., 2
San Luis Potosi, Sp. Mex., 21; Mex., in border proposals, 98
San Luis Rey de Francia, Sp. Cal., 35
San Mateo, Sp. Fla., 21, 35
San Matias, Gulf of, 4
San Miguel, Sp. Fla., 35
San Miguel Archangel, Sp. Cal., 35
San Miguel de Cuellar, Sp. Tex., 35
San Miguel de Gualdape, Sp. Tex., 35
San Rafael Archangel, Sp. Cal., 35
San Salvador, Sp. C.A., 21
San Sebastian, Sp. S.A., 21
San Xavier, Sp. Tex., 35
Sanders, route of, in the Seven Years' War, 34
Sandusky, Ohio, and Underground Railway, 146
Sandy Hook, N.J., in the Revolution, 48
Sangre de Cristo Mts., 2

All numbers refer to maps, not pages

[232]

All numbers refer to maps, not pages

All numbers refer to maps, not pages

All numbers refer to maps, not pages

All numbers refer to maps, not pages

All numbers refer to maps, not pages